中国非洲研究院首批资助课题“中国—南非青年参与社会发展机制及趋势研究”（CAI2017004）成果。

The first batch of research projects titled “China-South Africa youth participation in social development mechanism and tendency” (CAI2017004) that are funded by China-Africa Institute.

CHINA-SOUTH AFRICA

命运的共同体：

中国—南非青年社会发展参与研究

A COMMUNITY WITH A SHARED FUTURE: CHINA-SOUTH AFRICA YOUTH PARTICIPATION IN SOCIAL DEVELOPMENT

马 峰　颜炳文　著
FENG MA　BINGWEN YAN

中国社会科学出版社

图书在版编目（CIP）数据

命运的共同体：中国－南非青年社会发展参与研究／马峰，颜炳文著．—北京：中国社会科学出版社，2021.3

ISBN 978－7－5203－7649－5

Ⅰ.①命… Ⅱ.①马…②颜… Ⅲ.①青年—社会发展—参与管理—研究—中国、南非 Ⅳ.①D432.6②D434.786

中国版本图书馆CIP数据核字（2020）第257603号

出 版 人 赵剑英
责任编辑 刘凯琳 李凯凯
责任校对 侯聪睿
责任印制 王 超

出 版 中国社会科学出版社
社 址 北京鼓楼西大街甲158号
邮 编 100720
网 址 http://www.csspw.cn
发 行 部 010－84083685
门 市 部 010－84029450
经 销 新华书店及其他书店

印 刷 北京明恒达印务有限公司
装 订 廊坊市广阳区广增装订厂
版 次 2021年3月第1版
印 次 2021年3月第1次印刷

开 本 710×1000 1/16
印 张 19
插 页 2
字 数 318千字
定 价 109.00元

前言　中非青年携手构建更加紧密的中非命运共同体

举世瞩目的中非合作论坛北京峰会，为推动构建更加紧密的中非命运共同体擘划了发展蓝图。中非亲如一家、亲如兄弟的关系从为争取民族解放斗争的时候即已结成。六十多年来，中非命运休戚与共，中非人民相互依靠、相互理解、相互支持，纵使远隔万水千山，我们始终站在一起，发出共同的声音、追求共同的发展价值，为彼此的发展成绩而欢欣鼓舞。中非合作是南南合作的典范，更是不同文明合作和对话的典范。从摆脱殖民统治的民族解放运动到“两极格局”的第三世界团结协作，从冷战后的同舟共济到进入21世纪的紧密合作，从站起来、富起来到强起来，在不同的时代、不同的国际环境中，中非始终不离不弃，中非始终命运相依，中国的身后始终有非洲人民的支持，非洲的身后始终有中国人民的声援和鼎力相助，这是跨越了万水千山的友谊。坦赞铁路的轰鸣见证了六十多年来的坚守，蒙内铁路见证了新时代中非关系的新前景。

习近平主席指出：“根之茂者其实遂，膏之沃者其光晔。”① 历史有其规律和逻辑。中非双方基于相似的遭遇和共同使命，在过去的岁月里同心同向、守望相助，走出了一条特色鲜明的合作共赢之路。

青年是中非关系发展的未来，中非合作的成果惠及中非人民，更惠及中非青年。六十多年来，当年蓬勃的少年，中非关系的奠基人有的已

① 习近平：《携手共命运 同心促发展——在二〇一八年中非合作论坛北京峰会开幕式上的主旨讲话》，《光明日报》2018年9月4日第2版。

然逝去，有的已到耄耋之年，但是一代一代的中非青年薪火相传，接过中非友好的接力棒，不断将中非的亲情、友情传递下去。中非合作、中非友好是青春的友好，无论沧海桑田、世事变迁、时代转换，中非命运共同体始终休戚与共。在当今时代的发展背景下，面对世界发展纷繁复杂的形势，不确定性、不稳定性日益增加的国际环境，中非构建更加紧密的命运共同体有了新的时代内涵。当前，很多国家面临发展的压力、成长的烦恼，2008 年国际金融危机造成的影响远没有结束，单边主义的抬头，使以规则为基础的国际关系遭到严峻挑战，逆全球化潮流波涛涌起，这不单单是宏观国际形势的变化，世界发展的态势，更影响到每个人的切身利益。生活在地球村中的人，早就被全球化的潮流所席卷，以邻为壑，人为切断联系既是不可能的，也是不现实的。参与到全球化中的青年，在发展的机遇面前需要技能的培训，在发展的挑战面前需要良好的教育，在发展的前途与人生的抉择面前需要梦想以支撑，在发展的爬坡中需要看到发展的前途，而这些与发展的同频共振是青年所需要的。青年不缺少梦想，不缺少理想，不缺少奋斗的精神，缺少的是人生出彩的舞台。这舞台是经济的增长，这舞台是安定的社会，这舞台是公平的环境，这舞台是良好的教育，这舞台是谋生的技能，这舞台是发展的希望。少年强则国强，其实质点出的是青年有发展的动力，社会就有发展的活力，经济就有发展的能量，国家就会在“独行快”与“众行远”中奔腾向前。

习近平主席在访问非洲大陆时，提出“真、实、亲、诚”的对非政策主张，赢得非洲人民的广泛赞誉。

中非青年的合作发展，推动中非青年实现人生的出彩，不但是当前时代背景下中非共同面临的社会发展问题，也是需要共同推进的社会发展议程。从中非青年发展的视角，聚焦时代发展的命题和中非合作的新趋向，要努力促进中非青年共同发展，厚植中非青年友谊，解决中非青年发展问题。

青年发展是当今时代绕不过的主题，为青年发展厚植动力，促进青年就业是青年立足于社会的基本前提。让青年看到希望，社会才有希望，让青年拥有未来，社会才有前途。加强中非青年合作，让中非青年在中非发展中实现求进步、求发展的人生价值，书写中非青年携手发展，构建中非命运共同体的青春之歌，奉献中非友谊传承的青春力量。

习近平主席在2018年中非合作论坛北京峰会开幕式上的主旨讲话中指出："青年是中非关系的希望所在。我提出的中非'八大行动'倡议中，许多措施都着眼青年、培养青年、扶助青年，致力于为他们提供更多就业机会、更好发展空间。"① "'红日初升，其道大光。'我相信，只要中非友好的接力棒能够在青年一代手中不断相传，中非命运共同体就一定会更具生机活力，中华民族伟大复兴的中国梦和非洲人民团结振兴的非洲梦就一定能够早日实现！"②

携手青年，构建更加紧密的中非命运共同体，要让青年发展融入中非发展的大潮中，以就业为优先，以教育为动力，以职业培训、技能培养为切入点，以青春创业为中非青年合作的新亮点，搭建中非青年创业空间、发展平台，为中非青年搭建更多青春出彩的舞台，人生成长、发展的空间。

要实现中非青年梦想的对接。实现中华民族伟大复兴的中国梦是当代中国青年的共同价值追求，接过历史的接力棒，奋进在新时代新征程的新长征中，面向实现建成社会主义现代化强国的梦想，当代中国青年以新时代奋斗者的姿态，在奋斗中幸福，在奋斗中成长，在奋斗中发展，怀揣梦想，砥砺前进。实现团结振兴的非洲梦想，实现非洲大陆的现代化，是非洲青年的梦想和心声。在现代化中谋发展，在现代化中实现人生命运的翻转是中非青年的个人梦想。中非青年梦想的对接，是时代的要求，更是共同走向现代化的发展所需。培养青年、辅助青年，让青年在中非发展的快车道中找到发展的位置，是当代人对下一代人的

① 《携手共命运 同心促发展——在二〇一八年中非合作论坛北京峰会开幕式上的主旨讲话》，《光明日报》2018年9月4日第2版。

② 同上。

使命。

要实现中非青年创新的对接。当今时代惟创新者赢，惟创新者胜。青年是常新的，青年是敢想敢干敢闯的，这是创新的源泉，更是青年创新的驱动力。第四次工业革命的兴起，创新是核心，发展是目的。对青年既有挑战，也有机遇。青年要积极参与到第四次工业革命带来的全球新旧动能转换的发展之中，在新动能的发展中实现技能的提高和命运的翻转，成为新技术革命中的主干力量。让青年在发展中更好地与技术进步同步，与第四次工业革命同步，让青年成为社会发展的成果创造者、分享者。中非青年共同推动、共同参与“大众创业、万众创新”，让中非合作的成果更多惠及非洲普通青年。聚焦非洲的能力建设，“实施能力建设行动。中国决定同非洲加强发展经验交流，支持开展经济社会发展规划方面合作；在非洲设立 10 个鲁班工坊，向非洲青年提供职业技能培训；支持设立旨在推动青年创新创业合作的中非创新合作中心；实施头雁计划，为非洲培训 1000 名精英人才；为非洲提供 5 万个中国政府奖学金名额，为非洲提供 5 万个研修培训名额，邀请 2000 名非洲青年来华交流。”① 中非青年合作立足推动非洲自主发展，能力发展，为非洲长远发展积蓄青年人才的财富。

要实现中非青年命运共同体的对接。中非命运共同体，离不开青年的参与，中非友好的接力棒需要一代一代的中非青年传承下去。“一带一路”倡议是中非青年合作的重要平台，也是中非青年命运相依的发展平台。“一带一路”倡议将中国与非洲，中非与联合国可持续发展议程，中国与非洲各国的发展战略紧密相连。在发展中搭建互利共赢的发展新前景，而青年是其中的推动力量，更是参与力量。中非共同的创造力、凝聚力、行动力，将中非全面战略合作伙伴关系成功推向新的高度。

中非要携手打造责任共担的中非命运共同体，携手打造合作共赢的

---

① 习近平：《携手共命运 同心促发展——在二〇一八年中非合作论坛北京峰会开幕式上的主旨讲话》，《光明日报》2018 年 9 月 4 日第 2 版。

中非命运共同体，携手打造幸福共享的中非命运共同体，携手打造文化共兴的中非命运共同体，携手打造安全共筑的中非命运共同体，携手打造和谐共生的中非命运共同体。

中非携手，青年携手，在走向发展中国家实现现代化的进程中，中非青年携手以进、义利共担，将中非跨越六十多年的友谊传承下去。

课题组

2020 年 11 月于北京

Preface　Chinese and African Youth Work Together to Build an Even Stronger China-Africa Community with a Shared Future

The Beijing Summit of the Forum on China-Africa Cooperation, which attracts worldwide attention, has planned a blueprint for building a closer China-Africa community with a shared future. The brotherhood relationship between China and Africa was formed back at the struggle for national liberation. In the past 60 years, China and Africa have formed a community with a shared future. The Chinese and African people rely on each other, understand each other, and support each other. Even if we are far apart, we always stand together, have common voices, pursue common development values, and feel happy for each other's development achievements. China-Africa cooperation is a model of South-South cooperation and even a model for cooperation and dialogue among different civilizations. From the national liberation movements to free from colonial rule to the cooperation in the third world in the "bipolar structure", from the solidarity after the Cold War to the close cooperation in the new century, from standing up to becoming rich and to becoming strong, in different times and different international environments, China and Africa have always been inseparable and dependent on each other. China has always been supported by the African people and likewise, the African people have always had support and help from the Chinese people. This is a friendship that spans thousands of kilometers. The steam whistle of Tanzania-Zambia Railway witnesses the persistence of the past 60 years, and the Mombasa-Nairobi Standard Gauge Railway witnesses the new prospects of China-Africa relations in the new era.

President Xi Jinping pointed out: "Only with deep roots can a tree yield rich fruit; only filled with oil can a lamp burn brightly."① History follows its own rules and logic. With similar fate in the past and a common mission, China and Africa have extended sympathy to and helped each other throughout all the years. Together, we have embarked on a distinctive path of win-win cooperation.

The youth are the future of China-Africa relations. The achievements of China-Africa cooperation benefit the people, especially young people in China and Africa. In the past 60 years, some of the founders of China-Africa relations have already passed away, and some have already been at very old ages. However, the generations of Chinese and African young people have taken over the baton of China-Africa friendship and passed on their brotherhood friendship. China-Africa friendship is the friendship of youth. Regardless of the changes of the world, the China-Africa community with a shared future will always go through thick and thin together. In the development context of the current era, in the face of the complicated world situation of uncertainty and instability, the building of a closer China-Africa community with a shared future has new meaning of the era. At present, many countries are facing the pressure of development and troubles of growth. The impact of the 2008 international financial crisis is far from over. The rise of unilateralism and the rule-based international relations have been severely

① Xi Jinping, "Work Together for Common Development and a Shared Future—Keynote Speech at the 2018 Beijing Summit of the Forum on China-Africa Cooperation", Xinhuanet, http://www.xinhuanet.com/world/2018-09/03/c_1123373881.htm.

challenged and the anti-globalization tide is surging. This not only is the change of the macro international situation and of the world's development trend, but also has an impact on the personal interests of everyone. The people living in the global village have long been involved in the trend of globalization. Benefiting at others' expense and cutting off links with others is impossible and unrealistic. Young people involved in globalization need skills training in the face of opportunities for development, need good education in the face of development challenges, need dreams to support in the face of their future and choices of life, and need to see promising future in difficulties of development. The synchronization of these needs with development is what young people need. Young people do not lack dreams, ideals, or the spirit of struggle. What they lack is the stage to excel. This stage is economic growth, a stable society, a fair environment, a good education, a skill for making a living, and the hope of development. Strong youth lead to a strong country. If young people have the driving force for development, the society will have the vitality of development, the economy will have the energy to develop, and the country will move forward.

When General Secretary Xi Jinping visited the African continent, he put forward building relations with Africa based on "Sincerity, Real Results, Friendship, and Good Faith" and won wide acclaim from the African people.

The cooperative development of young people in China and Africa will make it possible for Chinese and African young people to excel in their life. It is not only the social development issue that China and Africa both face in the current era, but also the social development agenda that needs to be promoted together. From the perspective of the development of China-Africa youth, focusing on the proposition of the development of the times and the new trend of China-Africa cooperation, we will work hard to promote youth development for China and Africa, foster friendship between China and Africa, and solve the problem of youth development in China and Africa.

Youth development is the theme that cannot be circumvented in the current era. Injecting impetus for youth development and promoting youth employment are the basic premise for young people to establish themselves in society. Only if we make the youth know their life is promising, our society will be promising. Only if the youth master their future, our society will have a great future. Let's strengthen China-Africa cooperation on youth development, enable the young people of China and Africa to realize their life values for progress and development. Let's write the youthful song for Chinese and African young people to develop together in building a China-Africa community with a shared future, and contribute to the youthful strength for passing on the friendship between China and Africa.

In the keynote speech at the 2018 Beijing Summit of the Forum on China-Africa Cooperation, President Xi Jinping pointed out: "The future of China-Africa relations lies in our young people. Many of the measures in the eight initiatives I just outlined are designed to help young people in Africa. These measures will provide young Africans with more training and job opportunities and open up more space for their development."① "'The red rising sun will light up the road ahead.' I am confident that the baton of China-Africa friendship will be passed from one generation to the next and that China and Africa, working together, will build an even more vibrant community with a shared future. The day will surely come when the Chinese nation realizes its dream of national renewal and Africa realizes its dream of unity and invigoration!"②

We must join hands with young people to build a closer China-Africa

① Xi Jinping, "Work Together for Common Development and a Shared Future—Keynote Speech at the 2018 Beijing Summit of the Forum on China-Africa Cooperation", Xinhuanet, http://www.xinhuanet.com/world/2018-09/03/c_1123373881.htm.

② Ibid..

community with a shared future. We must integrate youth development into the tide of China-Africa development, giving priority to employment, taking education as the driving force, taking vocational training and skills training as the entry point, and taking youth entrepreneurship as new highlights of China-Africa youth cooperation. We must create space and build platforms for young entrepreneurs in China and Africa, and build more stages for them to excel in their personal progress and development.

We must link the dreams of Chinese and African young people. The Chinese dream of realizing the great rejuvenation of the nation is the common value pursuit of the contemporary Chinese youth. Holding the historical baton and forging ahead in the new long march of the new era and having the dream of building a socialist modernization power, the contemporary Chinese youth are making progress and developing in happiness and struggle positively in the new era. Achieving the African dream of unity and rejuvenation and realizing the modernization of the African continent are the dreams and aspirations of African youth. It is the personal dream of the young people of China and Africa to realize the development in modernization and realize the reversal of the destiny of life in modernization. Linking the dreams of young people in China and Africa is the requirement of the times and the need for realizing modernization. It is the mission of the present generation to the next generation to cultivate young people, support young people, and let young people find a place to develop in the fast lane of China-Africa development.

Chinese and African young people need to synergize in innovation. Innovators will win in the current era. Young people are innovative and have courage to make differences. This is the source of innovation and the driving force for youth innovation. In the rise of the fourth industrial revolution, innovation is the core and development is the goal. There are both challenges and opportunities for young people. Young people should actively participate in the development of the global replacement of old growth drivers by new ones brought about by the fourth industrial revolution, and realize the improvement of skills and the reversal of fate in the replacement of growth drivers and become the backbone of the new technological revolution. Young people need to better synchronize with technological progress in development, and with the fourth industrial revolution, so as to be creators and sharers of fruits in social development. The young people of China and Africa should jointly promote and participate in the "mass entrepreneurship and innovation", so that the achievements of China-Africa cooperation will benefit more ordinary African youth. We should focus on capacity building in Africa. "We will launch a capacity building initiative. China will share more of its development practices with Africa and support cooperation with Africa on economic and social development planning. Ten Luban Workshops will be set up in Africa to provide vocational training for young Africans. China will support opening of a China-Africa innovation cooperation center to promote youth innovation and entrepreneurship. A tailor-made program will be carried out to train 1000 high-caliber Africans. China will provide Africa with 50000 government scholarships and 50000 training opportunities for seminars and workshops, and will invite 2000 young Africans to visit China for exchanges."① China-Africa youth cooperation aims to promote Africa's independent development and capacity development, and accumulate the resources of young talents for the long-term development of Africa.

We should synergize in youth development of the China-Africa community with a shared future. A China-Africa community with a shared future is inseparable from the participation of young people. The Sino-African friendly

① Xi Jinping, "Work Together for Common Development and a Shared Future—Keynote Speech at the 2018 Beijing Summit of the Forum on China-Africa Cooperation", Xinhuanet, http://www.xinhuanet.com/world/2018-09/03/c_1123373881.htm.

baton needs to be passed down from generation to generation. The Belt and Road Initiative is an important platform for cooperation between China and Africa and a development platform for young people both in China and Africa. The Belt and Road Initiative links China and Africa, the UN Sustainable Development Agenda, and the development strategies of China and African countries. In the process of development, we will build a new prospect of mutual benefit and win-win development, and the youth are the driving force and also the participation force. The common creativity, cohesiveness and execution of China and Africa have successfully pushed China-Africa comprehensive strategic partnership to a new height.

China and Africa must work together to create a China-Africa community with a shared future of win-win cooperation, of shared happiness, of common cultural prosperity, of co-built security, and of harmonious coexistence.

In the process of modernization of developing countries, China and Africa, as well as their young people, join hands and work together to pass down the China-Africa friendship of over 60 years.

The Research Group

November 2020 in Beijing

目　　录

第一部分　中国青年与社会发展

第一章　中国青年参与社会发展政策及机制 ……………………………（3）

一　制定中长期青年发展规划促进青年参与社会发展 ………………………………………………………（3）

二　全面促进青年参与社会发展、实现自我价值 …………（6）

三　统筹全局设计青年社会发展参与机制 …………………（9）

第二章　中国青年参与社会发展的社会组织机制及人才战略 ……（15）

一　社会组织参与机制及人才发展 …………………………（16）

二　青年人才对参与社会发展的社会组织机制的环境需求 ………………………………………………………（18）

三　构建符合青年参与社会发展需求的社会组织机制及人才战略 …………………………………………………（21）

四　让社会组织成为青年参与社会发展“流动的广阔平台” ……………………………………………………（25）

第三章　中国青年参与社会发展的趋势变化 ……………………（26）

一　青年成长、社会发展与时代发展同步 …………………（26）

二　健康：青年参与社会发展的基础与前提 …………………（31）
三　教育、就业：青年参与社会发展的“起点公平”与“机会公平” ……………………………………………………（33）

第四章　百年变迁：“五四”精神激励中国青年在新时代民族复兴中追梦前行 ………………………………………（38）
一　青年是国家的未来、民族的希望 ……………………（38）
二　奋斗是青春最亮丽的底色 ……………………………（39）
三　做好新时代的青年工作 ………………………………（41）
四　新时代中国青年要有家国情怀、人类关怀 …………（43）

第二部分　南非青年与社会发展

第五章　南非青年参与社会发展政策及机制 ……………（47）
一　南非青年群体概况 ……………………………………（47）
二　青年发展与国家未来：南非青年参与社会发展政策 ……（48）

第六章　南非青年参与社会发展的影响因素及问题 ………（64）
一　就业状况 ………………………………………………（64）
二　教育状况 ………………………………………………（66）
三　技能培训 ………………………………………………（67）
四　青年工作框架 …………………………………………（69）
五　青年健康 ………………………………………………（69）
六　青年发展、社会凝聚力与志愿服务 …………………（72）

第七章　制定和形成更加积极的南非青年参与社会发展政策及机制 ……………………………………………………（76）
一　促进青年参与社会发展政策及机制转型 ……………（76）

二　国家与社会：建设发展与凝聚力的青年社会发展参与…………………………………………………………（82）
三　中非合作：关注非洲青年发展 …………………………（83）
四　南非青年参与社会发展的新希望 ………………………（86）

第八章　南非青年参与社会发展的价值观 ………………………（89）
一　南非青年参与社会发展的价值观取向 …………………（91）
二　南非青年参与社会发展的价值观选择 …………………（95）
三　南非青年参与社会发展的价值观分析…………………（101）
四　中国南非合作构筑青年发展新机遇……………………（103）

附　录 ……………………………………………………………（107）

后　记 ……………………………………………………………（115）

Contents

Part I Chinese Youth and Social Development

Chapter I Policies and Mechanisms for Chinese Youth's Participation in Social Development ………………… (119)

I Formulating medium-and long-term youth development plans and improving youth's participation in social development ………………………………………………… (119)

II Comprehensively promoting youth's participation in social development to achieve their self-worth …………………… (124)

III Coordinating the overall design of mechanisms for youth's participation in social development ……………………… (129)

Chapter II Social Organization Mechanisms and Talent Strategy of Chinese Youth's Participation in Social Development ……………………………………… (137)

I Participation mechanism of social organizations and talent development ……………………………………………… (138)

II Environmental requirements of young talents for the social organization mechanism involved in social development …… (142)

III Building a social organization mechanism and talent strategy that meet the needs of youth's participation in social development ……………………………………… (147)

IV Making social organizations a broad flowing platform for youth's participation in social development ……………………… (153)

Chapter III Changes in the Trend of Chinese Youth's Participation in Social Development ……………… (155)

I Synchronization of youth development, social development and national development ………………………………………… (155)

II Health: the basis and premise of youth's participation in social development ……………………………………………… (162)

III Education and employment: equity in starting point and opportunity for youth's participation in social development …………………………………………………… (165)

Chapter IV Changes in History: The Spirit of the May Fourth Movement Inspires Youth to Strive for Their Dreams in the National Rejuvenation in the New Era …… (173)

I The youth is the future of the country and hope of the nation ……………………………………………………………… (173)

II Struggle is the brightest tint of youth ……………………… (175)

III Doing a good job in youth work in the new era …………… (178)

IV Chinese youth in the new era should not only care about their family and country, but also have concerns for humanity ……………………………………………………… (181)

Part II South African Youth and Social Development

Chapter V Policies and Mechanisms for South African Youth's Participation in Social Development ………………… (187)

I Overview of South African youth groups …………………… (187)

II Youth development and national future: policies for South African youth's participation in social development ………… (189)

Chapter VI Influencing Factors and Problems of South African Youth's Participation in Social Development …… (209)

I Employment …… (209)

II Education …… (212)

III Skills training …… (213)

IV Youth work framework …… (215)

V Youth health …… (216)

VI Youth development, social cohesion and volunteer service …… (220)

Chapter VII Formulating and Forming More Active Policies and Mechanisms for South African Youth's Participation in Social Development …… (225)

I Promoting the transformation of policies and mechanisms for youth's participation in social development …… (225)

II State and society: building a developmental and cohesive youth's participation in social development …… (233)

III China-Africa cooperation: focusing on African youth development …… (235)

IV New prospect of South African youth's participation in social development …… (240)

Chapter VIII Values for South African Youth's Participation in Social Development …… (243)

I Value performance of South African youth's participation in social development …… (246)

II Value choice of South African youth's participation in social development …… (252)

III Value analysis of South African youth's participation in social development …… (259)

IV China and South Africa cooperate to create new opportunities for youth development …… (262)

Appendix …… (267)

Afterword …… (279)

第一部分

中国青年与社会发展

第一章　中国青年参与社会发展政策及机制

青年工作始终是党和国家工作的重要环节和组成部分。国家关注青年的发展，更关注青年成长成才。中华民族伟大的复兴事业需要一代代的青年接过历史的接力棒，走好每一代青年该走好的长征路。

一　制定中长期青年发展规划促进青年参与社会发展

党的十八大以来取得的发展成就，注定要载入中华民族走向复兴的历史。在这个过程中，伴随着国家整体的发展和理论、实践创新的推动，青年发展理论和实践也取得了新的发展，实现了新的突破，更加系统化、专业化和全面化。《中长期青年发展规划（2016—2025年）》的出台标志着中华人民共和国青年发展理论与实践新的发展高度。党和国家从全局的高度和视野关注青年发展，关爱青年进步，推动青年发展进入新的发展境界和历史方位。

党的十八大以来，习近平总书记围绕青年发展问题，先后发表系列讲话，针对青年发展中涉及的理想与信念、青年的价值观、青年的成长成才、搭建青年发展的舞台等青年关注、涉及青年对美好生活向往需求的重大问题，进行了科学的回答。习近平总书记站在实现“两个百年”奋斗目标的历史方位，结合中国特色社会主义进入新发展阶段特点，从新的伟大征程需要新时代的青年接过历史接力棒的角度，全面规划青年发展工作，为新时代开展青年工作，为青年社会发展参与理论和实践创新指明了方向和时代定位。

2013 年 5 月 4 日习近平总书记发表《在同各界优秀青年代表座谈时的讲话》，全面系统科学地回答了青年的理想与信念问题，将青年个人成长的人生梦想与实现中华民族伟大复兴中国梦的远大理想紧密相连。“中国梦是我们的，更是你们青年一代的。中华民族伟大复兴终将在广大青年的接力奋斗中变为现实。”① 习近平总书记指出：“展望未来，我国青年一代必将大有可为，也必将大有作为。这是‘长江后浪推前浪’的历史规律，也是‘一代更比一代强’的青春责任。广大青年要勇敢肩负起时代赋予的重任，志存高远，脚踏实地，努力在实现中华民族伟大复兴的中国梦的生动实践中放飞青春梦想。”② 他充满深情地鼓励青年人道：“青年朋友们，人的一生只有一次青春。现在，青春是用来奋斗的；将来，青春是用来回忆的。”③

2014 年 5 月 4 日，习近平总书记再次走到青年人中间，在北京大学发表了《青年要自觉践行社会主义核心价值观》的讲话，总书记讲话聚焦影响青年发展的重大理论和现实问题，特别是青年的价值观问题。价值观影响一个人的一生，而青年时期的价值观对于认识客观事物和社会发展是极其重要的，甚至影响一生。总书记指出：“我为什么要对青年讲讲社会主义核心价值观这个问题？是因为青年的价值取向决定了未来整个社会的价值取向，而青年又处在价值观形成和确立的时期，抓好这一时期的价值观养成十分重要。这就像穿衣服扣扣子一样，如果第一粒扣子扣错了，剩余的扣子都会扣错。人生的扣子从一开始就要扣好。”④ 聚焦影响青年发展的价值观问题，立足国家和社

① 习近平：《在同各界优秀青年代表座谈时的讲话》，《光明日报》2013 年 5 月 5 日第 2 版。

② 同上。

③ 同上。

④ 习近平：《青年要自觉践行社会主义核心价值观——在北京大学师生座谈会上的讲话》，《光明日报》2014 年 5 月 5 日第 2 版。

会的长远发展，着眼实现“两个一百年”的奋斗目标，从实现国家现代化的角度重视青年发展中的青年价值观问题，是习近平总书记关于青年思想的重要论述的新时代特征和闪光点。总书记从国家现代化的重要历史时间节点出发，科学分析指出：“现在在高校学习的大学生都是20岁左右，到2020年全面建成小康社会时，很多人还不到30岁；到本世纪中叶基本实现现代化时，很多人还不到60岁。也就是说，实现‘两个一百年’奋斗目标，你们和千千万万青年将全过程参与。”[①] 青年价值观的研究是青年发展的常态话题，但是站在实现国家现代化事业的高度，从进行新时代伟大斗争的角度，总书记对青年价值观问题给出了科学的回答。

2016年4月26日，在“五一”国际劳动节、“五四”青年节前夕，习近平总书记发表《在知识分子、劳动模范、青年代表座谈会上的讲话》，举办座谈会的对象主要是知识分子、劳动模范和青年代表。关于举办座谈会的目的，总书记指出：“这样安排，我们是有考虑的。我国是工人阶级领导的、以工农联盟为基础的人民民主专政的社会主义国家。知识分子是工人阶级的一部分，劳动人民是国家的主人，青年是中国特色社会主义事业接班人、是国家的未来和民族的希望。”[②] 总书记对知识分子、广大劳动群众、青年的发展提出了殷切的期望和要求。在谈到青年发展时，总书记从青年要有本领的角度，对青年在新时代的发展进行了科学的论述。总书记针对处于不同工作岗位的当代青年，在迈向现代化的进程中，如何练就过硬本领和实现自身发展与国家发展的同频共振，自觉奉献青春时，提出了明确的主张。总书记指出：“广大农村青年要在发展现代农业、建设社会主义新农村中展现现代农民新形象，广大企业青年要在积极参与生产劳动、产品研发、管理创新中创造

---

① 习近平：《青年要自觉践行社会主义核心价值观——在北京大学师生座谈会上的讲话》，《光明日报》2014年5月5日第2版。

② 习近平：《在知识分子、劳动模范、青年代表座谈会上的讲话》，《光明日报》2016年4月30日第2版。

更多财富，广大科研单位青年要在深入钻研学问、主动攻克难题中多出创新成果，广大机关事业单位青年要在提高为社会、为民众服务水平中建功立业。”①

总书记的讲话，清晰勾勒了处于不同岗位的当代青年发展的路径和实现“两个一百年”奋斗目标的青年目标、人生目标，是在对青年理想与信念、价值观作出重要论述和判断后，针对青年个人事业成长和进步的重要指向，明确了在新时代青年奋斗的目标和方向，同时也指明了青年规划理论和实践研究的方向和目标。

总书记针对青年发展的讲话，聚焦全面建成小康社会，立足实现现代化的战略定位，面向“两个一百年”的奋斗目标，从青年理想与信念、青年价值观、青年自身发展与青春奉献的视角，清晰、全面地勾勒了从宏观、中观到微观的青年发展思想，不但为青年制定自身的人生规划、职业规划指明了方向，而且为青年发展提供了从宏观、中观到微观的研究视角，最重要的是提供了面向“强起来”时代的研究视角、实践视角、创新视角。总书记围绕青年发展的一系列重要讲话是对当前及今后事业发展的科学总结和判断，是走好新时代的青年发展长征路的行动指南，具有重要的指导意义。

二　全面促进青年参与社会发展、实现自我价值

习近平总书记在党的十九大所做的政治报告中谈到青年时明确指出：“青年兴则国家兴，青年强则国家强。青年一代有理想、有本领、有担当，国家就有前途，民族就有希望。中国梦是历史的、现实的，也是未来的；是我们这一代的，更是青年一代的。中华民族伟大复兴的中国梦终将在一代代青年的接力奋斗中变为现实。全党要关心和爱护青

① 习近平：《在知识分子、劳动模范、青年代表座谈会上的讲话》，《人民日报》2016 年 4 月 26 日第 2 版。

年，为他们实现人生出彩搭建舞台。广大青年要坚定理想信念，志存高远，脚踏实地，勇做时代的弄潮儿，在实现中国梦的生动实践中放飞青春梦想，在为人民利益的不懈奋斗中书写人生华章！”① 这对青年发展提出了具体要求。首先，要聚焦青年与国家命运之间的关系。青年与国家的发展始终是同频共振的，而且青年对时代的变化也是最敏感的，青年是常新的，青年发展也是常新的。近代以来的青年发展，党成立以来的青年发展，中华人民共和国成立以来的青年发展，改革开放以来的青年发展，都是与国家、民族的命运紧密相连的。“国家好、民族好、大家才会好”②，“青年兴则国家兴，青年强则国家强”③。

其次，要培养、引导青年人“有理想、有本领、有担当”。理想决定信念，有理想就有战胜困难、挑战挫折的精神力量，就有远大的抱负和使命感。本领决定能力，有本领就有实践理想的本事，就有为人民服务，实现自身价值与国家、民族价值的能力和手段，就会实干而不空谈，努力而不退让。有担当就有大到为国家、为人民，小到具体工作、待人接物的责任感。培养青年、引导青年，让当代青年在发展中、成长中成为有理想、有本领、有担当的人，是为了让青年接过历史的接力棒，使“中华民族伟大复兴的中国梦终将在一代代青年的接力奋斗中变为现实”④。立足中国梦、青春梦，扎根新时代、新背景，为培养青年做好规划的理论和实践工作。

再次，要从“为他们实现人生出彩搭建舞台”的战略高度做好青年发展工作。让青年人生出彩是一个社会是否有希望的重要标志。青年人生不能出彩，青年就会失去对未来发展的希望。青年是最朝气蓬勃

① 习近平：《决胜全面建成小康社会夺取新时代中国特色社会主义伟大胜利——在中国共产党第十九次全国代表大会上的报告》，《光明日报》2017 年 10 月 28 日第 1 版。

② 《习近平：承前启后 继往开来 继续朝着中华民族伟大复兴目标奋勇前进》，新华网：http：//www. xinhuanet. com//politics/2012 - 11/29/c_ 113852724. htm。

③ 习近平：《决胜全面建成小康社会夺取新时代中国特色社会主义伟大胜利——在中国共产党第十九次全国代表大会上的报告》，《光明日报》2017 年 10 月 28 日第 1 版。

④ 同上。

的，也是最善于接受新事物的，青年始终是社会发展向前和变革的主要支持力量。青年人生要出彩，没有舞台，也就没有了出彩的途径。搭建舞台就是要为青年人生的出彩，青年的发展提供人人皆可成才、人人皆可尽其才的路径，这就要求我们在做青年发展工作时，要从全面深化改革的角度出发，为青年的发展做好对制度的研究，为青年实现梦想，实现命运翻转，提供理论和实践的成果，这也是青年发展的核心。“重要的是让青年人如何在浮华之风日盛的今日社会，在利益格局的篱笆日渐扎牢的今日社会，能够在忍受历史发展的巨大惯性和现实生存的压力之后，实现梦想、得到尊严。”①

党的十九大报告，为进入新时代的青年发展理论和实践研究提出新的要求和新的时代命题。习近平新时代中国特色社会主义思想，从科学的视角为进一步做好新时代的青年发展工作提供了更加全面的历史视野和发展境界，必将进一步推动当代青年发展工作，走向“强起来”的时代。

立足十九大报告对青年发展的论述，应该立足青年与国家的关系、对青年的引导与培养、为青年发展搭建人生出彩的舞台这三个方向做好青年发展的理论与实践，这三个方面与党的十八大以来习近平总书记关于青年发展的系列讲话一脉相承。青年与国家是理想与信念的问题，青年引导与发展是青年的价值观问题，为青年发展搭建人生出彩的舞台是青年的成长成才问题。其中为青年发展搭建人生出彩的舞台，聚焦青年最关心、最关注的问题，直接呼应青年在青年时期最需要的成长感和成就感，紧紧回应青年最关心最关注的问题，以人民有所呼，改革有所应的态度，推动青年发展和社会参与。“舞台”一词虽然小，但是点出了青年发展中涉及青年的一系列体制、机制问题，更是促进社会纵向流动的重要方面。“社会纵向流动性弱化，社会阶层日趋固化，是我国发展面临的重大挑战。阶层固化的社会，人们的社会地位往往由家庭背景因素决定，人们不断尝试通过自身的努力改变命运，但通道受阻会导致努

① 李春玲、马峰：《“空巢青年”：游走在“生存”与“梦想”间的群体》，《人民论坛》2017 年第 4 期。

力失败，因而产生挫败感。阶层固化还会导致阶层分裂，损害公平正义，加重社会戾气。”① 在这个领域做好青年发展的理论和实践研究是面向新时代关爱青年，为党和国家中心工作服务，提供决策参考和建议的重要方面。最重要的是要肯定人们，特别是青年人群的辛勤劳动的价值，引导更多年轻人通过勤劳致富，通过勤劳改变命运，形成有利于优秀人才和劳动力向上流动的社会环境和舆论氛围，形成多元化和多维的青年向上流动机制和发展机制。

三　统筹全局设计青年社会发展参与机制

从战略高度统筹设计青年社会发展参与机制。青年社会发展的参与机制研究，重点是在中国特色社会主义进入新时代的背景下，其更需要与新时代同频共振。按照新时代“两步走”发展战略规划，今天的青年人将全程参与国家走向基本现代化和建成社会主义现代化强国的整个过程。这个过程主要涉及“80后”“90后”和“00后”三代人，他们是当代青年的主力。涉及人群既有在农村工作的，也有在企业、科研单位和机关事业单位的，更有在新业态新经济领域就业的。面对不同的青年就业群体，不同的代际，其不同的利益诉求和发展诉求在迈向现代化进程的统一目标和大时代背景下，成为新时代青年发展的新课题。要聚焦新时代青年与时代发展的同频共振，要关注不同青年的利益诉求，要从宏观着眼，从面向2035年和2050年两个阶段的战略高度，提出前瞻性的成果，聚焦青年理想信念的宏观导向。从宏观高度实现青年的理想信念与实践和国家战略规划对接，明确基本实现现代化阶段是当代青年理想信念，特别是实现个人第一阶段发展与国家发展同步的重要衔接，明确建成社会主义现代化强国阶段是当代青年实现人生成长，实现伟大的中国梦与实现青年个人青春跳动的青春梦的重要连接。青年个人成功

① 《党的十九大报告学习辅导百问》，党建读物出版社2017年版，第143页。

之梦与中华民族伟大复兴的中国梦是紧密相连的，更是中国梦的重要组成部分。

从宏观视角设计青年社会发展参与机制，聚焦培养青年现代化事业的接班人。当代青年是实现中国梦的重要参与者和推动力量，更是这一代人的历史使命。走好新一代人的长征路，要聚焦人才培养和新时代的接班人，这不是一两个行业的问题，而是全局性、全盘性的问题。到2050年时，20世纪80年代出生的人群都已60多岁，因此，在从建党一百年到中华人民共和国成立一百年的过程中，青年人是顶梁柱，这贯穿青年生命历程和职业生涯的全部。因此，要增强研究的战略性、紧迫感，不能脱离青年、脱离实际、脱离时代。

立足新时代我国社会主要矛盾，针对性地研究青年对美好生活向往的需求问题。对美好生活的向往在青年群体中反应总是最强烈的，青年处于人生的奋斗和成长的阶段，对美好生活的向往是青年成长、进步、奋斗的动力，更是青年发展、成长的人生目标。青年求学、工作、远离故乡，从学校走向社会，从农村走向城市，从国内走向国外，从沿海走向内地，从青涩走向成熟，希望人生出彩，希望美好生活是不同时代青年人的共同底色。满足青年对美好生活向往的需求，帮助青年在新时代成长和发展，引导青年在我国发展进入新的历史方位的重大历史阶段，找准人生定位的历史方位，实现自身发展方位与国家发展方位的对接，与全体人民一起“撸起袖子加油干”①，这是这个时代推动青年社会发展参与的重点。

实现青年成长和发展美好生活需求的主要方向是人生出彩。人生出彩是青年向往美好生活奋斗的主要动力，更是其人生观价值观与国家发展相衔接，正确认识社会发展的重要基础，关键是要在影响青年成长和发展的重要阶段，为青年搭建人生出彩的“舞台”。这个舞台既是机会，也是全面深化改革，要以极大的政治勇气破除利益固化的藩篱，让

① 《国家主席习近平发表二〇一七年新年贺词》，《光明日报》2017年1月1日第1版。

青年能够出得来，动起来，促进机会公平，这对青年是最重要的。“防止社会阶层固化，关键是深化改革、促进机会公平。”① 党的十九大报告指出：“破除妨碍劳动力、人才社会性流动的体制机制弊端，使人人都有通过辛勤劳动实现自身发展的机会。”② 这句话深刻阐释了促进社会流动，破除妨碍流动的体制和机制弊端对我国社会稳定和社会发展，特别是对青年融入社会发展意义重大。让人人都有通过辛勤劳动实现自身发展的就会，这是中国特色社会主义制度的巨大制度优势，也是为改革开放四十多年来的实践所证明的发展成就。“如果说30多年前我国用‘让一部分人先富起来’激发了社会活力、促进了社会流动，那么，今天我们正在用全面深化改革来激发社会活力、促进社会流动。在全面深化改革的进程中，每一个人都有人生出彩的机会。”③

实现青年成长和发展美好生活需求的关键是就业。就业是民生之本，更是刚刚踏入社会的青年的安身立命之本。今后一段时期，我国青年发展中最大的生存需求、对美好生活需求的重点是就业。在党的十九大第五场记者招待会上，人力资源和社会保障部部长尹蔚民指出：“今后一个时期，我们就业面临着两个方面的矛盾，一方面是总量压力依然很大，在未来的三年，也就是全面建成小康社会的过程当中，城镇每年需要安排的就业人员仍然超过1500万人，总量压力很大。这1500万人大多是青年学生。高校毕业生从明年开始要突破800万人，而且在800万人以上的高位上还要持续一段时间。另外还有500万左右的中等职业学校的毕业生和技校的学生，还有一部分初中高中毕业以后不再继续升学的学生，每年需要就业的总量压力很大。”④ 要立足中国经济从数量

① 马峰：《用全面深化改革激发社会活力正确看待社会流动问题》，《人民日报》2017年7月20日第7版。

② 习近平：《决胜全面建成小康社会夺取新时代中国特色社会主义伟大胜利——在中国共产党第十九次全国代表大会上的报告》，《光明日报》2017年10月28日第1版。

③ 马峰：《用全面深化改革激发社会活力正确看待社会流动问题》，《人民日报》2017年7月20日第7版。

④ 尹蔚民：《高校毕业生从明年开始要突破800万人》，新华网：http：//news. xinhuanet. com/politics/19cpcnc/2017 - 10/22/c_ 129724609. htm。

导向型向质量导向型的转变，深入研究影响青年发展的就业问题，从就业市场的结构性矛盾入手，当前我国“劳动力就业市场‘招工难’与‘就业难’两难现象并存，产业结构与就业结构错配，‘硕士博士满街跑，高级技工难寻找’，结构性失业突出等”①。高校毕业生、青年学生对高质量就业岗位的需求，正是这个时代青年对美好生活向往的主要体现，也是当前社会主要矛盾发生变化在青年群体身上的体现，一方面我国对劳动力的需求依然比较大，另一方面高质量的就业岗位，满足知识青年需求的岗位发展还不平衡不充分，因此要立足这个新时代的现实问题，有针对性地解决好青年社会发展参与中的就业问题。社会主要矛盾的变化，使得针对我国青年社会发展参与方向要更加聚焦主要矛盾，抓住“牛鼻子”。

实现青年成长和发展美好生活需求的基础是教育。教育是阻断贫困代际传递的治本之策。党的十九大报告指出：“努力让每个孩子都能享有公平而有质量的教育。”“健全学生资助制度，使绝大多数城乡新增劳动力接受高中阶段教育、更多接受高等教育。”② 让绝大多数城乡新增劳动力接受高中阶段教育、更多接受高等教育是国家发展的重大战略，其影响极其深远。如果绝大多数新增劳动力可以接受高中教育，并且可以接受高等教育，这不但会改变我国人口素质结构，而且将极大提高我国人口的质量结构，为中国经济换挡升级，为中国社会发展换挡升级，提供源源不断的人才红利，为青年改变命运，摆脱贫困，阻断代际贫困传递，实现起点公平奠定坚实的基础。这是针对目前在校或即将踏入学校的新时期青年的重大举措，可以垫高他们面向实现现代化时代的发展平台，符合新时代发展的素质要求。教育始终是青年社会发展参与的重要方面，青年的教育要与时代同步，面向新发展阶段、面向现代化的青年社会发展参与。

---

① 《党的十九大报告学习辅导百问》，党建读物出版社 2017 年版，第 141 页。

② 习近平：《决胜全面建成小康社会夺取新时代中国特色社会主义伟大胜利——在中国共产党第十九次全国代表大会上的报告》，《光明日报》2017 年 10 月 28 日第 1 版。

立足国家治理体系和治理能力现代化，推动青年社会发展参与机制建设。“全面深化改革总目标是完善和发展中国特色社会主义制度、推进国家治理体系和治理能力现代化。”① 党的十八大以来青年发展取得了新的突破，构建了新时代青年参与社会发展的体系和机制。在国家走向强起来的时代背景下，伴随着国家走向基本实现现代化，建成社会主义现代化强国的历史征程，中国特色社会主义制度也将更加成熟、更加定型，国家治理体系和治理能力也将更加现代化。青年治理是解决青年发展问题的根本出发点和落脚点。实现青年社会发展参与治理现代化，完善青年社会发展参与治理体系和能力，是促进青年社会发展参与机制的根本出发点。青年社会发展参与的根本就是实现青年参与治理机制的现代化，并为青年有序参与社会治理服务。宏观的理想信念、中观的价值观、微观的青春奉献与成长，这些涉及青年发展的关键问题和重要环节，归根结底是青年的治理问题。满足青年对美好生活的向往，实现机会公平，促进起点公平，为青年青春出彩搭建舞台，靠的是青年社会发展参与方面治理能力的提高和治理体系的完善。

让青年有理想信念，让青年树立正确的价值观，让青年与时代发展同步，说到底就是要让青年看到发展的希望，分享到发展的成果，让青年能够有成长成才的渠道、路径，而这根本上要依靠的是国家的发展，关键是发展中的青年社会发展参与方面治理能力的提高。

青年是党和国家的宝贵财富，更是民族的未来和国家的希望。国家发展到今天就是一代代的青年人从风华正茂到耄耋之年奋斗的结果，更是一代代的青年人接过历史的接力棒奋斗的结果，在这个过程中青年成长、进步、发展，国家成长、进步、发展。青年从国家的发展中获得成功，反过来更加促进国家的进步与发展，两者始终是互动的关系。

党领导一切，党管青年工作是我们的最大特色，也是青年社会发展参与得以实现的保障。“中国特色社会主义最本质的特征是中国共产党

① 习近平：《决胜全面建成小康社会夺取新时代中国特色社会主义伟大胜利——在中国共产党第十九次全国代表大会上的报告》，《光明日报》2017年10月28日第1版。

领导，中国特色社会主义制度的最大优势是中国共产党领导，党是最高政治领导力量。”[①] 促进青年参与社会发展要立足青年成长，面向实现“两个一百年”的奋斗目标，满足青年对美好生活向往的需求，为青年人生出彩搭建舞台，形成新时代中国特色青年社会发展参与机制。

① 习近平：《决胜全面建成小康社会夺取新时代中国特色社会主义伟大胜利——在中国共产党第十九次全国代表大会上的报告》，《光明日报》2017 年 10 月 28 日第 1 版。

第二章　中国青年参与社会发展的社会组织机制及人才战略*

党的十八大以来，从国家到地方都加大了对社会组织培育扶持力度，社会组织呈蓬勃发展态势，截至2017年年底，全国共有社会组织76.2万个，比上年增长8.4%；吸纳社会各类人员就业864.7万人，比上年增长13.2%。① 社会组织发展态势良好，作为社会治理主体的作用日益明显，已成为提供基层公共服务的重要载体。任何一个行业的蓬勃发展都离不开人力资源的充分供给，社会治理领域也不例外。人才是社会组织最宝贵的资源，并且社会组织将越来越成为吸引优秀人才的重要通道。然而，事实上，当前社会组织在发展中却面临着人才供给不足、专业性缺失、流动性高等短板，本文认为人才问题的长期存在是由于社会组织的人才环境不足以满足青年的职业发展需求。而社会组织可以根据人才的需求，做出改革和探索，构建适宜的人才环境，建立一支规模宏大、结构合理、素质优良的人才队伍，这是构建与社会组织发展相适应的人才发展机制的内在要求，也是社会治理创新的重大举措。

---

* 姜宁宁博士对本章的写作做出了重要的贡献。简介如下：姜宁宁，讲师，公共管理学博士，中国社会科学院社会学博士后，现就职于中国矿业大学（北京）文法学院行政管理系。主要研究领域为合作治理理论、合作型组织。曾在《中国行政管理》《南京社会科学》《行政论坛》等CSSCI期刊发表论文，并负责、参与三项国家级课题。

① 数据来源：中华人民共和国民政部《2017年社会服务发展统计公报》。

一　社会组织参与机制及人才发展

国务院多次发文安排部署创业就业工作，其中特别强调要发挥社会力量的作用。在经济下行压力加大的背景下，社会组织已成为吸纳就业的新洼地。应当说，社会组织目前面临着既迫切地需要人才，又缺乏吸引人才的环境的矛盾。尽管我国社会组织作为新常态下解决就业问题的重要选择，社会组织人才队伍建设环境不断优化，人才总量逐年攀升，但依然面临以下几个方面的现实困境。

一是社会组织人才总量不足、人才结构不合理。虽然近年来社会中从业人员的数量在不断增长，但比起庞大的社会需求来说，其总量依然不足。在人才结构方面，则面临着专职人员偏少、行业分布不均衡、缺乏专业职称支持等问题，不能有效满足推进社会治理创新的需求。同时还存在晋升空间有限，以及薪酬水平偏低、员工认同度不高等问题。据调查，全国性社会组织中60%以上的从业人员认为其工资水平低于或远低于经济发展水平，只有30%左右的社会组织从业人员认为目前工资水平能调动工作积极性；[①] 另有调查显示，高校应届毕业生认为社会组织吸引力强的比例仅为2.26%。[②] 这些因素都成为制约社会组织发展的重要瓶颈。

二是社会组织教育相对滞后，人才培养与人才需求错位问题较为突出。近年来，社会组织教育发展较快，由高职到本科再到研究生，社会组织人才教育体系已初步形成，但与社会组织发展需要相比还相对滞后。社会组织人才培养力度不够，培训资源少，专门的社会工作人才培训教育机构较少，师资不足，导致从业人员继续教育机会减少，影响职业发展。此外，现有的社会组织教育与实务工作缺乏深层次对接，高等院校社会组织专业办学模式僵化、封闭，理论与实际脱离，人才在知识

---

① 王爱敏、董志超：《社会组织人才薪酬激励政策研究》，《第一资源》2014年第2期。

② 詹成付：《中国社会组织发展舆情报告（2014—2015）》，中国社会出版社2016年版。

结构、能力结构方面难以适应社会组织相关岗位的任职要求。

三是社会组织人才队伍建设政策贯彻难度大。近年来中央组织部、民政部等部门就社会组织人才队伍建设出台了一系列指导性政策文件，但目前还尚未建立社会组织方面的专业职称，从业人员无法在社会组织中参与职称评定，社会组织人才与党政人才、企业经营管理人才、专业技术人才队伍相比，在政策落地支持层面还存在较大差距。

总之，社会组织的人才问题实际上从各个角度反映了社会组织发展所面临的瓶颈。要解决这个问题，首先应当尊重这些新型组织的特点。应当说，自重构人际关系开始，组织结构就进入变革的过程之中。全球化和后工业化的力量将人们置于越来越有关联性的、共通的环境中去。当人们面临共同的风险时，就意味着人有共生共在的愿望，参照工业社会中人类发明的管理的方式，后工业社会中的个体行动者和集体行动者需要用合作的方式来面对新的风险，因此，这种状况要求人们尽快地用新型的组织模式取代管理型组织。一种全新的集体行动模式“合作制组织”将以其灵活性而在应对各种各样的危机事件中表现出优势。

习近平总书记指出：“新经济组织、新社会组织中的知识分子，如律师、会计师、评估师、税务师等专业人士，是改革开放以来快速成长起来的社会群体。目前看，这些人主要在党外、体制外，流动性很大，思想比较活跃，做他们的工作，一般化的方式不太管用。经了解，这些人往往根据自己的职业或兴趣加入了各种社会组织。我们要注意通过他们所在的组织了解情况、开展工作，对其中的代表人士更要重点培养，引导他们发挥积极作用。我们党历来有一个好办法，就是组织起来。新形势下，组织起来不仅要注重党政机关、企事业单位、人民团体等，而且要注重各类新经济组织、新社会组织。”① 在社会组织这种新兴的领域中去开辟符合青年人才特征的环境，创造符合青年职业发展需求的社会组织人才发展战略，成为新时期社会组织进一步壮大的重要保障。

---

① 《习近平谈统战工作：本质要求是大团结大联合》，人民网：http：//cpc. people. com. cn/xuexi/n1/2017/1122/c385476 -29660701. html。

二　青年人才对参与社会发展的社会组织机制的环境需求

从社会组织中存在的人才问题中，我们可以得知，在社会组织的实践中，青年人才的流动与岗位设置滞后之间存在矛盾、人才的纵向晋升与职业体系之间存在矛盾、青年人才的专业化需求与培训学习体系之间存在矛盾。反之，这些问题的存在也反映出社会组织在职业供给方面存在着诸多不足，而这些不足恰恰是青年选择其作为长期职业的几项重要指标。人的职业活动是非常复杂的社会活动，无论是选定一个行业、选择一种职业还是最终确定一个职位，都是由社会整体的发展状况、行业和组织的供给情况以及个人的生存发展需求来共同决定的。社会服务行业是专门修复和拓展人的社会关系或社会能力的行业，它是人对人的服务，这些职业活动不可能被机械化的管理行动或是新兴的 AI 技术所取代。所以，这种职业带来的职业满足感和职业焦虑感也是传统的生产制造行业中所没有的。对于社会服务的从业者来说，他们的选择可以被称为“自我决定论”[①]。也就是说，求职者追求“自我一致性”，要求自己追求目标的理由与自己的兴趣及核心价值观要相一致。如果他追求目标的理由是自己内在的兴趣或理想，那么他实现目标的可能性更大，即便最终没有实现目标，他们也会很高兴。因为，努力的过程本身就充满乐趣。[②] 并且，由于内在原因而追求工作目标的人对自己的工作更为满意，他们认为自己与组织更合得来，而且还能表现得更好。[③] 因此，利

---

① E. Deci and R. Ryan eds., *Handbook of Self-determination Research*, NY: University of Rochester Press, 2002.

② K. M. Sheldon, A. J. Elliot, and R. M. Ryan, “Self-concordance and Subjective Well-being in Four Cultures”, *Journal of Cross-cultural Psychology 35*, No. 2, 2004, pp. 209 – 223.

③ J. E. Bono and T. A. Judge, “Self-concordance at Work: Toward Understanding the Motivational Effects of Transformational Leaders”, *Academy of Management Journal* 46, No. 5, 2003, pp. 553 – 571.

用自我决定论来分析青年求职者对于组织和职业环境的期许，可以为社会组织人才战略提供一些基本思路。

根据对社会组织行业的调查了解，以及对以往社会工作者的基本求职情况的分析，我们可以总结出青年人才对于社会组织职业环境存在着组织管理规范和行业前景可持续的基本需求。

首先，拟进入社会组织行业的求职者通常是青年人，更重要的是他们是具有特定的社会理想和价值观的社会人。他们致力于通过艰苦卓绝的努力，实现某些社会目标，促进社会问题的解决，推动社会的发展。也就是说，求职者的道德理想和社会责任感是其求职的源动力。当然，这既是青年群体具有的主动性、创造性特征，也是社会组织的人才战略与青年发展息息相关的根源。

“人的主动性和创造性决不是人的抽象能力，不是单纯在科学学习、知识增长甚至职业训练中能够达到的，而是人的本质的外显，是治理者作为职业活动者的完整人的本质的实现。所以，在面向未来而进行社会治理体系建构的过程中，我们所要追寻的是，去建构起一个能够让社会治理者的本质得以实现的社会治理平台，要把社会治理活动转化为有益于人的本质实现的前提。”① 所以，人的社会性与道德性需求是社会组织人才战略应当率先确立的基础。

其次，求职者对于组织发展状况具有一定的需求。求职者决定在公益行业就业时，通常受到某些社会理想的驱动，对于自身的兴趣、核心价值观、职业观以及组织的目标之间的匹配度具有较高的要求。然后，在选取具体的项目和机构时，首先关注的是用人单位的薪酬、待遇，以及社会组织自身的建设，团队结构，团队的执行力和凝聚力、组织文化等。虽然大家对公益行业的薪资待遇期待较低，但这一情况在求职者入职之后却成为人才流失的最大隐患，加之当前社会组织人力资源管理水平较弱，部分社会组织每年的离职人数接近半数。通常，组织环境中的

① 张康之：《论伦理精神》，江苏人民出版社 2010 年版，第 96 页。

激励因素成为青年求职者最常考虑的因素，也是求职者对于其岗位和职业选择的基本需求之一。

从组织管理的角度来看，在当前的组织管理实践中经常出现人才供需不均衡、权责不匹配的问题。这是因为工作分析将组织岗位“颗粒化”，也就是不断分解组织的功能，分解行动者角色，导致组织对于自身行动及其成员的背叛：这种分解导致了组织无法形成合力应对环境的不确定性和复杂性，也导致了个体行动者整体角色的碎片化、权责碎片化。在复杂环境中，行动者往往需要综合的能力、复合的角色去处理复杂问题，因此，组织变革的重要战略之一就是重构人力资源的开发和利用模式，不仅要建立权责匹配的岗位，更重要的是要发挥人的主动性。发现组织中的人，在中观的组织层面就意味着要改变以往组织管理中的因岗定人，要因人定岗。原因就在于，组织是社会人的集合，发挥人的合力，因此要尊重人的社会属性和本质特征，组织的制度安排和结构设置都应该以此为出发点进行设计，把人的主动性、他在性、个人的追求、价值目标与组织的行动目标协调起来，建构总体性的行动结构。行动主义原则中的组织人力资源管理，本质上是对人的合作能力的培养与行动能力的引导。因此，在社会组织中，个体成员不仅有表达和实现个人社会价值追求的空间，也有学习知识、变革自我、建构社会网络的长期的个人发展愿景，个体的发展与组织的行动，是能够结合起来的。①

最后，基于社会服务行业的特殊性以及求职者的道德性，相比于其他成熟的行业，求职者还看中社会组织的整体发展前景、行业的发展前景，以及自身的职业发展前景等宏观的职业因素，并对于这些要素具有较高的需求，但是这些因素都与社会组织的发展状况和社会治理的发展水平密切相关。在我国，社会治理职业宏观环境由于其复杂性和丰富性，既成为青年对于社会组织职业的基本需求内容，但同时也成为社会组织行业的瓶颈式问题。

---

① 姜宁宁：《社会治理结构变迁中的社会组织角色研究》，博士学位论文，中国人民大学，2016 年。

众所周知，社会组织经历了从合法性身份的获得到自主治理者角色抗争的过程，这个过程同时也是社会治理结构经历重大变革的过程。所以，无论是政府在社会组织的管理制度方面的改革还是组织自身的内部治理结构改革，都需要建立新的理论基础和行动原点，这个基点就是组织结构的网络化、组织行动的合作化。

总之，人才问题的存在是社会组织本身和社会治理环境的双重困境造成的，由于组织管理瓶颈和行业发展瓶颈造成的“年轻人留不住、高素质人才不愿来、高技能人才引不来”① 的局面，需要从战略思维上进行整合，通过法律、公共政策、行业规则以及组织变革等多种途径来解决。

三　构建符合青年参与社会发展需求的社会组织机制及人才战略

以社会组织为主体的第三产业还是一个比较新兴的领域，社会服务也是新兴的行业，整体来看人才储备状况比较薄弱。所以，社会组织的人才构成以不断涌入和流出的青年为主体。社会组织显然正在为新的就业创业模式做出贡献。我们应当从尊重组织任务的临时性和流动性方面去探索新的组织管理模式和职业发展路径，以支持社会组织人才战略的建构。“青年人是社会上最富活力、最具创造性的群体，理所当然应该走在创新创造的前列，做锐意进取、开拓创新的时代先锋。”② 所以，最大限度地配置青年人才资源、做好激励青年的工作，鼓励青年为国家治理和社会治理贡献更多的智慧与能量，需要国家的宏观政策和社会组织主动做出如下探索。

① 马树梅：《中国社会组织人才供需指数及专业人才需求趋势分析研究》，中国社会组织公共服务平台“中国社会组织建设与管理理论研究课题成果 2016 年”：http：//www. chinanpo. gov. cn/700106/newswjindex. html。

② 习近平：《在同各界优秀青年代表座谈时的讲话》，《光明日报》2013 年 5 月 5 日第 2 版。

（一）开辟社会组织青年人才的渠道，建立人才储备库

一个行业的发展需要源源不断的人才供给，而社会治理领域是一个复杂领域，探索多元的人才渠道，建立丰富的人才储备库是夯实社会服务行业基础，促进社会组织可持续发展的最根本措施。比如说挖掘在公共卫生、国际关系、医疗、社会工作、工程、政治科学和传媒等领域深造的人才；培养高度专业化、经过训练等持相关专业证书的专业人员（社会工作者）；鼓励曾经在政府部门或企业界具有较高声誉、较大影响力的人群参与社会事务；发掘掌握多种语言，拥有广泛游历经历，在国外学习、生活和工作过的人，在特定事件所处地区或环境工作过，对其特点及事件影响力有充分了解的人参与社会服务；培养主动性和参与感强、常常参加志愿活动、对特定服务人群及相关组织有极强奉献精神的人从事更加专业的社会治理事务。

在筹建人才库的基础上，加大对社会组织人才统计工作的力度，各级登记管理机关应依据社会组织人才资源统计指标体系，将社会组织人才统计工作纳入新的《全国社会组织中长期人才发展规划纲要》之中，建立社会组织人才资源的预测、跟踪监测体系，掌握社会组织人才的基本数据，做好人才需要预测体系。

（二）建立具有复合专业能力的人才体系，探索青年人才培养方案

社会组织的专业人才培养是个系统工程，既需要传统的专业学历教育，也需要完善丰富的职业培训，还需要建立符合人才成长规律的职称体系。

学历教育的周期较长、系统性强，对于夯实社会组织人才的知识基础，培养专业素养具有基础性作用。王名建议，通过修订与完善国务院学位委员会、教育部制定的《学位授予和人才培养学科目录》，在我国高等学校本科教育专业设置中的“管理学”门类一级学科“公共管理”下设立二级专业目录“社会组织管理”，逐步建立社会组织专业的高

职、本科、硕士、博士等不同层次的人才培养体系。完善以能力培养为本位，以专业教学为基础，以工作过程为主导的“岗—课—证”相融通的项目化课程体系。[①]

在学历教育的基础上，丰富职业培训也是社会组织人才培养的必然要求。“职业教育是国民教育体系和人力资源开发的重要组成部分，是广大青年打开通往成功成才大门的重要途径，肩负着培养多样化人才、传承技术技能、促进就业创业的重要职责，必须高度重视、加快发展。”[②] 职业培训的周期较短，时效性强、实践性强。职业培训可以满足已经踏入社会组织实践领域的从业者的需求。职业培训是对专业学历教育的补充，是将理论知识转化为实践智慧的重要方式，同时也是提升社会组织人才专业化程度和实践能力的重要方式。在职业培训体系中，应当注重不同机构、不同行业、不同岗位之间的交流与了解程度，从根本上增强专业人才的综合能力，这包括理论的能力和实践的能力。“要牢牢把握服务发展、促进就业的办学方向，深化体制机制改革，创新各层次各类型职业教育模式，坚持产教融合、校企合作，坚持工学结合、知行合一，引导社会各界特别是行业企业积极支持职业教育，努力建设中国特色职业教育体系。”[③]

另外，健全社会组织职业资格认证体系，推进持证上岗和职称评定等工作。进一步规范与明确社会组织专职人员岗位设置、建立社会组织职业制度、健全社会组织人才继续教育制度，实现专业人才培养与职业资格的衔接。[④]

总之，通过探索理论与实践并轨的培养模式，建立符合复杂社会治理事务需求的具有综合能力的青年人才体系，这样才能将潜在的人力资

---

① 王名：《建立健全社会组织人才培养体系》，《政协第十二届全国委员会第二次会议提案》，2014 年 3 月 3 日。

② 《习近平就加快发展职业教育作出的指示》，《人民日报》2014 年 6 月 24 日第 1 版。

③ 同上。

④ 王名：《建立健全社会组织人才培养体系》，《政协第十二届全国委员会第二次会议提案》2014 年 3 月 3 日。

源转化为人才，并真正发挥社会治理的作用。同样，良好的人才培养体系也将为青年的发展提供保障，吸引更多青年人才加入社会组织的行业中来。

（三）探索社会组织合作机制，建立符合人才流动规律的职业发展平台

社会治理的事务庞杂而广泛，因此社会组织也随之深入各个社会领域中，而社会组织的人才体系包容性则更大、流动性也更强。假如公共领域是一个“市场”，那么社会组织就是其中的生产性组织，它的资源、产品需求以及生产成本来源于社会，产品供社会消费、“盈利”所得的社会资本供社会部门从事再生产。社会组织内部将以不同的服务领域为范围形成一定的行业体系和行业规则，要建立公益共同体，需要不同行业的支持和相对成熟的社会发展状态。

迈克尔·波特的价值链理论指出：企业的全部生产活动，包括设计、生产、销售、发送等活动集合在一起，就是一条价值链，企业的竞争力的强弱取决于组织内部价值链的完善程度，因此，价值链的存在是为企业组织的效率和竞争力服务的。但这其中蕴含了另一种隐喻：组织行动系统的行动、观念和价值连续性的重要意义，实际上包含着合作的理念。社会组织所处的社会服务行业同样是一个巨大的价值链，其中每个组织、每个个人都在为该行业最终的价值产出做出贡献。虽然在行业价值链中存在着同类主体间的竞争，但行业链为组织和个人的发展提供了支持性的条件，因此，组织具有良好的环境可以专注于服务，进行良性的竞争，创造社会资源。例如，在公益行业，公益价值链包括金融、实业、研发以及咨询。如果价值链足够通畅，那么，社会组织的人力资源将摆脱晋升途径之困。

基于价值链，社会组织的人才战略应当注重对平台的运用，比如说建立行业共同体、职业共同体、专业共同体等，探索促进人才交换、流动的机制，促进人才的复合化、专业化，拓展晋升空间。不仅要建立组

织内的流动机制，还要建立行业间的、跨行业的职业资质认证、岗位流动机制、完善的人力资源流动机制等。实现人才的流动，也就实现了资源的流动。具体而言，要实现同能力等级组织成员的水平流动，实现人力资源的垂直流动。我国公务员制度中采用的借调、挂职等方式，其思路也许可作为社会组织人力资源流动体系的参考。

四　让社会组织成为青年参与社会发展“流动的广阔平台”

当今时代，随着全球化、后工业化进程的加速，跨界带来的行业边界模糊等一系列挑战，使得各类组织的生存和发展都面临着诸多掣肘因素。在这种艰难的背后，存在一个本质性的问题：组织的绩效不再由内部的因素约定，而是由围绕在组织外部的因素决定，比如环境的不确定性、合作伙伴、跨界的对手、全新的技术等。社会组织尤其如此，就其在社会治理中越来越重要的角色来看，它需要对情境因素有更好的把握、整合更多的资源。当然，从管理的角度来看，社会组织是一种新型的合作制组织，它具有任务型、扁平化、灵活性、合作性等特征，在新的组织格局中，组织需要每个成员突破自己固有的优势和行为习惯、拥有开放学习的心态和行动、展开信息共享以及培训学习。并且，在合作制的组织中，领导是引导者，以“无我”打造组织大系统的协同价值环境，并为每一个组织成员赋能。所以，社会组织能够成为各类社会资源汇聚的平台，也具有建立人才流动平台的天然禀赋。这就需要研究者和实践者充分理解新时代的特征、把握社会组织的新属性、把握新时代青年的职业需求，并将这些因素综合考虑，做好社会组织行业发展的规划，统筹设计符合各方特征与需求的社会组织人才战略。

第三章　中国青年参与社会发展的趋势变化

一　青年成长、社会发展与时代发展同步

从中华人民共和国成立之初的“一穷二白”到中国 GDP 总量跃居世界第二位，我国经济社会发展不断取得新成就，这为青年发展事业奠定了坚实的物质基础和发展的前提，青年事业的发展与国家进步同频共振，与人民生活条件不断改善、物质生活水平提高同频共振。1949 年，城镇居民家庭人均现金收入不足 100 元，农村居民人均纯收入仅为 44 元。1978 年，城镇居民人均可支配收入达到 343 元，农村居民人均纯收入达到 134 元，分别比 1949 年名义增长 2.4 倍和 2.0 倍，年均增长 4.3% 和 3.9%。[①] 2018 年，城镇居民人均可支配收入 39251 元，农村

表 3 - 1　中华人民共和国成立七十年主要时间节点居民收入变化

年份	城镇居民	农村居民
1949	人均现金收入不足 100 元	人均纯收入仅为 44 元
1978	人均可支配收入达到 343 元	人均纯收入达到 134 元
2018	人均可支配收入 39251 元	人均可支配收入 14617 元

数据来源：国家统计局。

① 中华人民共和国国家统计局编：《新中国六十五年》，中国统计出版社 2014 年版，第 112 页。

居民人均可支配收入 14617 元。①

随着国家总体经济实力的增长和人民物质生活水平的提高，青年发展事业，特别是针对青年个人的成长发展和人生规划，也使很多不可能变成了可能，使很多看似不可能实现的青年发展梦想，变成了很多普通家庭的青年也可以享受到的发展机会，这跟居民收入的增加，国家的开放进步有着密切的、直接的，甚至是根本的关系。例如：从出国留学人员和学成回国留学人员情况来看，中华人民共和国成立之初，从 1950 年开始有统计的出国留学人员是 35 人，从 1953 年开始有统计的学成回国留学人员是 16 人。1978 年之前，出国留学人员最多的年份是 1956 年，为 2401 人。② 在国家建设起步的发展阶段，出国留学更多的是公派，在人均收入很低，甚至没有达到温饱的情况下，自费出国留学对亿万中国青年来说是不现实的。十一届三中全会后，随着国家的发展，人民生活水平的提高，特别是国家放开自费留学后，除了国家公派的途径外，出国留学也可以成为很多普通青年人的自主选择，让诗和远方成为青年求知、发展梦想的可能。截止到 2017 年，我国出国留学人员 608400 人，学成回国留学人员 480900 人，创历史新高。③

表 3－2　**改革开放以来留学生人数统计④**　单位/人

年份	出国留学人员	学成回国留学人员
1978	860	248
1979	1777	231
1980	2124	162

① 《中华人民共和国 2018 年国民经济和社会发展统计公报》，国家统计局：http：//www.stats.gov.cn/tjsj/zxfb/201902/t20190228_1651265.html。

② 中华人民共和国国家统计局编：《新中国六十五年》，中国统计出版社 2014 年版，第 292 页。

③ 《改革开放 40 年》编写组编：《改革开放 40 年》，中国统计出版社 2018 年版，第 438 页。

④ 同上。

续表

年份	出国留学人员	学成回国留学人员
1981	2922	1143
1982	2326	2116
1983	2633	2303
1984	3073	2290
1985	4888	1424
1986	4676	1388
1987	4703	1605
1988	3786	3000
1989	3329	1756
1990	2950	1593
1991	2900	2069
1992	6540	3611
1993	10742	5128
1994	19071	4230
1995	20381	5750
1996	20905	6570
1997	22410	7130
1998	17622	7379
1999	23749	7748
2000	38989	9121
2001	83973	12243
2002	125179	17945
2003	117307	20152
2004	114682	24726
2005	118515	34987
2006	134000	42000
2007	144000	44000
2008	179800	69300

续表

年份	出国留学人员	学成回国留学人员
2009	229300	108300
2010	284700	134800
2011	339700	186200
2012	399600	272900
2013	413900	353500
2014	459800	364800
2015	523700	409100
2016	544500	432500
2017	608400	480900

数据来源：国家统计局。

尽管目前能够出国留学的青年人数创历史新高，但是我们依然要看到出国留学的青年人数相对于我国庞大的青年群体依然是较少的，人生有很多选择，青年不一定要靠出国留学才能实现诗和远方。新时代的"追梦人"在越来越开放、越来越走向世界的国家发展大潮中，与时代共进步，与国家共发展，以更加自信的态度走向世界，以更加理性的思维思考中国在世界发展大潮中的作用和意义，在时代发展的大潮中勇立潮头，在国际交流与交往的进程中更加落落大方，更加挥洒自如。近年来，我国出境旅游人数持续增长，青年是其中的主力。1995 年至 2016 年，随着人民生活水平的改善，我国出境旅游支出也大幅提高。1995 年我国出境旅游支出居世界第 25 位，2000 年上升到世界第 8 位，2013 年居世界第 2 位，2014—2015 年稳居世界第 1 位。2016 年，我国出境旅游支出额为 2611 亿美元，比 1995 年的 37 亿美元，提高了 2574 亿美元，增长 69. 6 倍。①

中国青年随着国家的进步而走出去，有的成为中外交往的佳话，更

① 《改革开放 40 年》编写组编：《改革开放 40 年》，中国统计出版社 2018 年版，第 69—70 页。

有的构成了中外交往的中国故事，中国青年的故事。2013 年习近平主席访问非洲，在坦桑尼亚尼雷尔会议中心发表的题为“永远做可靠朋友和真诚伙伴”演讲中，习近平总书记讲述了亲如一家的中非青年故事：“我听说了一个故事，有一对中国年轻人，他们从小就通过电视节目认识了非洲，对非洲充满了向往。后来他们结婚了，把蜜月旅行目的地选在了坦桑尼亚。在婚后的第一个情人节，他们背上行囊来到了坦桑尼亚，领略了这里的风土人情和塞伦盖蒂草原的壮美。回国后，他们把在坦桑尼亚的所见所闻发布在博客上，得到了数万次的点击和数百条回复。他们说，我们真的爱上了非洲，我们的心从此再也离不开这片神奇的土地。这个故事说明，中非人民有着天然的亲近感，只要不断加强人民之间的交流，中非人民友谊就一定能根深叶茂。”①

习近平总书记讲述的这个中国青年故事，所折射的是中国青年在国家发展与国际交流中不断书写的国家好、民族好、大家才会好的真实情景。青年需要发展、需要进步，但前提是国家的发展与进步。青年在发展的机遇面前需要技能的培训，在发展的挑战面前需要良好的教育，在发展的前途与人生的抉择面前需要以梦想为支撑，在发展的爬坡中需要看到发展的前途，而这些与发展的同频共振是青年所需要的。青年不缺少梦想，不缺少理想，不缺少奋斗的精神，缺少的是人生出彩的舞台。这舞台是经济的增长，这舞台是安定的社会，这舞台是公平的环境，这舞台是良好的教育，这舞台是谋生的技能，这舞台是发展的希望。青年发展是当今时代绕不过去的主题，为青年发展厚植动力，促进青年就业是青年立足于社会的基本前提。让青年看到希望，社会才有希望，让青年拥有未来，社会才有前途。

少年强则国强，其实质点出的是青年有发展的动力，社会就有发展的活力，经济就有发展的能量，国家就会在“众行远”中奔腾向前。中华人民共和国成立七十多年，改革开放四十多年来，中国青年事业的

---

① 习近平：《永远做可靠朋友和真诚伙伴——在坦桑尼亚尼雷尔国际会议中心的演讲》，《光明日报》2013 年 3 月 26 日第 2 版。

发展与国家发展同频共振，国家发展的无限可能，给中国青年发展提供了无限的可能，给民族复兴提供了无限的可能。

在2019年的新年致辞中，习近平总书记讲道："我注意到，今年，恢复高考后的第一批大学生大多已经退休，大批'00后'进入高校校园。"① 从"两弹一星"功勋奖章获得者那一代青年人，到今天恢复高考后第一批大多已经退休的大学生，再到大批进入高校校园的"00后"，中华人民共和国七十多年来代代青年，薪火相传，将中国特色社会主义事业不断传承、发展下去。中国特色社会主义进入新时代，为今天的青年人奋斗人生，奋斗未来开辟了更广阔的发展未来。"近代以来我国历史告诉我们，只有社会主义才能救中国，只有中国特色社会主义才能发展中国，才能实现中华民族伟大复兴。坚持好、发展好中国特色社会主义，把我国建设成社会主义现代化强国，是一项长期任务，需要一代又一代人接续奋斗。我们的今天就是这样走过来的，我们的明天需要青年人接着奋斗下去，一代接着一代不断前进。"②

二　健康：青年参与社会发展的基础与前提

党的十九大报告明确提出实施健康中国战略。"人民健康是民族昌盛和国家富强的重要标志。"③ 青年是国家的希望和民族的未来，青年健康是青年成长、成才的根本前提和基础。中华人民共和国成立七十多年来，伴随着国家经济成长和进步，我国医疗事业取得了显著的进步，人民健康水平显著提高，从吃饱穿暖到快乐健康生活实现了历史性转变，生活要小康，全民要健康的理念深入人心。我国居民平均预期寿命1949年前为35岁，改革开放之初的1978年为68.2岁，到2017年为

① 《国家主席习近平发表二〇一九年新年贺词》，《光明日报》2019年1月1日第1版。

② 习近平：《在北京大学师生座谈会上的讲话》，《光明日报》2018年5月3日第2版。

③ 习近平：《决胜全面建成小康社会夺取新时代中国特色社会主义伟大胜利——在中国共产党第十九次全国代表大会上的报告》，《光明日报》2017年10月28日第1版。

76.7 岁，较 1949 年前增加了 41.7 岁；婴儿死亡率由 1949 年前的 200‰下降到 2013 年的 9.5‰，2017 年的 6.8‰；孕妇死亡率由 1949 年前的 150/10 万下降 1989 年的 94.7/10 万，再到 2010 年的 23.2/10 万，截止到 2017 年下降到 19.6/10 万。[①] 青年健康水平的显著提高为国家的经济社会发展提供了重要的人力资源，为改革开放四十年来人口红利的持续发挥和释放提供了重要前提和基础。

医疗事业的发展为我国人民健康、青年健康提供了重要的保障。除此以外，全面健康事业也取得历史性的发展成就，健康中国战略深入推进。目前，我国各类体育场地已超过 100 多万个，是中华人民共和国成立初期的 240 倍以上。2010 年，全国达到《国民体质测定标准》"合格"以上标准的人数比例为 88.9%。[②] 而且，2017 年全年共有 1113 万人次享受了生育保险待遇，首次突破 1000 万人次，比 2012 年增加 760 万人次，年均增长 25.8%。2017 年生育保险人均待遇水平为 18126 元，比 2012 年增加 6839 元，年均增长 9.9%。[③] 在竞技体育方面，1949 年到 2013 年，我国运动员共获得世界冠军 2902 个，其中 1978 年到 2013 年共获得世界冠军 2876 个，占中华人民共和国成立以来总数的 99.1%。[④] 自 2014 年到 2017 年，我国又获得世界冠军 438 个。自 1978 年到 2017 年，我国累计获得世界冠军 3314 个。[⑤] 体育产业从无到有，并发展壮大，青年体育发展事业取得丰硕成果。根据《2018 年全国时间利用调查公报》显示："居民健身锻炼的平均时间为 31 分钟，其中城镇居民 41 分钟，农村居民 16 分钟。按 10 岁为组距分组，75—84 岁居民健身锻炼的平均时间

① 中华人民共和国国家统计局编：《新中国六十五年》，中国统计出版社 2014 年版，第 157 页；《改革开放 40 年》编写组编：《改革开放 40 年》，中国统计出版社 2018 年版，第 250 页。

② 中华人民共和国国家统计局编：《新中国六十五年》，中国统计出版社 2014 年版，第 159 页。

③ 《改革开放 40 年》编写组编：《改革开放 40 年》，中国统计出版社 2018 年版，第 288 页。

④ 中华人民共和国国家统计局编：《新中国六十五年》，中国统计出版社 2014 年版，第 159 页。

⑤ 《改革开放 40 年》编写组编：《改革开放 40 年》，中国统计出版社 2018 年版，第 444 页。

最长，为 64 分钟；25—34 岁居民时间最短，为 14 分钟。居民健身锻炼的参与率为 30. 9% ，其中城镇居民 38. 7% ，农村居民 18. 7% 。”①

从站起来、富起来到强起来，百年来青年发展事业在奋斗中前行。国家关注青年发展，家庭关注孩子成长。从健康、锻炼为了救国救民，到健康与全面小康，国民素质的提高，折射的是百年来中国发展方位的历史性变革。各行各业的青年，以健康的心态，健康的身姿，健康、阳光的面貌，健康的生活，健康的行为融入国家建设、民族复兴的伟大征程中。今天，健康的中国青年，在国家健康事业的保障和推动下，不但艰苦训练永争上游，力夺世界冠军，为国争光，而且扎根边疆、山村、荒野、隔壁，有的远赴国外在艰苦战乱地区维护世界和平。他们以良好的中国青年形象，诠释中国国家形象。人均预期寿命的大幅提高，孕妇死亡率的大幅降低是中华人民共和国健康事业发展的最好证明。一代代的青年，接过历史的接力棒，砥砺奋进，在“健康”中，见证中国青年发展事业健康发展。

三　教育、就业：青年参与社会发展的“起点公平”与“机会公平”

教育和就业是青年发展事业的重要指标，更是青年“追梦”和“圆梦”的重要前提和路径。中华人民共和国成立以来，我国教育事业、就业发展取得了巨大成就，多彩的青春，在多彩的中国，织就出多彩的梦想，汇聚成青春的中国梦。习近平总书记指出：“广大青年既是追梦者，也是圆梦人。追梦需要激情和理想，圆梦需要奋斗和奉献。广大青年应该在奋斗中释放青春激情、追逐青春理想，以青春之我、奋斗之我，为民族复兴铺路架桥，为祖国建设添砖加瓦。”②

中华人民共和国成立之初，全国 80% 的人口是文盲，农村的文盲率

---

① 《2018 年全国时间利用调查公报》，国家统计局：http：//www. stats. gov. cn/tjsj/zxfb/201901/t20190125_ 1646796. html。

② 习近平：《在北京大学师生座谈会上的讲话》，《光明日报》2018 年 5 月 3 日第 2 版。

高达95%，适龄儿童入学率不足20%，中华人民共和国成立后特别是改革开放以来，我国实现了由文盲大国向人力资源大国的转变，人口受教育水平不断提高。1982年，我国15岁及以上的人口平均受教育年限为5.3年，2013年达到9.3年，劳动年龄人口的平均受教育年限达到9.3年。[①] 2016年我国劳动年龄人口人均受教育年限达到10.35年，2017年新增劳动力平均受教育年限达到13.25年，接受过高等教育的比例超过45%，[②] 截止到2018年年底，我国高中阶段毛入学率为88.8%。[③]

在中华人民共和国成立七十年取得的巨大发展成就基础上，坚持以人民为中心的发展思想，本着发展为了人民，发展的成果由人民共享，聚焦青年发展事业的长远未来，党的十九大报告提出普及高中阶段教育。健全学生资助制度，使绝大多数城乡新增劳动力接受高中阶段教育、接受更多高等教育。[④] 李克强总理在十三届人大二次会议上所做的政府工作报告中提及要推进高中阶段教育普及。[⑤]

教育事业的发展，特别是高中阶段教育、高等教育、职业教育的发展为青年的发展夯实了“追梦”的基础，有力地促进了机会的公平和发展的公平。教育是社会公平的底线，像阳光、空气一样，是最普惠的公共产品，提供这一公共产品是政府义不容辞的责任。《中长期青年发展规划（2016—2025年）》提出，力争到2025年，青年受教育权利得到更好保障，基本公共教育服务均等化逐步实现，教育公平程度明显提升。新增劳动力平均受教育年限达到13.5年以上，高等教育毛入学率达到50%以上。[⑥] 这必将为青年发展提供更公平的发展环境，更优越的发展基础，

---

① 中华人民共和国国家统计局编：《新中国六十五年》，中国统计出版社2014年版，第131页。

② 《改革开放40年》编写组编：《改革开放40年》，中国统计出版社2018年版，第274页。

③ 《中华人民共和国2018年国民经济和社会发展统计公报》，国家统计局：http://www.stats.gov.cn/tjsj/zxfb/201902/t20190228_1651265.html。

④ 习近平：《决胜全面建成小康社会夺取新时代中国特色社会主义伟大胜利——在中国共产党第十九次全国代表大会上的报告》，《光明日报》2017年10月28日第1版。

⑤ 李克强：《政府工作报告——2019年3月5日在第十三届全国人民代表大会第二次会议上》，《光明日报》2019年3月17日第1版。

⑥ 《中长期青年发展规划（2016—2025年）》，中国政府网：http://www.gov.cn/zhengce/2017-04/13/content_5185555.htm#1。

为2035年基本实现现代化提供更加可持续、稳定的人才供给。

在就业层面，就业多元化、个性化是时代发展最显著的特征，也昭示着青年就业的巨大进步。中华人民共和国成立初期到改革开放前，我国城镇就业经历了由快速增长到徘徊不前的状态。1949年年末，全国城镇就业人员为1533万人，474.2万人失业，失业率为23.6%。1978年年末，全国就业人员增加到40152万人，其中城镇就业人员9514万人。[①] 2017年年末，就业人员总量达到77640万人，比1978年增加32948万人，增长了346%，平均每年增长845万人。[②] 截止到2018年年末，全国就业人员77586万人，其中城镇就业人员43419万人。[③]

就业是民生之本，促进就业始终是党中央、国务院工作的重中之重，青年就业被摆在重要的位置。"我们的劳动力资源近9亿人，就业人员7亿多，受过高等教育和职业教育的高素质人才有1.7亿，每年大学毕业生有800多万。"[④] 这些为我国的长远发展提供了可靠的保障。

此外，教育事业与青年就业实现了联动发展，极大地改善了就业人群，特别是青年群体的结构，为我国劳动力市场的发展提供了大量的高素质人才和劳动力，大量留学人员回国也进一步提升了就业人员素质。从1982年到2017年，我国大专及以上文化程度者所占比重由0.9%上升到19.5%；小学及以下文化程度的比重由62.6%下降到19.2%。1978—2017年，已有313.2万留学人员选择回国发展，占已完成学业留学群体的83.73%。[⑤]

在从高速增长阶段向高质量增长阶段迈进的过程中，我们始终把就

---

① 中华人民共和国国家统计局编：《新中国六十五年》，中国统计出版社2014年版，第107页。

② 《改革开放40年》编写组编：《改革开放40年》，中国统计出版社2018年版，第200页。

③ 《中华人民共和国2018年国民经济和社会发展统计公报》，国家统计局：http：//www.stats.gov.cn/tjsj/zxfb/201902/t20190228_ 1651265.html。

④ 《国新办举行2018年国民经济运行情况发布会》，国新网：http：//www.scio.gov.cn/xwfbh/xwbfbh/wqfbh/39595/39709/index.htm。

⑤ 《就业总量持续增长就业结构调整优化——改革开放40年经济社会发展成就系列报告之十四》，国家统计局：http：//www.stats.gov.cn/ztjc/ztfx/ggkf40n/201809/t20180912_ 1622409.html。

业列为优先发展战略，实施积极的就业政策，并且把就业与货币、财政共同列为宏观政策，在经济下行压力大的情况下，能够更好地促进“稳就业”。2019 年 1—2 月，全国城镇调查失业率分别为 5.1%、5.3%，低于 5.5% 左右的预期目标，据人力资源和社会保障部数据，1—2月份城镇新增就业 174 万人。① 当前，我国就业形势总体稳定，就业质量稳步提高。但是在发展的过程中，我国就业还面临结构性的矛盾，就业难、招工难并存的结构性矛盾更加突出，部分高校毕业生面临就业难，另一方面企业急需的技术人才短缺现象严重，无论是沿海还是中西部地区，部分企业都发生了技工、熟练工和新型人才短缺的现象，据人力资源和社会保障部数据，近年来技能劳动者求人倍率一直在 1.5 以上，高级技工求人倍率甚至在 2.0 以上。② 这就需要我们加大政策调整力度，立足经济发展的阶段性特征和长期性战略目标，深入推进“稳就业”政策，将青年就业，特别是破解青年就业的结构性问题列为重要的优先政策选项，扩大就业政策与教育政策的联动，推进就业供给侧结构性改革。

中华人民共和国成立七十多年，改革开放四十多年为我们推进就业供给侧结构性改革，加大就业与教育联动牵引，发挥教育、培训促进就业，改善就业人员素质、技能奠定了坚实的物质基础、发展基础。2019 年，实施职业技能提升行动，从失业保险基金结余中拿出 1000 亿元，用于 1500 万人次以上的职工技能提升和转岗转业培训。同时，改革完善高职院校考试招生办法，鼓励更多应届高中毕业生和退役军人、下岗职工、农民工等报考，今年大规模扩招 100 万人。“我们要以现代职业教育的大改革大发展，加快培养国家发展急需的各类技术技能人才，让更多青年凭借一技之长实现人生价值，让三百六十行人才荟萃、繁星璀璨。”③

---

① 李希如：《就业形势总体稳定　结构性矛盾需要关注》，国家统计局：http：//www.stats.gov.cn/tjsj/sjjd/201903/t20190314_1653894.html。

② 同上。

③ 李克强：《政府工作报告——二〇一九年三月五日在第十三届全国人民代表大会第二次会议上》，《光明日报》2019 年 3 月 17 日第 1 版。

可以说，从“文盲大国”到人力资源大国，从就业为了解决温饱，到高质量就业，到教育与就业联动发展，破解就业结构性矛盾，中华人民共和国七十多年青年教育与就业始终相伴而行，在“追梦”与“圆梦”中稳定发展。党的十九大报告指出：“提供全方位公共就业服务，促进高校毕业生等青年群体、农民工多渠道就业创业。破除妨碍劳动力、人才社会性流动的体制机制弊端，使人人都有通过辛勤劳动实现自身发展的机会。”①

教育和就业是引导青年参与社会发展的重要形式和路径，也是青年社会化完成的重要阶段。促进教育事业发展，根本是为民族的长远发展储存最本质的不竭动力。促进就业发展，不断改善就业环境，为青年发展提供进身之阶，发展之梯，根本是为国家的长远发展蓄积磅礴之力。从人口红利的持续发挥，到人才红利的不断蓄积，我国青年的素质结构发生了历史性的变化。进一步推进全面深化改革，按照党的十九大做出的战略部署，破除妨碍劳动力、人才社会性流动的体制机制弊端，必将开辟新时代青年事业发展的崭新未来，让青年在“追梦”中，不断“圆梦”，在“圆梦”中，不断缔造中国发展新的奇迹。追人生发展之梦，圆人生发展之梦，归根结底是追民族复兴之梦，圆民族复兴之梦。“一个流动的中国，充满了繁荣发展的活力。我们都在努力奔跑，我们都是追梦人。”②

---

① 习近平：《决胜全面建成小康社会夺取新时代中国特色社会主义伟大胜利——在中国共产党第十九次全国代表大会上的报告》，《光明日报》2017 年 10 月 28 日第 1 版。

② 《国家主席习近平发表二〇一九年新年贺词》，《光明日报》2019 年 1 月 1 日第 1 版。

第四章　百年变迁："五四"精神激励中国青年在新时代民族复兴中追梦前行

一　青年是国家的未来、民族的希望

习近平总书记在党的十九大报告中精辟地指出："青年兴则国家兴，青年强则国家强。青年一代有理想、有本领、有担当，国家就有前途，民族就有希望。中国梦是历史的、现实的，也是未来的；是我们这一代的，更是青年一代的。"①

青年是国家的未来和民族的希望，近代百年来，中国青年融入历史发展大潮，融入国家命运、民族发展希望之中。百年发展历程，中国青年投身于党领导的人民事业、民族复兴事业，投身民族解放、抵御外辱、"两弹一星"奋斗、改革开放奋进的每一个历史阶段，书写了青春中国奋斗的每一个历史瞬间。面向下一个30年，到2035年基本实现现代化，到2050年建成社会主义现代化强国，新时代的青年人，要接过民族复兴的历史接力棒，跑出一个好未来。

当前，世界正经历百年未有之大变局，百年历史犹如沧海一粟，但是百年来中国青年为国家、民族、人民的伟大奋斗历程，却在五千年的中华民族历史发展进程中占据重要的地位。"五四"运动是中国青年、

---

① 习近平：《决胜全面建成小康社会夺取新时代中国特色社会主义伟大胜利——在中国共产党第十九次全国代表大会上的报告》，《光明日报》2017年10月28日第1版。

中国社会、中国人民伟大觉醒的开始。"五四"运动是鲜活的，为"五四"奋斗的青年是鲜活的，奋斗于"五四"的青春是鲜活的，百年来未曾改变。因为，为人民谋幸福、为民族谋复兴是一代代中国青年不变的初心，无悔的青春底色。

百年前的中国青年，投身民族复兴、拯救民族危亡是人生唯一的选择，"为中华之崛起而读书"激励了一代青年人砥砺奋斗于"站起来"的时刻；"团结起来振兴中华"成为"富起来"时代青年发展最深刻的烙印，感染了一代青年人争做八十年的新一辈；我们都是"追梦人"成为"强起来"时代青年发展最本真的底色，鼓励一代青年人，接过历史的接力棒，勇立潮头，踏浪前行，砥砺奋斗在追梦路上。百年前，百年后，党的领导，与时代同行，与人民同行，与民族同行，是中国青年奋斗的不变底色，是最亮丽的青春之色。

习近平总书记指出："新时代中国青年要勇做走在时代前列的奋进者、开拓者、奉献者，毫不畏惧面对一切艰难险阻，在劈波斩浪中开拓前进，在披荆斩棘中开辟天地，在攻坚克难中创造业绩，用青春和汗水创造出让世界刮目相看的新奇迹！"①

二　奋斗是青春最亮丽的底色

无奋斗，不青春！青春的代名词是奋斗。没有奋斗的青春是不完整的人生。习近平总书记指出："今天，我们的生活条件好了，但奋斗精神一点都不能少，中国青年永久奋斗的好传统一点都不能丢。"②

时代发展不同，青年的追求和价值观也时刻发生着巨大的变化，但奋斗的青春是中国青年不变的底色，是奋斗的中国最亮丽的色彩。从革命战争年代，到社会主义革命和建设时期，再到改革开放历史新时期，

---

① 习近平：《在纪念五四运动100周年大会上的讲话》，《光明日报》2019年5月1日第2版。

② 同上。

青年在民族振兴中奋斗前行，广大青年响应党的号召，投身到祖国建设的各行各业、方方面面，用实际行动践行团结起来振兴中华的时代强音。

从“两弹一星”功勋奖章获得者那一代青年人，到今天恢复高考后第一批大多已经退休的大学生，再到大批进入高校校园的“00后”，中国青年薪火相传，将中国特色社会主义事业不断传承、发展下去。中国特色社会主义进入新时代，为今天的青年人奋斗人生，奋斗未来开辟了更广阔的发展空间。

更具个性，更加自我，更强调参与性、主动性成为这个时代青年发展的显著特征。同时，工作、家庭、婚恋、育儿、养老的压力，也让当代青年承受着事业上升和发展的压力，其人生观、世界观、价值观的波动也十分明显。每一代青年都有每一代青年的奋斗群像，每一代青年都有每一代青年不同成长、发展的时代背景和时空背景。但是积极向上、阳光进取、奉献友爱的中国青年奋斗群像如夜空中最亮的星，始终璀璨夺目。

当时代发展要求将民族复兴事业传递到“80后”“90后”“00后”手中时，他们没有逃避时代赋予的责任，历史赋予的重担，在青春奋斗中实现自身价值与担负民族责任的统一，有的甚至为党和人民的事业过早地付出了青春年华。2019年在四川木里森林火灾中，27位牺牲的消防队员，其中大部分是“90后”甚至是“95后”，两位是“00后”，他们的事迹在这个共和国第七十个年头的春天定格在人民的心中，全国人民对他们的离去感到惋惜、心痛，他们用实际行动证明当代青年人是靠得住的，是可以信赖的。王勇国务委员代表党中央、国务院在木里森林火灾扑救中英勇牺牲烈士悼念活动中指出：“在这场血与火、生与死的考验面前，全体参战人员视灾情为命令，以保卫森林资源、维护生态安全为己任，用鲜血和生命忠实践行了‘不畏艰险、不怕牺牲，为维护人民生命财产安全、维护社会稳定贡献自己的一切’的铮铮誓言。这次牺牲的英烈就是其中的典型代表，是新时代学习的楷模！烈士们的

英雄事迹将永远载入共和国的史册！"① 这些为人民和国家逝去生命的青年，他们是新时代最可爱的人。

面向未来，发展任务将会更加艰巨，前进的路上依然需要保持艰苦奋斗的作风。"在实现中华民族伟大复兴的新征程上，必然会有艰巨繁重的任务，必然会有艰难险阻甚至惊涛骇浪，特别需要我们发扬艰苦奋斗精神。奋斗不只是响亮的口号，而是要在做好每一件小事、完成每一项任务、履行每一项职责中见精神。"国家的发展不能没有青年的参与，民族的复兴不能没有青年的砥砺奋斗。在千帆并进、百舸争流的时代，奋斗在民族复兴征程中的当代青年，以青春、汗水迎接挑战，踏实工作，将奋斗的青春底色擦得更亮、更闪耀。

三　做好新时代的青年工作

以习近平同志为核心的党中央高度重视青年发展事业，关心青年、关爱青年。习近平总书记多次就青年发展事业发表重要讲话，构成了新时代青年事业发展工作的行动指南。党的青年工作，在新时代聚焦基本实现现代化、建成社会主义现代化强国的历史使命和责任，为党和人民的事业培养合格的接班人。习近平总书记指出："中国共产党自成立之日起，就始终把青年工作作为党的一项极为重要的工作。"② "中国共产党立志于中华民族千秋伟业，必须始终代表广大青年、赢得广大青年、依靠广大青年，用极大力量做好青年工作，确保党的事业薪火相传，确保中华民族永续发展。"③

推动新时代青年发展事业不断开创新局面，要以习近平新时代中国特色社会主义思想为指导，贯彻落实总书记关于青年发展的系列重要论

---

① 《四川举行木里森林火灾扑救中英勇牺牲烈士悼念活动》，中央政府网：http://www.gov.cn/xinwen/2019-04/05/content_5379813.htm。

② 习近平：《在纪念五四运动100周年大会上的讲话》，《光明日报》2019年5月1日第2版。

③ 同上。

述，弘扬青年文化，立足青年实际，解决青年难题，不断为青年发展打造人生出彩的舞台，为党和人民的事业培养合格的建设者和接班人，让新时代的新青年走好属于这一代人的长征路。习近平总书记寄语当代青年，指出："青年朋友们，人的一生只有一次青春。现在，青春是用来奋斗的；将来，青春是用来回忆的"。"只有进行了激情奋斗的青春，只有进行了顽强拼搏的青春，只有为人民作出了奉献的青春，才会留下充实、温暖、持久、无悔的青春回忆。"①

青年阶段是人生的起始阶段，也是人生的奋斗阶段，幸福是靠奋斗得来的，也只有在奋斗中得到的幸福才是真正的幸福，是人民的幸福，更是民族复兴进程中的幸福。总书记强调："青年的人生目标会有不同，职业选择也有差异，但只有把自己的小我融入祖国的大我、人民的大我之中，与时代同步伐、与人民共命运，才能更好实现人生价值、升华人生境界。"② 面向新时代青年发展事业，要落实好国家中长期青年发展规划纲要，聚焦青年就业、教育、住房、平台等一系列现实性问题；要聚焦青年成长的价值观、人生观、世界观问题，加强引导和指导，让青年融入国家发展、社会进步，实现自身价值；要聚焦影响青年长远健康发展的社会问题，为青年发展营造良好的经济环境、社会环境、虚拟世界环境；要聚焦青年可持续发展能力培养，加大职业教育力度，助力青年脱贫，透过青年扶持创业计划，打通青年上升的通道。

青年是新时代的未来，也是民族的未来。新时代中国特色社会主义事业的成功实践在青年。百年来青年发展事业的历史将告诉我们，新时代是近代百年来最好的发展时代，同时也是接近民族复兴曙光的时代，民族复兴不是简简单单敲锣打鼓就能实现的，近代百年以来，一代代仁人志士的接续奋斗、流血牺牲，才有了今天的幸福生活和发展局面，只

① 习近平：《在同各界优秀青年代表座谈时的讲话》，《光明日报》2013 年 5 月 5 日第 2 版。

② 习近平：《在纪念五四运动 100 周年大会上的讲话》，《光明日报》2019 年 5 月 1 日第 2 版。

有中国特色社会主义道路，才是适合中国青年发展的根本道路。我们要按照党的十九大做出的战略部署，破除妨碍劳动力、人才社会性流动的体制机制弊端，开辟新时代青年发展的崭新未来，让青年在"追梦"中，不断"圆梦"，在"圆梦"中，不断缔造中国发展新的奇迹。追人生发展之梦，圆人生发展之梦，归根结底是追民族复兴之梦，圆民族复兴之梦。"一个流动的中国，充满了繁荣发展的活力。我们都在努力奔跑，我们都是追梦人。"①

四　新时代中国青年要有家国情怀、人类关怀

新时代的中国，其所处的国际地位和发展环境已经实现根本性的转变。作为世界第二大经济体、联合国安理会常任理事国的中国，在全球治理体系与能力建设中，参与、引领全球化的国际角色发生重要转换，中国成为多边主义发展的重要"一边"。"一带一路"倡议的推进，获得国际社会的广泛支持，青春的"一带一路"，青年的人类命运共同体让世界和平发展事业接续而行。青年是国家的，是民族的，也是世界的。中国年轻维和士兵，参与到维护地区和世界和平的行动中；中国年轻的建设者，参与到"一带一路"沿线国家的基础设施建设与开发中；中国年轻的医疗工作人员，参与到非洲人民的医疗事业中；中国年轻的学者们，参与到世界青年的知识交流中，推动"一带一路"民心相通。

习近平总书记指出："新时代中国青年，要有家国情怀，也要有人类关怀，发扬中华文化崇尚的四海一家、天下为公精神，为实现中华民族伟大复兴而奋斗，为推动共建'一带一路'、推动构建人类命运共同体而努力。"②

---

① 《国家主席习近平发表二〇一九年新年贺词》，《光明日报》2019 年 1 月 1 日第 1 版。

② 习近平：《在纪念五四运动 100 周年大会上的讲话》，《光明日报》2019 年 5 月 1 日第 1 版。

家国情怀，是“五四”精神留给中国青年最闪亮的价值。“五四”运动的核心精神是爱国主义。这是中华民族千年不辍的精神价值传承。它高尚而圣洁，传承于每一个炎黄子孙的灵魂与血脉之中，爱国是每一个炎黄子孙自然的感情流露。习近平总书记深刻地总结道：“一个人不爱国，甚至欺骗祖国、背叛祖国，那在自己的国家、在世界上都是很丢脸的，也是没有立足之地的。对每一个中国人来说，爱国是本分，也是职责，是心之所系、情之所归。对新时代中国青年来说，热爱祖国是立身之本、成才之基。”①

人类关怀，是新时代的中国青年奋斗发展的新精神内涵。这与国家发展、时代脉动紧密相连。中国的发展离不开世界，世界的发展需要中国的鼎力支持。新时代中国青年的人类关怀的情怀是中国人自古“先天下之忧而忧，后天下之乐而乐”精神的传承，是中国共产党人致力于推动人类发展事业的精神的体现。发展的世界，需要各国青年携手而行，承担更多人类社会的发展责任。走到十字路口的人类社会发展，向前行，还是向后退，不能离开对青年需求的关注，不能离开对青年愿望的体察。青年是未来，青年的未来在哪里，人类社会的发展希望就在哪里，中国青年的人类情怀，将中国人民的发展事业追求与促进全人类事业发展的追求紧密结合在一起，让青春的中国点亮世界青年携手构建人类命运共同体的前程。

不驰于空想，不骛于虚声，新时代的中国青年，接过“五四”精神的接力棒，将青春奋斗在新时代的追梦路上。“我们都是追梦人”是这个时代中国青年的奋斗群像！

---

① 习近平：《在纪念五四运动100周年大会上的讲话》，《光明日报》2019年5月1日第1版。

第二部分

南非青年与社会发展

第五章　南非青年参与社会发展政策及机制

一　南非青年群体概况

总体来说，青年人口没有广义的定义。从传统意义的认知来看，“青年”被定义为从童年到成年的过渡时期。[①] 在2009年《非洲青年报告》（以下简称AYR）中，“青年”被定义为15岁至39岁的人。[②] 但是，一些非洲国家对青年人口的定义不同。例如，加纳、坦桑尼亚和南非将青年人口定义为15岁至35岁之间的人口；尼日利亚和斯威士兰将其定义为12岁至30岁之间的人口；博茨瓦纳和毛里求斯将其定义为14岁至25岁之间的人口。[③] 针对青年人口的这些不同定义，我们难以有效地讨论影响非洲青年的一般问题并对各国的青年信息进行比较。

根据联合国人口司经济和社会事务部2030号人口报告，联合国大会将青年描述为15岁至24岁的人口。[④] 在南非，根据《国家青年委员会法》（1996年）和《国家青年发展政策框架》（2002年）的授权，

---

① United Nations Economic Commission for Africa（UNECA），*African Youth Report*（*AYR*）：*Expanding Opportunities for and with Young People in Africa*，June 2009，https：//www. uneca. org/sites/default/files/PublicationFiles/africanyouthreport_ 09. pdf.

② Ibid. .

③ Ibid. .

④ Ibid. .

《国家青年政策（2015—2020）》将青年定义为年龄在15岁至35岁之间的年轻人。为了保护延长的年龄类别，国家青年委员会（NYC）1996年法案的陈述是："其实质是，在许多年长的青年中，大多数因反对种族隔离的斗争而处于不利地位，需要被纳入青年发展倡议"[①]。因此，此项法案从很大程度上将许多年长的人员纳入了青年的范畴。

然而，尽管自1994年民主运动以来，年轻人的社会状况发生了很大变化，但35岁年龄限制的动机尚未改变，因为南非的历史不平衡问题尚未得到充分解决。[②] 这也符合《非洲青年宪章》对青年的定义（该宪章也将青年定义为年龄在15岁至35岁之间的青年）。《国家青年政策（2015—2020）》认识到年轻人不是一个同质群体，因此采取了差异化的方法，针对其根据年龄群体和特定群体实施的干预措施，以其广泛的"青年"定义来解决年轻人的具体情况和需求。[③]

这种差异化的方法使《国家青年政策（2015—2020）》有可能将相关立法和政策中规定的其他定义考虑在内。例如《国家青年发展政策框架》和《儿童法》中关于18岁以下儿童的定义，刑事司法系统提到年龄在14岁至25岁之间的年轻罪犯，以及其区分"孩子"和"成年青年"之间的差异化，[④] 后者被视为不需要特殊培养计划的专业群体。

二　青年发展与国家未来：南非青年参与社会发展政策

（一）青年发展政策及背景

南非是非洲为数不多的几个在过去几十年中制定并试图实施全面青年政策的国家之一。

---

① National Youth Development Agency（NYDA），*National Youth Policy*（*NYP*）*2015 - 2020*，April 2015.

② Ibid. .

③ Ibid. .

④ Ibid. .

由于南非独特的历史，青年政策已成为其提供社会正义和公平发展政策的一个组成部分。在后种族隔离时期，南非采取了一系列青年政策，包括2000年的《国家青年政策》，2002—2007年的《国家青年发展框架》（NYDF）和2009—2014年的《国家青年政策》。[①] 此外，南非政府于1996年通过了《全国青年委员会（NYC）法案》，并成立了相关委员会。《国家青年政策（2009—2014）》侧重于四个干预领域：教育、健康和福祉、经济参与和社会凝聚力。[②] 特别关注的青年团体包括年轻女性、残疾青年、失业青年、失学青年、农村青年和面临风险的青年。该政策为每个目标提供具有可衡量基准的具体干预措施，其实施将涉及政府、私营部门和非政府组织。《国家青年政策（2009—2014）》呼吁在每个政府部门或部门之间设立青年单位或管理委员会，并且建立一个机制，对南非的青年方案进行影响评估。鉴于南非的青年失业率很高，《国家青年政策（2009—2014）》高度重视为青年提供就业机会。[③] 为了达到更好的实施效果，任何政策都需要经过精心设计和战略计划，同时也需考虑到环境中的所有因素。

自1994年以来，南非政府已经对各种战略和方案进行了概念化测试和实施，以促进南非的青年发展。虽然做了很多努力，青年发展研究也取得了一些进展，但在青年发展过程中的一些影响因素仍然阻碍了南非青年的发展。这些因素包括失业率、辍学率、技能发展不足、缺乏体育和文化机会、社会凝聚力和志愿服务、青年工作框架不足等。[④]

为了应对这些影响因素，2015年4月，南非政府制定了《国家青年政策（2015—2020）》。该政策是为南非所有年轻人制定的，重点是迎接该国青年的具体挑战和解决青年的迫切需求。该政策通过涉及南非青年面临的新挑战，改进并更新了以前的政策，同时承认要解决在第一

---

① Presidency of South Africa, *National Youth Policy 2009 - 2014*, Presidency, Pretoria, http: //www. thepresidency. gov. za/download/file/fid/122.

② Ibid. .

③ Ibid. .

④ Ibid. .

个“国家青年政策”里所发现的挑战，还有很多工作要做。《国家青年政策（2015—2020）》旨在创造一种环境，使南非的年轻人能够尽最大可能去发挥他们的潜力。[①] 该政策概述了干预措施，以促进青年人的最佳发展，使他们无论是作为个人还是作为南非社会的成员，都能成为促进经济发展和国家治理的新动力。

《国家青年政策（2015—2020）》参考了南非宪法、联合国相关文件及其后的《世界青年行动纲领》（1995 年）、《非洲青年宪章》（2006 年）、《国家发展政策》（2012 年）和其他各种政策。该计划旨在到 2030 年建立一个包容性的社会和培养其积极的公民能力。《国家青年政策（2015—2020）》赞同这一愿景，其基础是确保南非在未来 20 年具有消除贫困和减少不平等的潜力和能力。这需要一种新的方法，即一种从被动的社会转向经济包容的社会，在这种社会中，人民是有效政府的拥护者，同时政府也是公民自身发展的积极支持者。[②]

青年人是社会发展的主要人力资源，往往也是社会变革、经济扩张和创新的关键引领者。他们的想象力、理想、能量和愿景对于社会的不断发展起到至关重要的作用。《国家青年政策（2015—2020）》旨在确认年轻人在国家建设中发挥的重要作用，确保有一些流程和机会，使年轻人能够发展和发挥他们的潜力。该政策拒绝了快速解决方案，将注意力转移到需要解决的复杂制度和系统问题上。[③] 它寻求将发展能力作为长期解决方案的一部分，这将为青年人提供社会参与以及利用南非政府所提供的发展机遇的契机。

（二）青年发展与展望

在讨论青年发展与展望之前，需要分析一下南非的人口群体和性别

① National Youth Development Agency (NYDA), *National Youth Policy (NYP) 2015 - 2020*, April 2015.

② Ibid..

③ Ibid..

分类。南非统计局2018年的数据（表5-1）显示了按人口群体和性别分类的年中人口估计数。年中人口总数估计约为5773万；非洲黑人人口占大多数（4668万），约占南非总人口的81%；白人人口估计为452万，有色人口约为507万，印度/亚洲人口约为145万；[①] 男性人口占人口总数的49%（2818万），女性人口刚好超过51%（2955万）。[②]

表5-1　**按人口群体和性别分类的年中人口估计数（2018年）**

分组	男性		女性		总计	
	人口数	占所有男性人数百分比（%）	人口数	占所有女性人数百分比（%）	人口数	占总人数百分比（%）
非洲黑人	22786200	80.9	23896700	80.9	46682900	80.9
有色人种	2459500	8.7	2614800	8.9	5074300	8.8
印度/亚洲人	740200	2.6	708100	2.4	1448300	2.5
白人	2194200	7.8	2325900	7.9	4520100	7.8
总计	28180100	100.0	29545500	100.1	57725600	100.0

注：由于数据为四舍五入得出，存在大于、小于100%的情况。

资料来源：南非统计局，2018年。

下面的图5-1显示，南非人口的增长率在2002年至2018年有所增加。估计的总体增长率从2002—2003年的约1.04%增加到2017—2018年的1.55%。[③] 南非老年人的比例正在增加，这表明随着时间的推移，估计的增长率从2002—2003年的1.21%上升到2017—2018年的3.21%。鉴于生育率随时间的波动，0—14岁儿童的增长率在2002—2012年增加，在2013—2018年出现停滞。[④]

① Statistics South Africa (Stats SA), *Mid-2018 Population Estimates*, 2018, Pretoria.

② Ibid..

③ Ibid..

④ Ibid..

南非统计局估计年中人口总数为 5773 万（2018 年 7 月估计）。① 但是，目前没有详细的与 2018 年青年就业有关的人口结构的统计数据。因此，这里使用了 2017 年的数据。2017 年，南非统计局估计年中人口为 5652 万。②

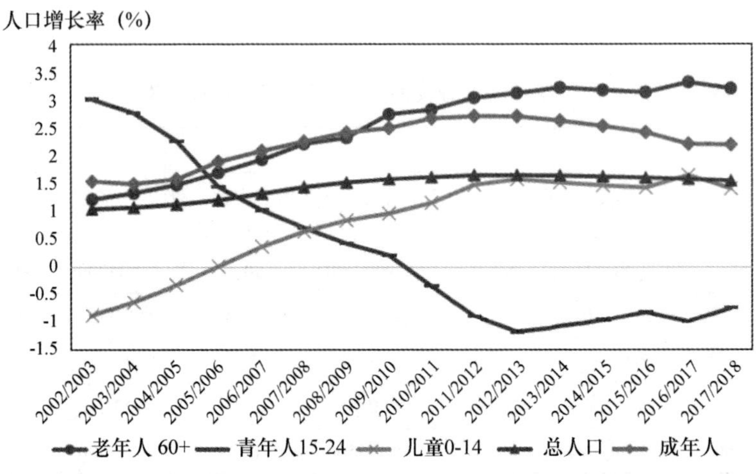

图 5－1　2002—2018 年所选年龄组的人口增长率

资料来源：南非统计局，2018 年。

根据表 5－2，2017 年青年人口总数（15—35 岁）约为 2040 万，约占其总人口的 36.08%。③ 这本身就是青年发展政策的一个独特情况。这意味着南非的青年发展不仅仅是青年部门的优先事项，如果青年要实现增长和发展，这应该成为一个国家的优先事项。

表 5－3 显示了南非人口的年增长率从 2002 年到 2017 年有所增加。估计的总体增长率从 2002 年至 2003 年的约 1.17% 增加到 2016 年至 2017 年的 1.61%。④

① Statistics South Africa (Stats SA), *Mid－2018 Population Estimates*, 2018, Pretoria.

② Ibid..

③ Ibid..

④ Statistics South Africa (Stats SA), *Mid－2017 Population Estimates*, 2017, Pretoria.

表 5－2　　南非青年人口（15—35 岁）

年龄	非洲黑人			有色人种			印度/亚洲人			白人		
	男性	女性	总计	男性	女性	总计	男性	女性	总计	男性	女性	总计
15—19	1911064	1934788	3845852	205394	203685	409079	44979	42742	87712	126279	123069	249348
20—24	2100859	2128984	4229843	215112	214307	429418	54761	50943	105704	133602	132703	266305
25—29	2326453	2350758	4677212	217062	217516	434577	66283	57990	124273	141495	140748	282243
30—34	2208498	2202074	4410572	198595	201063	399659	74584	62150	136734	153579	306769	460348
总计	8546874	8616604	17163479	836163	836571	1672733	240607	213825	454432	554955	549709	1104664

资料来源：南非统计局，2017 年。

表 5－3　　2002—2017 年估计的年人口增长率

年份	儿童（0—14 岁）	青年（15—34 岁）	中老年（60＋）	合计
2002—2003	－0. 85	2. 48	1. 34	1. 17
2003—2004	－0. 50	2. 35	1. 45	1. 20
2004—2005	－0. 16	2. 18	1. 60	1. 23
2005—2006	0. 21	1. 96	1. 74	1. 26
2006—2007	0. 45	1. 73	1. 87	1. 29
2007—2008	0. 58	1. 61	2. 11	1. 32
2008—2009	0. 74	1. 49	2. 30	1. 35
2009—2010	0. 84	1. 36	2. 46	1. 38
2010—2011	0. 94	1. 24	2. 59	1. 41
2011—2012	1. 23	1. 02	2. 69	1. 45
2012—2013	1. 39	0. 87	2. 75	1. 48
2013—2014	1. 46	0. 78	2. 90	1. 51
2014—2015	1. 44	0. 68	2. 95	1. 54
2015—2016	1. 54	0. 32	2. 98	1. 58
2016—2017	1. 56	0. 18	2. 99	1. 61

资料来源：南非统计局，2017 年。

尽管整个南非人口增长率在过去 20 年中有所下降，但青年人口继续以高于一般人口的速度增长。生育率也明显低于非洲地区的其他国家。对南非人口群体生育率的分析也表明非洲黑人的生育率较高，占白人总生育率的80%以上。[①] 图5－2描绘了南非人口的结构，清楚地显示了青年人口的显著隆起。[②]

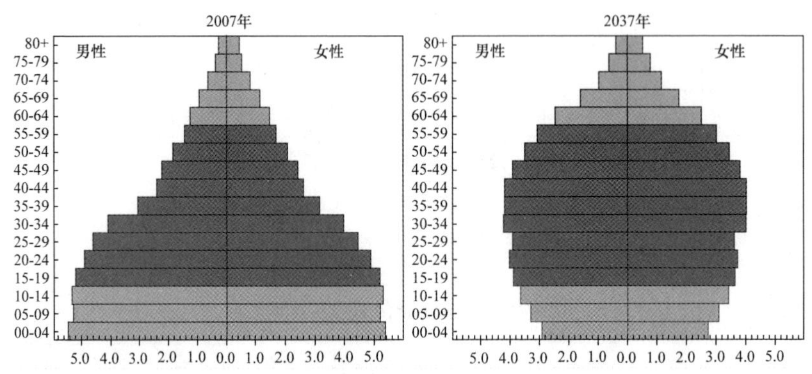

图5－2　南非人口的年龄和性别结构（2007—2037年）

资料来源：南非统计局，2017年。

仔细研究南非的情况会发现，目前普遍存在的情况与常态略有不同，依赖程度并不像预期的那么低，因此资源的转移也不会那么自动。此外，尽管自1994年以来经济增长在过去几年一直保持稳定，在经济方面投入相对充足，但青年人依旧失业，经济上不独立。根据图5－2所示的预计人口结构，到2037年，南非政府需要首先制定应对当前青年挑战的创新性计划和战略，利用好人口红利。[③]

根据南非统计局2018年统计数据，大约29.5%的人口年龄小于15岁，约8.5%是60岁及以上。15岁以下的人居住在豪登省（21.1%）和夸祖鲁—纳塔尔省（21.0%）的比例相似；在60岁及以上的老年人中，居住在豪登省的人最多，为24.0%。[④] 随着生活条件及医疗水平的

---

① Statistics South Africa（Stats SA），*Mid*－2017 *Population Estimates*，2017，Pretoria.

② Ibid..

③ Ibid..

④ Ibid..

提高，60 岁及以上年龄段的老年人比例随着时间的推移而增加。

回顾过去 20 年，总体来说，南非青年的经济参与状况不容乐观，而且失业率高，创业水平低。截至 2011 年，南非的失业率为 25%，大约 70% 的失业者是青年（14—35 岁）。[①] 15 岁至 24 岁年龄组的青年失业率较高，这种失业模式在多年来一直保持不变，非洲土著人和有色人种青年受影响最大。[②]

失业可以说不仅取决于国家经济吸收劳动力的能力，而且也取决于年轻人的受教育水平、个人技术和技能以及工作经验。年轻人被边缘化的状况主要表现在青年失业率高。这亟须政府出台以青年为目标的干预措施，使南非青年能够积极参与社会和经济活动。在工作机会稀缺的环境中，找到工作对年轻人来说尤其困难，这不仅仅是一个地方性的问题。

根据国际劳工组织（ILO）2013 年估计，在全球范围内，有 7340 万想要工作并且正在积极寻找工作的年轻人无法正常就业；每两个年轻人中就有一个（52.9%）是失业者或沮丧的求职者。[③] 国际劳工组织的同一份报告指出，世界正面临着日益恶化的青年就业危机，年轻人失业的可能性是成年人的三倍。南非不能幸免于这一全球趋势。[④] 根据南非 2014 年 6 月的劳动力调查，年龄在 15 岁至 35 岁之间的年轻人中有 36.1% 失业，这几乎是 35 岁至 64 岁失业者比例（15.6%）的两倍。[⑤] 与此同时，成人的劳动吸收率为 57.8%，几乎是年轻人（30.8%）的两倍。年轻女性面临更高的失业率，约 34.5% 的年轻女性既没有就业

---

① South Africa's Ministry of Finance, Facing Youth Unemployment: South Africa's Policy Choices, 2011.

② Ibid..

③ Assaad, R. & Levison, D., Employment for youth—A Growing Challenge for the Global Economy, Commissioned Paper for the High-Level Panel on Post – 2015 UN MDG Development Agenda Employment and Economic Growth, University of Minnesota, 2013, p. 166.

④ Ibid..

⑤ Statistics South Africa, *Labor Force Survey*, Season 2, 2014, Pretoria.

也没有上学，这包括继续教育和高等教育，而年轻男性则为 29.9%。[①] 虽然年轻人比成年人受雇的可能性更小，但他们通常有更多的学校教育年限。从这个角度来看，拥有大学学历的年轻人将会有更好的就业机会。

根据南非统计局资料，年轻人占南非全国人口的 37%。[②] 如果青年得到支持并能够成为社会和经济发展的积极成员，他们将为国家提供强大的人力资源。南非国家青年发展署表示："拥有一定数量相对年轻的人口对国家可能是有利的，只要大部分符合工作年龄的年轻人都有工作及收入……挑战就在于如何将其转化为人口红利。只有在具备工作年龄的青年人数符合生产活动时才能实现这一目标。"[③] 然而，社会规范继续支持南非的年轻人，将政治和经济参与视为成年人及老年人的特权，这就是为什么仍然需要有意关注青年问题的政策和实施框架的原因所在。

根据南非统计局 2018 年公布的最新劳动力季度情况调查，南非的失业率在 2018 年第四季度与 2018 年第三季度相比下降了 0.4 个百分点，降至 27.1%；[④] 与同年第三季度相比，2018 年第四季度的工作年龄人口增加了 149000 人或 0.4%；与 2017 年第四季度相比，未就业、未接受教育或培训的 15—34 岁年龄段的人数比例在 2018 年同期从 38.4% 增加到 38.9%，增加了 0.5 个百分点。[⑤]

基于上述情况，南非亟须制定一项具体的针对年轻人的青年政策，以防止失业对个人和社会造成负面的影响。无法谋生的年轻人很难离开父母，独立自我维持生计。[⑥] 他们经常被社区边缘化，无法找到与社会

---

① Statistics South Africa, *Labor Force Survey*, Season 2, 2014, Pretoria.

② Statistics South Africa, *Mid-year Population Estimates for 2014*, Pretoria.

③ National Youth Development Agency (NYDA), *National Youth Policy (NYP) 2015 - 2020*, April 2015.

④ Statistics South Africa, *Quarterly Labour Force Survey 2018*, Quarter 4, 2018, Pretoria.

⑤ Ibid..

⑥ National Youth Development Agency (NYDA), *National Youth Policy (NYP) 2015 - 2020*, April 2015.

有效的接触方式。在南非，年轻人通常不符合领取失业保险基金的资格，因为保险基金只涵盖以前有过工作的人。这迫使相当一部分年轻人成为家庭的负担并沦为“啃老族”。

虽然有许多年轻人在积极推动社区和相应青年发展倡议，并致力于改善他人的生活，然而，有些年轻人既是犯罪的受害者，也是犯罪者。安全研究所2003年的研究表明，“与南非其他年龄组相比，12岁至21岁年龄组的犯罪者和受害者人数最多；年轻人的危险行为导致高发病率和死亡率，即他们面临最高的艾滋病毒/艾滋病感染率；艾滋病毒感染率在30岁至34岁的女性中达到峰值（36.8%）。[①] 2013年，南非5698名与流动人口有关的死亡人数中有2515人是年轻人。同样，69%的因殴打致死和59%的因故意自伤的案例是在15岁至34岁年龄组之间发生的。”[②]

《国家青年政策（2015—2020）》考虑到自1994年以来取得的进展，以先前的青年政策的一些成功实施业绩为基础，进一步阐明了国家发展政策针对青年的具体建议。它加强了现有的干预措施、引入了新的干预措施，并摒弃了那些尚未奏效的措施。该政策旨在提高所提供服务的质量，扩大覆盖面并增加影响，试图通过新方法解决差距，并坚定地迎接顽固的挑战。[③]《国家青年政策（2009—2014）》在指导政府关于青年发展的思想方面发挥了重要作用。该政策为国家机关提出了他们对这一重要领域的规划和贡献并提供了实施指南。同时，它还为国家青年发展署（NYDA）创建了一个协调平台，并推动了协调机构，如青年发展部门委员会，以促进国家机关的参与力度。[④]

总的来说，过去几年，年轻人的社会经济状况有所改善。虽然这

---

① National Youth Development Agency（NYDA），*National Youth Policy（NYP）2015－2020*，April 2015.

② Ibid..

③ Ibid..

④ Ibid..

些改进可能不一定归功于《国家青年政策（2009—2014）》，但该政策为其他政策提供了框架和空间，有助于青年发展。[1] 尽管取得了这些进展，但仍有许多工作要做。例如，南非青年获得受教育和技能发展的机会有所改善，但教育质量和教育成果仍然是一项挑战。[2] 目前，南非国内仍有大量未受教育、就业或培训的年轻人。虽然国家机关在参与青年发展方面取得了一些进展，但私营部门在这方面却做得很少，这可能部分归因于青年发展论坛的消亡，该论坛协调了私营部门在这一领域的参与。将青年发展纳入国家机关和私营部门的工作并将其纳入主流并非最佳选项，民间社会在青年发展方面发挥的作用也是有限的，主要原因是缺乏资金来源、政府领导力的丧失以及相关部门的开支有限。[3]

青年经济参与（通过创业及参与劳动力市场）是一个需要认真关注的领域。为改善年轻人的就业机会和技能而采取的各种干预措施仍然缺乏影响力。青年健康和福祉要得到改善，还需要做更多工作来减少艾滋病毒感染率和发病率、药物滥用、暴力和危险行为，以及改善营养和鼓励健康生活方式。[4]

在社会凝聚力方面，越来越多的年轻人正在参加体育项目和社区组织的活动。但是，青年参与改善种族关系和公民参与（如投票）的努力需要引起注意。虽然国家青年服务署为青年发展提出主要方案并取得了积极成果，但也受到目前协调机制的限制。该计划没有设立专门的资金，这意味着它的实施取决于实施者的善意。此外，负责协调的机构能力也有限。[5]

导致《国家青年政策（2009—2014）》影响不佳的可能因素之一是

---

① National Youth Development Agency (NYDA), *National Youth Policy (NYP) 2015 - 2020*, April 2015.

② Ibid..

③ Ibid..

④ Ibid..

⑤ Ibid..

“青年发展综合战略”，该战略旨在为公共部门、民间社会和私营部门提供蓝图，以实施青年发展计划，应对国家青年政策的目标。游说和倡导制订能够响应政策目标的计划的工作也很有限。[①]

根据《国家青年发展机构法》（2008 年）第 75 条法案，这意味着它不会影响各省。[②] 这制约了组织和部门有效倡议和协调省级青年发展的能力。缺乏青年工作监管框架在限制政策实施方面发挥了重要作用。

《国家青年政策（2015—2020）》还提出了战略政策干预措施，填补了以往政策的空白和缺陷，满足了青年的需求。该政策旨在确定新的干预措施；巩固青年发展作为关键角色参与者，特别是政府角色参与者开展的项目中的主流化；制定并评估政策实施进展的过程；明确问责制和持续改进干预措施的监测和评估机制。[③]

南非的青年发展概念受到塑造国家及其民主目标的历史条件的影响，它基于社会和经济正义、人权、赋权、参与、积极公民身份、促进公共利益以及分配和自由价值观的原则。[④] 青年发展决定了南非的未来，应该成为国家青年政策发展议程的核心。

《国家青年政策（2015—2020）》响应了 21 世纪全球和区域发展的社会和经济力量的影响，特别是国际金融危机的后果。它旨在使年轻人的发展与政府解决贫困和不发达问题的方法保持一致，正如新民主党所诊断的那样。[⑤] 因此，必须通过有效的体制和政策赋予弱势青年权利，以克服对他们不利的条件。同样，边缘化青年和那些已经脱离教育、社会和经济主流的青年必须通过第二次机会和其他支持性行动使他们能重新融入社会。[⑥] 这将需要采取多部门合作的方法，让公共部门、民间社

---

① National Youth Development Agency (NYDA), *National Youth Policy (NYP) 2015 - 2020*, April 2015.

② Ibid. .

③ Ibid. .

④ Ibid. .

⑤ Ibid. .

⑥ Ibid. .

会和私营部门的利益攸关方参与进来，共同努力促进青年发展和为青年提供服务。

《国家青年政策（2015—2020）》与《国家青年发展政策框架》的愿景保持了一致。根据《国家青年政策（2015—2020）》，南非青年发展愿景是“整体和可持续的青年发展，意识到历史的不平衡和当前的不平衡，结合当前现实，建立一个非性别歧视、非种族主义、民主的南非。年轻人及其组织不仅在社会、经济和政治领域能充分发挥其潜力，而且还承担起他们为所有人创造更美好生活的责任”①。

《国家青年政策（2015—2020）》的方针是巩固青年倡议，增强年轻人改变经济和社会的能力。② 这将通过满足他们的需求来实现，并致力于发展为所有年轻人，特别是为社会、政治和经济主流之外的年轻人提供必要的支持。③

根据《国家青年政策（2015—2020）》，南非的青年发展目标是：巩固将青年发展纳入政府政策、计划和国家预算的进程；加强关键青年发展机构的能力，确保在提供青年服务方面的整合与协调能力；提高年轻人的能力，使他们能够通过获取资产和发挥潜力来掌控自己的福祉；加强对年轻人的爱国主义教育，帮助他们成为照顾家庭和社区的负责任的成年人；培养民族凝聚力，明确鼓励青年积极参与不同的青年倡议、项目和国家建设活动，培养其爱国主义精神。④

《国家青年政策（2015—2020）》是《南非共和国宪法》的总体立法和政策框架的一部分，该政策以综合方式响应各种立法和政策，并与之互动。《南非共和国宪法》确立了所有南非人必须坚持的具体权利、

---

① National Youth Development Agency (NYDA), *National Youth Policy (NYP) 2015 - 2020*, April 2015.

② Presidency of South Africa, *National Youth Policy* 2009 - 2014, Presidency, Pretoria, http://www.thepresidency.gov.za/download/file/fid/122. Accessed on 12 June, 2019.

③ National Youth Development Agency (NYDA), *National Youth Policy (NYP) 2015 - 2020*, April 2015.

④ Ibid..

责任和原则，它为青年经济赋权奠定了基础，并在“权利法案”中规定了人民（包括青年）的权利，确认了人的尊严、平等和自由的价值观。①

南非国家发展计划提供了 2030 年南非的理想愿景，并提出以下建议：为孕妇和幼儿提供营养干预措施，确保普及儿童早期发展教育并改善学校系统，提高学生成绩，加强教师培训。加强青年服务计划并推出新的社区计划，为青年人提供生活技能培训、创业培训和参与社区发展计划的机会。加强和扩大继续再教育和培训（FET）学院的数量，将学生参与率提高到25%，将 FET 学院的毕业率提高到 75%，为贫困家庭的学生提供全额资助，并建立社区安全中心以防止犯罪。为雇主制定税收激励措施，以减少雇用年轻劳动力市场进入者的初始成本，为安置单位提供补贴，以准备和安排大学毕业生进入工作岗位。提高青年学习能力，直接向求职者提供培训券。将公共服务引入正式的毕业生招聘计划，以吸引高技能人才，同时，扩大国有企业在培训工匠和技术专业人员中的作用。鼓励健康和积极的生活方式。②

《新增长之路》（2011 年）强调国家需要通过直接就业计划、有针对性的补贴和扩张性的宏观经济一揽子计划创造就业机会；支持吸收劳动力的活动，特别是在农业、轻工制造业和服务业，以促进大规模就业；同时，建立一套激励措施和支持机制，鼓励私营部门投资新企业，扩大现有业务。③ 成功的主要指标是就业情况（创造就业机会的数量和质量）、增长情况（增长率、劳动强度和经济增长的构成）、公平程度（低收入不平等和贫困）和环境成果。④

贸易和工业部的“工业政策行动计划”确定了可以优先利用工业和基础设施扩大发展机会的部门。“工业政策行动计划”和“新增长道

① National Youth Development Agency (NYDA), *National Youth Policy (NYP) 2015 - 2020*, April 2015.

② Ibid. .

③ Ibid. .

④ Ibid. .

路”都承认青年在创造就业机会和加强企业家精神方面具有优先地位的重要性。[①] 一个新的市场，一个创造性的和盈利的商业模式将创造供应链，为以前的微型和小型企业提供进一步的就业机会。[②]

由企业、政府、劳工、民间社会和非政府组织（NGO）签署的《青年就业协议》（2013 年）和《技能协议》（2011 年）旨在改善年轻人的工作条件，并使经济运行情况能敏锐反映年轻人的就业需求。[③]《国家青年发展署法案》（2008 年）要求国家青年发展署制定南非综合青年发展战略，并启动、设计、协调、评估和监督旨在将青年融入整个经济和社会的所有计划。[④] 该法案指示国家青年发展署促进所有国家机关、私营部门和非政府组织对青年发展采取统一的方法。

《基于广泛的黑人经济赋权法》（2003 年）规定政府和私营部门的所有领域都应努力实现宪法规定的平等权利，促进黑人在经济活动中的广泛和有效参与，增加就业并促进更公平的收入分配；它还要求制定一项基础广泛的关于黑人经济赋权的国家政策，以促进国家的经济统一、保护共同市场、促进机会平等和平等获得政府服务。[⑤] 修订后的法规以政府公报的形式公布（公报 800 号，2012 年），并征询公众意见。[⑥]

《非洲青年宪章》（2006 年）是一份政治和法律文件，作为一个战略框架，它为非洲大陆、区域和国家各级的青年赋权和发展指明方向。该宪章于 2006 年 5 月通过，并于 2006 年 7 月得到非洲联盟国家元首的认可，包括南非。[⑦] 它确定了以下优先事项：教育、技能发展、就业和可持续生计、青年领导和参与、健康和福利、和平与安全、环境保护以及文化和道德价值观。《非洲青年宪章》的所有条款都符合该国目前和

---

① National Youth Development Agency (NYDA), *National Youth Policy (NYP) 2015 - 2020*, April 2015.

② Ibid. .

③ Ibid. .

④ Ibid. .

⑤ Ibid. .

⑥ Ibid. .

⑦ African Union, *African Youth Charter*, 2006.

设想的社会经济方案。[①]《国家青年政策（2015—2020）》通过支持将青年带入经济和社会主流的行动和流程，共享宪章旨在使年轻人全面发展的目标。

《国家青年政策（2015—2020）》还通过了以下千年发展目标（MDG）：消除贫困和饥饿（MDG1）、实现普及初等教育（MDG2）、降低儿童死亡率（MDG4）、改善孕产妇健康状况（MDG5）。[②]

《国家青年政策（2015—2020）》呼应了联合国2000年及其后的世界青年行动纲领和联合国年度青年行动纲领。[③] 联合国确定了十多项优先事项以应对青年面临的挑战，包括教育、就业、饥饿和贫困、健康、环境、药物滥用、青少年犯罪、休闲、女孩和年轻妇女的参与、全球化、信息和通信技术、艾滋病毒/艾滋病、青年和冲突以及代际关系。[④] 这些优先领域中的每一个方面都是根据主要问题、具体目标以及各方为实现这些目标而拟采取的行动提出的。

---

① National Youth Development Agency (NYDA), *National Youth Policy (NYP) 2015 - 2020*, April 2015.

② Ibid. .

③ Ibid. .

④ Ibid. .

第六章　南非青年参与社会发展的影响因素及问题

一　就业状况

南非的青年失业率几乎是一般成年人失业率的两倍，从全球比较的角度来看，南非总体失业率也非常高。① 此外，自 1994 年向民主过渡以来，高失业率一直是南非经济的一个长期特征。失业率在 1994 年之前的相当长的一段时间内可能也非常高，但是由于缺乏那个时期适当的数据，所以要想精确衡量那个时代的失业率是不可能的。② 2013 年，1/3 的南非人获得了社会补助金，预计在不久的将来，将有超过 1600 万人依赖政府财政拨款。这种经济边缘化给政府资源带来压力，同时也引发了人们对社会稳定的担忧。③

1996 年，国际劳工组织对南非劳动力市场开展了审查，他们的报告提出，大多数分析家都认为，南非失业率在 20 世纪 70 年代急剧上升，并且持续到 20 世纪 80 年代和 90 年代。④

根据《国家统计局劳动力调查》2014 年的报告，如图 6 - 1 所示，

---

① "Social Grants Reach Almost One Third of South Africans", 19 June 2014, http://www.southafrica.info/about/social/grants-190614.htm#.VlWwdXYrLDc.

② Mlatsheni, C and Ranchhod, V. 2017, "Youth Labor Market Dynamics in South Africa: Evidence from NIDS 1 - 2 - 3. REDI3x3", working paper 39, July 2017.

③ National Youth Development Agency (NYDA), *National Youth Policy (NYP) 2015 - 2020*, April 2015.

④ Mlatsheni, C and Ranchhod, V. 2017, "Youth Labor Market Dynamics in South Africa: Evidence from NIDS 1 - 2 - 3. REDI3x3", working paper 39, July 2017.

无论是使用狭义还是广义的失业定义，南非青年失业率都很高，并且即使在国家经济增长的情况下也并未改善。①

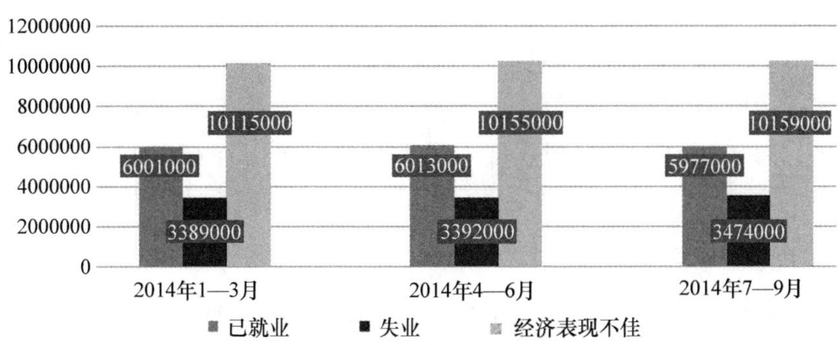

图 6 - 1　青年（15—34 岁）已就业、失业和经济表现不佳的情况

资料来源：国家统计局劳动力调查，2014 年。

南非统计局 2014 年劳动力调查第二季度报告指出，南非的青年失业率从 2018 年第三季度的 52.80% 增加到 2018 年第四季度的 54.70%；南非的青年失业率从 2013 年到 2018 年平均为 52.15%，最高时达 55.90%；2017 年第二季度和 2014 年第四季度为 48.80%，创最低纪录。②

研究表明，阻碍年轻人参与主流经济的主要挑战是失业、贫困和不平等。③ 如果不加以解决，其对社会经济的影响将是可怕的，包括犯罪率增高、经济表现不佳、高失业率和贫困，以及政治不稳定的可能性增加。在此背景下，《国家青年政策（2015—2020）》将创造就业置于青年发展干预的中心。④

青年失业率达到惊人的 36.1%，而成年人失业率则为 16.3%，青年和成年人的就业吸收率分别为 30.7% 和 57.6%。⑤ 说这些数字令

---

① Statistics South Africa, *Labor Force Survey*, Season 2, 2014, Pretoria.

② Ibid..

③ National Youth Development Agency (NYDA), *National Youth Policy (NYP) 2015 – 2020*, April 2015.

④ Ibid..

⑤ Mtwesi, A., "An Overview of Youth Policy", *Helen Suzman Foundation Magazine*, Iss. 74, November 2014.

人失望，只是轻描淡写，实际上，年轻人的高失业率早已被描述为“毒品”和“嘀嗒作响的定时炸弹”。①

从南非统计局2018年发布的数据（图6－2）可以看出，在2018年第三季度失业人数增加127000人之后，2018年第四季度失业人数减少了70000人。② 从图6－2中可以看出，南非失业人数自2013年以来，每年第四季度出现下降。最大跌幅纪录出现在2017年第四季度，下降了33万，随后是2014年第四季度下降了24.2万，2015年第四季度下降了22.5万。③

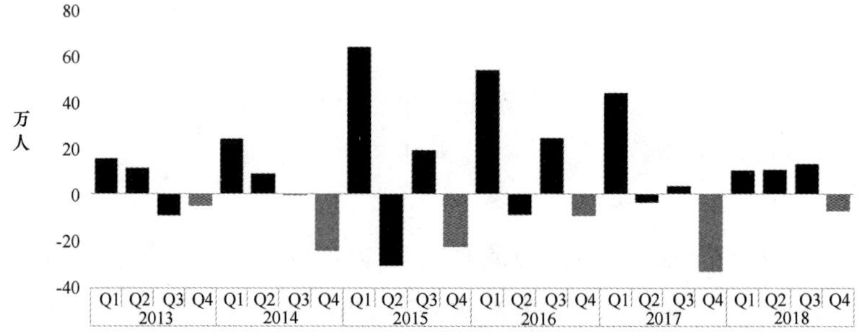

图6－2　2013年第一季度至2018年第四季度的失业变化

资料来源：南非统计局，2018年。

二　教育状况

南非教育系统的各级教育质量低下，这抵消了学校教育参与率的提高带来的积极影响。技能培训渠道充斥着破坏劳动力市场公平以及阻碍获取就业机会的不利因素。④

---

① Mtwesi, A.,“An Overview of Youth Policy”, *Helen Suzman Foundation Magazine*, Iss. 74, November 2014.

② Statistics South Africa, *Quarterly Labour Force Survey 2018*, Quarter 4, 2018, Pretoria.

③ Ibid..

④ National Youth Development Agency（NYDA）, *National Youth Policy（NYP）2015－2020*, April 2015.

南非小学生的识字和算术技能远低于国际平均水平。12年级的学生数学和科学的考试通过率低，这抑制了高等教育的增长，特别是在工程、科学和技术方面。南非22岁至25岁的人中约有47%读完了12年级，而大多数发展中国家的这一比例为70%。

大量学习者在没有获得国家高级证书、没有读完12年级，或者未完成进一步的教育和培训（Further Education and Training，FET）以及成人基础教育和培训资格的情况下退学。每年大约有100万年轻人退出教育系统，其中65%的人没有获得12年级证书。

虽然近些年FET机构的参与率显著增加，但它们的数量和质量仍然不足以满足经济发展的技能需求。只有少数离开学校系统的人进入技术职业教育和培训（TVET）学院或接受某种培训。2011年，只有11.5万人参加了FET学院的一般职业课程。[①]

高等教育的低入学率影响了高水平、技能熟练的毕业生的供应。学校毕业生获得学前教育和培训的机会有限，而且由于提供的教育和培训质量差，获得这些机会的人往往没有为工作做好充分准备。南非教育面临的挑战是如何找到正确的方法来帮助绝大多数没有资格直接进入高等教育或就业的毕业生获得技能。[②]

三　技能培训

提高年轻人的技能水平将增加他们就业的机会。南非青年失业率高的主要原因是青年的技能短缺。2011年，只有31%的年轻人完成了12年级教育。[③] 2013年的综合住户调查估计，当年有983698名学生入读高等教育机构，这些学生中有66.4%是黑人、22.3%是白人、6.7%是有色人种、4.7%是亚洲人。[④]

---

① National Youth Development Agency（NYDA），*National Youth Policy（NYP）2015 – 2020*，April 2015.

② Ibid..

③ Ibid..

④ Ibid..

尽管大多数学生都是黑人，但与亚洲人和白人群体相比，该群体的学生参与率仍然相对较低。2013 年，约有 4.3% 的 18 岁至 29 岁的青年在南非的高等教育机构注册，比 2002 年的 4% 有所增加。[①] 估计这一年龄组的白人占 18.7%，亚洲人占 9.2%。[②] 在高等教育机构注册的有色人种和黑人人口的人数分别为 3.1% 和 3.2%；没有接受任何学校教育的人口比例从 2002 年的 10.6% 下降到 2013 年的 5.6%。[③] 这表明上学的机会正在增加，但是没有足够的学龄前阶段的年轻人参加其所需的技能培训。

大量年轻人过早退出教育系统，缺乏专业或技术技能，致使他们失业。大约 60% 的 35 岁以下待业青年从未工作过。[④] 如果没有针对性的干预措施，他们将继续被排除在经济参与之外。因此，南非需要采取多种方法来加强基础教育并降低现有学生的辍学率。同时，必须为毕业生创造可行的途径，以获得学习机会，并解决失学青年缺乏技能和工作经验的问题。

南非青年失业率居高不下，大学毕业生就业率低，年轻人持续感染艾滋病毒/艾滋病，学校和高等教育机构辍学率持续居于高位。这些现象使人们认为，现有的青年发展机构有较大的改进空间。

青年发展机构表现不佳的主要原因包括：缺乏明确的任务，导致责任重复和领域重叠。例如，全国青年理事会和总统府青年理事会的任务似乎有相当大的重叠；缺乏对现有计划的协调及其对实施计划的问责、监测、评估的影响；缺乏能力，例如，国家青年发展署是青年计划的主要推动者，但它没有足够的能力。[⑤]

总之，提高年轻人的技能水平将增加他们获得有偿职业的机会，提高其参与社会发展的能力。

---

① National Youth Development Agency (NYDA), *National Youth Policy* (*NYP*) *2015 - 2020*, April 2015.

② Ibid..

③ Ibid..

④ Ibid..

⑤ Ibid..

四　青年工作框架

青年工作是一个专注于年轻人整体发展的实践领域。在南非，青年工作专业化的过程始于20世纪80年代后期。2008年成为南非青年工人协会的青年从业者宣传小组制定了“猎人休息宣言”和青年工作政策草案，并提交给青年问题部际委员会。[①] 南非青年工人协会与青年工作联合会进行了磋商和合作，以促进青年工作专业化进程。

《国家青年政策（2015—2020）》提出，为了使青年工作蓬勃发展，需要采取以下措施：建立关于青年工作的立法框架，成立青年工人数据库等。[②]

国家青年发展署和南非青年工人协会制定了2013年全国青年工人道德守则草案，其中的一项主要决议是南非应该立法规定青年工人的专业化。[③] 据此，国家青年发展署制定了青年工作专业法案草案，并将根据《国家青年政策（2015—2020）》的要求继续开展这项工作。[④]

五　青年健康

根据《国家青年政策（2015—2020）》所述，南非青年面临的健康挑战不仅仅是医疗风险，不健康的生活方式也对身体状况有着重要的影响。虽然慢性疾病，特别是那些与不健康的生活方式有关的疾病，在年轻人中相对来说并不常见，但是年轻人在青春期的许多不健康的行为，使这些疾病在他们中的一些人的晚年生活中将逐步表现出来。[⑤]

---

① National Youth Development Agency（NYDA），*National Youth Policy（NYP）2015 - 2020*，April 2015.

② Ibid..

③ Ibid..

④ Ibid..

⑤ Ibid..

南非年轻人面临的最大挑战之一是性健康和生殖健康问题。2011—2012 年度第三次青少年风险行为监测由医学研究委员会与各部门联合进行。这项研究从 9 所公立学校中选取 8—11 年级学生作为样本，结果发现有 36% 的学生有过性行为，12% 的学生报告他们首次性行为时年龄未满 14 岁。[①] 在发生过性行为的学生中，47% 的人有两个或两个以上的性伴侣，18% 的人在饮酒后发生性行为，13% 的人在服用药物后发生性行为，33% 的人使用一次性安全套，18% 的人怀孕；只有 1/7 的学生报告其接受过学校的艾滋病毒/艾滋病教育。[②]

缺乏高质量的卫生设施导致产妇死亡率高，艾滋病毒流行率高。据《拯救母亲报告》，孕产妇死亡的五个主要原因是：非妊娠相关感染，主要是艾滋病（34. 7%）；产科出血和高血压的并发症（30. 4%）；产科出血（产前和产后出血）（12. 4%）；与妊娠有关的败血症（9. 0%）；预先存在的孕产妇疾病（11. 4%）。[③]

同一份报告指出，这些死亡案例中本有 60% 是可以避免的，[④] 但是由于产前、产时和产后的护理质量差，这一情况并未改善。一些确定的问题包括临床评估不佳，转诊延迟，不遵循标准方案，并且在监测患者期间没有对异常做出反应。缺乏经过适当培训的医生和护士分别导致 15. 6% 和 8. 8% 的孕产妇死亡。孕妇的患病率随着年龄的增长而增加，从 14 岁儿童的 0. 7% 上升到 19 岁青少年的 12. 1%。[⑤]

据 News 24 报道，青少年怀孕率上升令人担忧，年龄在 15 岁至 19 岁的女孩占全世界出生人口的 11%。[⑥] 在这 11% 中，几乎所有新生儿（95%）都在中低收入国家，包括南非。[⑦] 世界卫生组织声称，除了健康

---

① National Youth Development Agency (NYDA), *National Youth Policy (NYP) 2015 - 2020*, April 2015.

② Ibid. .

③ Ibid. .

④ Ibid. .

⑤ Ibid. .

⑥ Jyothi Laldas, "Concerns about Rising Teenage Pregnancies", *News 24*, October 17, 2018.

⑦ Ibid. .

状况不良和贫困之外，少女怀孕仍然是母婴死亡的主要原因。尽管政府和非政府组织持续努力提高民众认识并采取威慑手段，但青少年怀孕仍是一个主要问题。每年约有1600万15岁至19岁的女孩怀孕，有大约100万15岁以下的女孩分娩，每年还有300万女孩接受不安全的堕胎。[①]

根据南非统计局2018年统计，南非人口的艾滋病毒感染率约为13.1%。2018年，艾滋病病毒感染者总人数约为752万。15—49岁的成年人中，估计有19.0%感染艾滋病毒。[②]

滥用药物已成为南非严重的问题，特别是酒精滥用导致的暴力行为和造成的机动车事故。西开普省的酒精消费者比例最高，为46.15%，其次是北开普省（37.3%）、豪登省（34%）、东开普省（24.1%）、自由州（20.8%），[③] 越来越多的年轻人开始尝试毒品和酒精。2011—2012年度青少年风险行为监测研究发现，33%的受访者报告说，他们曾被一个酗酒的人所驱使，13%的人报告说他们曾经因为饮酒而醉卧街头。[④] 大约28%的学生报告曾吸过香烟。在从未吸过香烟的学习者中，43%的人表示过去一周曾被动吸烟，20%的人有吸烟的父母或监护人；大约32%的受访者表示在调查前一个月内饮酒过量，25%的受访者表示在过去一个月内曾酗酒；大约13%的学习者吸食过dagga（一种非洲具有危险性的吸食毒品），12%使用过吸入剂，5%使用过可卡因，6%使用了结晶药，5%使用过镇静片。[⑤]

综上所述，南非许多社会现象表明年轻人面临产生心理健康问题的风险，例如贫困、暴力犯罪以及艾滋病毒/艾滋病导致的死亡等。滥用酒精、烟草和毒品也会导致年轻人的心理健康问题。

南非体育和娱乐部（SRSA）负责监督和管理南非体育和娱乐的发

---

① Jyothi Laldas, "Concerns about Rising Teenage Pregnancies", *News 24*, October 17, 2018.

② Statistics South Africa (Stats SA), *Mid-2018 Population Estimates*, 2018, Pretoria.

③ National Youth Development Agency (NYDA), *National Youth Policy (NYP) 2015-2020*, April 2015.

④ Ibid..

⑤ Ibid..

展。该部门致力于增加体育和娱乐设施的可及性，这有助于实现国家发展计划，提升社会凝聚力和推进健康的民族生活方式。该部门计划鼓励民众参加体育和娱乐活动，促进体育和娱乐的转型，并支持有才能和高水平的运动员在国际体育舞台上取得成功。[①]

南非体育和娱乐部通过各种活动，给大众提供参与体育和娱乐的机会，例如国家青年营、Big Walk（与 loveLife 建立伙伴关系以鼓励积极的生活方式选择），以及土著游戏。[②] 它将继续把资源用于弱势群体，以促进其参与并增加体育和娱乐设施的使用度。该部门将协助 60 个国家联合会以支持学校体育计划，并改善体育设施的使用情况，促进黑人运动员的发展。[③] 年轻人将有机会在国家学校锦标赛等活动中展示自己的技能，从而使全国联合会更广泛地接触南非体育人才。

体育和文化活动可以创造健康和积极的公民，培养公民的民族自豪感，促进社会和经济变革。因此，南非体育和娱乐部需要转移重点，以便从现有和计划的体育、娱乐以及艺术、文化计划和倡议中获得最大利益。南非体育和娱乐部有可能为南非的经济增长做出贡献，并且对南非青年尤其具有吸引力。因此，这一部门有可能帮助青年发展技能，为其提供就业和创业机会，并帮助年轻人参与国家建设。[④]

六　青年发展、社会凝聚力与志愿服务

根据 2014 年人文科学研究委员会（HSRC）选民参与调查，大多数南非人都是爱国的：86% 愿意成为南非公民，而不是其他任何国家的公民。[⑤] 公众清楚地认识到一系列核心民主原则的重要性，包括自由

① National Youth Development Agency（NYDA），*National Youth Policy（NYP）2015 – 2020*，April 2015.

② Ibid..

③ Ibid..

④ Ibid..

⑤ Ibid..

和公正的选举、集会和示威的权利、协商民主、选举问责制、言论自由和政治宽容。自由和公正的选举仍然是评价最高的民主理想。[①] 但年轻人感到被社会排斥，主要是由于高失业率和无法参与经济活动。

腐败是公众关注的问题，2013 年公众对腐败的关注度达到 25%，而 2003 年只有 9%。服务提供也成为一个紧迫的问题，2013 年公众对其关注度是 24%，2003 年则是 12%。[②]

南非公民对国民政府的信任度从 2009 年的 61% 下降到 2013 年的 44%。[③] 只有 44% 的人信任他们的省政府，34% 的人信任他们的地方政府，而不到 25% 的人信任政党或政治家。[④] 独立选举委员会的信任度在 2012 年至 2013 年略有改善（从 60% 升至 63%）。[⑤] 近 73% 的人不知道南非人在 16 岁时可以登记投票。[⑥] 虽然 16 岁至 19 岁的人比普通人更倾向于知道这一点，但是这个年龄段的大多数人仍然没有意识到登记年龄的重要性。[⑦] 这是独立选举委员会未来选民教育的一个潜在重点领域。16 岁及以上的人中有 68% 赞成将最低投票年龄保持在 18 岁，17% 的人认为应该降低投票年龄，而只有 11% 的人主张提高投票资格标准。[⑧]

约有 7.5% 的南非人口（2870130 人）患有某种残疾，其中残疾人流行率在年轻人中最低（年龄段在 15—34 岁）（见图 6－3）。[⑨]

根据南非财政部 2011 年的研究报告，年轻人的生产率和入门级工资之间存在很大差距。技能不匹配导致的实际工资与生产率之间的这种差距，使教育和技能发展成为政府的长期优先事项，这也是缓解青年失业的必要条件。[⑩] 干预措施对于提高基础教育和高等教育的质量，以及

---

① National Youth Development Agency (NYDA), *National Youth Policy (NYP) 2015 - 2020*, April 2015.

② Ibid..

③ Ibid..

④ Ibid..

⑤ Ibid..

⑥ Ibid..

⑦ Ibid..

⑧ Ibid..

⑨ Ibid..

⑩ National Treasury, *Confronting Youth Unemployment: Policy Options for South Africa*, 2011, Pretoria.

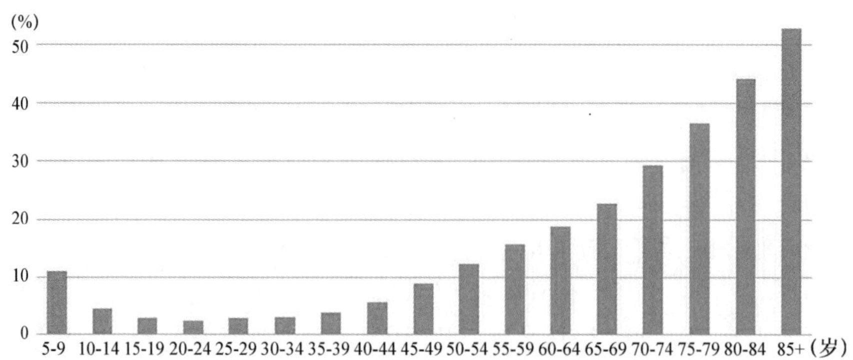

图 6－3　按年龄组分类的残疾人流行率

资料来源：南非国家统计局，2011 年。

提供不仅培养学术技能而且培养职业技能的环境至关重要，纠正这些技能问题的教育干预措施需要时间来实施并产生效果，特别是考虑到开始但未完成中学教育的年轻南非人的数量。①

如果劳动力需求疲软，离校生将继续难以融入劳动力市场，因为雇主无法充分判断年轻人的生产力和工作适应能力。增长委员会的任务是提供对快速和持续的经济增长以及减贫的基本政策及战略的最佳理解，承认教育和提升技能对就业增长的重要性，同时强调提高劳动力需求带来的巨大好处。②

南非目前的劳动力市场政策侧重于通过扩大公共工程计划支持技能开发和直接公共就业，私营部门几乎没有参与。但是，绝大多数青年工人受雇于私营部门，这对于低技术工人来说尤其如此。③

青年面临的就业挑战的严重程度以及刺激劳动力需求的迫切需要意味着私营部门在加速就业增长方面发挥着关键作用，这使得针对私营部门创

① National Treasury, *Confronting Youth Unemployment: Policy Options for South Africa*, 2011, Pretoria.

② Ibid..

③ Ibid..

造就业的激励措施成为政府就业政策的必要支柱。① 青年就业补贴的重点是刺激劳动力需求，同时利用基本的工作经验和在职培训提供就业前景。这可以孤立地进行，但有一些干预措施可以补充就业补贴并可能提高其效力。例如，对就业补贴计划的评估强调，这些补贴在与培训相结合时往往更有效。

《国家青年政策（2015—2020）》特别关注年轻人面临的挑战。情况分析表明，该政策应该能够促进经济参与和转型，发展技能，促进风险较低的行为，改善健康，并增强不同种族和阶级之间的信任。同时，也有必要建立处理不平等和排斥等社会现象所需的长期契约。② 因此，该政策的最终重点是增强国家建设能力和社会凝聚力。

---

① National Treasury, *Confronting Youth Unemployment: Policy Options for South Africa*, 2011, Pretoria.

② National Youth Development Agency (NYDA), *National Youth Policy (NYP) 2015 - 2020*, April 2015.

第七章　制定和形成更加积极的南非青年参与社会发展政策及机制

一　促进青年参与社会发展政策及机制转型

（一）经济社会发展转型与青年参与

减少南非青年的高失业率需要走上一条吸收劳动力的经济增长道路。这需要对经济重新定位以提高劳动力需求，供应方面也需要有相应的改善。再工业化和经济多样化也是促进就业的必要条件，这些因素是新民主党的新增长之路和工业政策行动计划（部门战略和支持经济转型的其他计划）的核心。①

公共部门采取的措施，如基础设施投资，促进了青年在建筑业的就业。扩大的公共工程计划提升了年轻人的入学率和参与度。推出的就业税激励措施鼓励私营部门雇用新进入劳动力市场的人。高等教育和继续教育的情况有所改善。②

在过去几年中，有许多南非学者关注评估立法，特别是关注政府为解决该国青年面临的挑战而制定的政策。

一些研究国家青年发展署的学者关注的是为青年赋权的具体

---

① National Youth Development Agency（NYDA），*National Youth Policy*（*NYP*）*2015 - 2020*，April 2015.

② Ibid. .

计划。[①] 国家青年发展署补助金计划主要关注年轻企业家，它试图在经济上赋予青年权利。在政治上或经济上赋予青年权利是迈向社会发展参与的重要一步。工业发展公司和小企业融资机构共承诺投入 27 亿兰特资金，用于资助青年企业。[②] 国家青年发展署还为一系列青年企业和合作社提供支持。许多青年拥有的企业已从国家和私营部门的采购和企业发展计划中受益。

2013 年签署的《青年就业协议》是一个重要的里程碑。该协议为社会伙伴之间的合作设定了一个框架，以解决青年失业问题并支持青年创建的企业。[③]《青年就业协议》旨在改善年轻人的教育和技能水平，帮助他们找到工作或开办自己的企业。作为协议的一部分，政府致力于增加公共部门的就业人数，而某些行业则制定了青年发展目标。所有党派、各级政府、有组织的劳工、有组织的企业、社区和青年组织一致同意实施经过协调的青年就业战略。[④]

（二）支持青年参与社会发展的社会政策

1. 积极的就业

这项干预方案分两个阶段实施，以支持青年人就业。在短期内，果断干预将为失业和贫困的年轻人提供收入和社区服务以及经济参与的机会。从中长期来看，经济措施将用于促进年轻人可持续就业的增长。政府需要改善公共就业计划，以提供更好的可能性。[⑤] 国家青年发展署将

---

① Fatoki, O. and Chindoga, L., "An Investigation into the Obstacles to Youth Entrepreneurship in South Africa", *International Business Research*, Vol. 4, No. 2, 2011, pp. 161 – 169; Hartley, S. and Johnson, H., Learning to co-operate: "Youth Engagement with the Co-operative Revival in Africa", *The European Journal of Development Research*, Vol. 26, No. 1, 2014, pp. 55 – 70; Malebana, M. J., "The Effect of Knowledge of Entrepreneurial Support on Entrepreneurial Intention", *Mediterranean Journal of Social Sciences*, Vol. 5, No. 20, 2014, p. 1020.

② National Youth Development Agency (NYDA), *National Youth Policy (NYP) 2015 – 2020*, April 2015.

③ Ibid..

④ Ibid..

⑤ Ibid..

与国家青年服务中心合作，将在两年内让至少100万年轻人参与其中。

此外，要为失业者提供临时的、对社会有用的工作来增加收入，确保大多数机会流向年轻人，并动员年轻人帮助社区，赚取收入并获得宝贵的工作经验。①

2. 培养年轻的企业家

政府需要改善公共就业计划，该计划应为年轻人开设社区工作项目，每周提供两天的就业以及公众参与选择和塑造项目的机会，以便更多地获取有关信息。它还应该鼓励青年积极主动地决定优先事项，并确定哪些年轻人可以成为供给目标。应重新配置国家青年事务处，将修订后的青年目标纳入社区工作方案，以突出社区卫生工作者方案对吸收更多年轻人的贡献，并制定一项国家青年志愿者方案，吸引失学青年参加志愿服务。②

经济发展部应与企业合作，有效实施协议。应通过实施青年就业协议的经验教训来了解这一过程。应该要求企业为年轻人创造就业机会。贸易和工业、经济发展、公共工程、合作治理和传统事务、能源和国家财政部门应制定措施，实现青年就业目标。③ 虽然这将在中长期产生影响，但必须在整体新增长路径的就业驱动因素计划、产业政策行动计划和农业政策行动计划中确定吸收年轻人的潜力最大的部门。必须制定支持创造就业机会和监测与评估框架的措施。此外，经济部门应与能源和环境部门合作，制定青年参与绿色经济的战略。信息和通信技术（ICT）战略必须由电信和邮政部领导的经济部门制定。④

经济发展部应制定青年参与创意产业、旅游、体育和娱乐的战略，需要确定学习者为工作实践做好准备所需的技能。教育和经济发展部门

① National Youth Development Agency (NYDA), *National Youth Policy (NYP) 2015 - 2020*, April 2015.

② Ibid. .

③ Ibid. .

④ Ibid. .

应该与企业就如何为工作场所培养青年做好准备，还必须咨询雇主以了解他们的观点和需求。[①]

3. 积极的技能培训

缺乏工作经验限制了年轻人找工作。有许多公共和私营部门的举措可以将求职者与工作岗位相匹配，包括劳工部、国家青年发展署。[②]

证据表明，雇主，特别是小企业主，不愿意努力培训新人。[③] 中小企业确实面临一些制约因素，但只要有适当的支持和有利的经济条件，它们就可以为创造新的就业机会做出重大贡献。高等教育部需要制定战略，支持这些小公司培训和雇用年轻人。就业前服务可以最大限度地降低为公司雇用新员工产生的交易成本，并为工作场所的潜在员工做好准备。[④]

4. 扶持青年企业和合作社

许多年轻人已经开办了自己的企业或合作社，但南非青年拥有和控制的企业数量并不为人所知，[⑤] 因为所有权在采购或供应链流程中不会按年龄或性别细分。南非正在实施一些举措，在财务、业务技能和市场方面支持青年人的公司。《国家青年政策（2020）》提出，无论遇到什么挑战，都不应拒绝参与技术革命。为促进技术进步，发展中国家应对青年人的优质教育进行投资，并为工人和管理人员提供持续的技能培训，确保在整个社会中尽可能广泛地分享知识。[⑥]

贸易和工业部以及小企业发展部启动了青年企业发展战略，以促进大规模青年企业发展，例如，向青年公司提供抵押补助金。国家青年发展署已经实施了支持青年企业融资、培训和市场联系的计划，许多政府部门和市政当局也在自己的空间内实施企业发展计划。[⑦]

---

① National Youth Development Agency（NYDA），*National Youth Policy*（*NYP*）*2015 – 2020*, April 2015.

② Ibid. .

③ Ibid. .

④ Ibid. .

⑤ Ibid. .

⑥ Ibid. .

⑦ Ibid. .

5. 推动农村发展和土地改革

自 1994 年以来，农村发展面临的主要挑战是穷人的边缘化。为应对这些情况，需要改变获取资源（土地、水、教育和技能）的方式，改善农村基础设施。贫穷国家发展农村和提高农业收入的传统方法是通过支持农产品加工帮助农民向价值链上游转移。[①] 然而，在南非，玉米、小麦、糖、葵花籽油、茶叶、面粉、花生酱、香烟、啤酒、果汁和罐头食品等主要产品已经存在于高度集中、纵向一体化的农产品加工部门。[②]

农村发展往往与土地改革密不可分，通过提高农业产量的农村发展战略，可以提高农村地区的就业率，支持小农扩大土地所有权，并投资水、交通和其他网络基础设施。一项实施良好的农业产出战略到 2030 年可创造 100 万个就业岗位。[③]

生活在农村地区的年轻人由于缺乏土地，再加之经济和社会基础设施薄弱，常常难以参与经济发展，他们在农村经济中也面临着二元论。[④] 因此，农村发展战略还需要考虑全国农村地区缺乏同质性的特点。[⑤]

6. 青年的职业培训

教育应该有助于年轻人提升能力并发挥他们的潜力。青年发展署概述了南非的教育愿景，即到 2030 年南非人应该获得尽可能高质量的教育和培训，从而显著改善学习成果。南非学习者在国际标准化考试中的表现应与具有相似发展水平的国家的学习者表现相当。

《国家青年政策（2015—2020）》建议，教育系统应该迎合不同的群体，培养高技能人才。南非大学和学院的毕业生应具备满足国家当前和未来需求的技能和知识。创新对于解决南非面临的紧迫挑战、将新产

---

① National Youth Development Agency (NYDA), *National Youth Policy (NYP) 2015 - 2020*, April 2015.

② Ibid..

③ Ibid..

④ Ibid..

⑤ Ibid..

品引入市场以及更有效地生产产品和服务至关重要。应大力扩展研究与开发，以支持创新和竞争力。

教育系统将在建设包容性社会、提供平等机会和培养所有南非人以充分发挥其潜力方面发挥更大作用，特别是那些以前因种族隔离政策而处于不利地位的人。为实现这一愿景，职业技术教育与培训部门需为约25%的年轻人提供机会，这意味着到2030年培训岗位将从目前的约30万增加到125万。

南非需要熟练的劳动力来促进经济增长，包括工程师以及卫生专业人员，以提供高质量的医疗保健服务。此外，研究人员和创新者在创造新产品和更有效地生产现有产品的新方法中发挥关键作用，包括提供公共服务。为了实现这些目标，研究机构以及国家科学和创新体系必须协作，学前教育和培训部门应该提高教育的公平与质量。①

7. 推进青年健康计划

南非的卫生系统以初级卫生保健和地区卫生系统为基础。建立国家医疗保险制度是一个重要目标。② 其成功有四个先决条件：提高公共卫生保健的质量，降低私人护理的相对成本，在公共和私营部门招聘更多的专业人员，以及建立公共和私营卫生服务提供者的卫生信息系统。③ 此外，青年健康结果还受到卫生系统以外的因素的影响，如生活方式、饮食和营养水平、教育、性行为、运动、交通事故和暴力程度。④ 为了确保青年普遍获得高质量的医疗保健水平，政府将建立一个公共资助和管理的国家健康保险（NHI）基金，以推动NHI计划的推出。NHI资助模式将实现NHI的三个关键原则：提供优质医疗保健水平，通过交叉补贴实现社会团结，以及公平。⑤ 为实现这一目标，

① National Youth Development Agency (NYDA), *National Youth Policy (NYP) 2015 - 2020*, April 2015.

② Ibid..

③ Ibid..

④ Ibid..

⑤ Ibid..

政府将在未来五年内通过 NHI 法案，最终确定 NHI 基金的资助模式（包括地区初级卫生保健和个人卫生服务的预算重新分配），并在 2016—2017 年之前创建该基金。该基金旨在确保设施清洁、安全和可靠，并确保患者得到尊重并维护其权利。[①]

到 2030 年，卫生系统应向所有人提供优质护理，并在服务点免费提供。医院应该高效地为有需要的人提供优质的二级和三级医疗服务。应增加卫生专业人员数量，特别是在贫困社区。[②]

二　国家与社会：建设发展与凝聚力的青年社会发展参与

南非政府为公民提供基本服务并提升其发展能力。发展能力的方法侧重于人们能够做什么，包括人们监督政府的能力，这是国家建设进程的一个基本要素。[③] 确保南非人能够跨越种族和阶级进行互动将有助于增强社会凝聚力。[④]

《国家青年政策（2015—2020）》旨在缩小社会差距，应对既有挑战并提出新措施，以改善和加速青年政策的实施，具体包括以下四个方面：教育、健康和福祉、经济参与和社会凝聚力。[⑤] 青年发展署预测，到 2030 年，南非人将生活在一个更具凝聚力的社会中，这个社会可以弥合种族、性别、空间和阶级的分歧，更接受人民的多重身份。[⑥] 年轻人必须带头实现创造一个统一、非性别歧视、非种族歧视、民主、繁荣和平等的社会梦想。

---

① National Youth Development Agency（NYDA）, *National Youth Policy*（*NYP*）*2015 - 2020*, April 2015.

② National Planning Commission（NPC）, *National Development Plan 2030*（*NDP 2030*）: *Our Future-Let It Work.*

③ National Youth Development Agency（NYDA）, *National Youth Policy*（*NYP*）*2015 - 2020*, April 2015.

④ Ibid..

⑤ Ibid..

⑥ Ibid..

南非自身的历史和其他国家的经验表明，团结和社会凝聚力是实现社会和经济目标的保障。如果南非在不减少贫困和不平等的情况下在减少所有权和经济控制权方面取得进展，那么其转型将是浅层次的。同样，如果在没有明显改变所有制模式的情况下减少贫困和不平等，进展将是动荡和脆弱的。①

至少在未来十年，就业公平应该主要集中在为历史上处于不利地位的社区中的年轻人提供机会。更具体地说，种族和性别应继续是选择的主要决定因素，这将确保社会能够利用该国的全部人力资源，并有助于提高社会凝聚力。因此，建立一个更加强大和有效的监测和执法系统至关重要。②

安全和保障的实现与社会经济发展水平以及社会平等直接相关。一个安全可靠的国家通过提供有利于创造就业、改善教育和健康以及加强社会凝聚力的环境来鼓励经济增长和转型。③

南非宪法是建立团结的起点，宪法包含的价值观包括尊严、非性别歧视、非种族主义和法治。这些价值观为南非的新身份奠定了基础，南非可以在这种身份中建立一个以平等、自由和尊严为基础的社会。徽章和国花等国家象征有助于增强公民的共同身份意识，因此应该为年轻人所知。“国家象征通常不仅代表国家的一般概念，也会凝聚与一个国家相关的知识、价值观、历史和记忆”。④

三　中非合作：关注非洲青年发展

习近平主席在中非合作论坛北京峰会开幕式的主旨讲话中指出，中非合作“八大行动”绘制了新时代中非发展新蓝图，揭开了新时期中

---

① National Youth Development Agency（NYDA）, *National Youth Policy*（*NYP*）*2015 - 2020*, April 2015.

② Ibid. .

③ Ibid. .

④ Butz, D. , “The National Symbol was the Promoter of Psychological and Social Change”, *Political psychology*, Vol. 30, No. 5, 2009.

非合作的宏伟篇章。[①] 以建设新型国际关系和人类命运共同体为基础的“八大行动”，坚持真诚的诚信观，正确的利益观，广泛深入地寻求中国和非洲各界人士的意见和建议。密切关注“合作共赢，携手构建更加紧密的中非命运共同体”的主题，共同构建“一带一路”、联合国2030年可持续发展议程、非盟《2063议程》，促进非洲国家的发展。[②] 该战略的重点是帮助非洲培养内生增长能力，创新合作理念，推动中非合作向更高层次发展。

根据联合国统计，目前非洲人口为13亿，其中40%不到15岁，70%不到30岁。[③] 非洲处于人口红利潜力期，迫切需要提高青年劳动技能，增加有效就业，将潜在的人口红利转化为现实生活发展动力，以此有效促进非洲国家的社会稳定和经济发展。非洲联盟的《2063年议程》明确指出，支持青年成为振兴非洲的动力。[④] 长期以来，中国积极协助非洲国家培养各类人才，加强人力资源开发合作，提供大量政府奖学金和培训场所，为增强非洲国家的自主发展能力发挥积极作用。鉴于此，中国将在实施“八大行动”中重点关注与非洲青年的合作，重点培养各类人才，支持青年创新创业。

根据《中非合作论坛—北京行动计划（2019—2021年）》的规划，在培养各类人才方面，中国将协调各方资源，进一步深化与非洲国家在人力资源开发领域的合作，重点关注培养非洲国家的政府官员、政党干部、专家学者、技术人员等行业和部门。[⑤] 2019—2021年，中国将向非洲国家提供5万个研修培训名额和5万个中国政府奖学金名额。[⑥] 中方

---

① 习近平：《携手共命运　同心促发展——在二〇一八年中非合作论坛北京峰会开幕式上的主旨讲话》，《光明日报》2018年9月4日第2版。

② 同上。

③ United Nations, Department of Economic and Social Affairs, Population Division, *Population 2030: Demographic Challenges and Opportunities for Sustainable Development Planning*, 2015.

④ Ibid..

⑤ 《中非合作北京行动计划论坛（2019—2021）》，外交部：https://focacsummit, mfa. gov. cn/chn/hyqk/t1592247. html。

⑥ 同上。

还将邀请2000名非洲青年来中国进行讨论和交流，继续派遣青年志愿者前往非洲国家，加强中非青年之间的友谊，增进相互了解。[①]

南非总统西里尔·拉马福萨于2018年9月3日举行的2018年中非合作论坛北京峰会开幕式上致辞，拉马福萨总统称赞中国取得了“出色的经济成就”，包括让数百万人摆脱贫困。[②] 他强调，“非洲可以从中国令人印象深刻的增长模式中学到许多宝贵的经验，特别是利用生产能力和自然资源来作为经济增长的催化剂。”[③]

《贸易经济学》资料显示，南非的失业率从上一时期的27.5%下降至2018年第四季度的27.1%；失业人数减少7万至614万，就业人数增加14.9万至1653万。[④] 由于节日期间工作活动增加，失业率通常在每年最后一个季度下降。从2000年到2018年，南非的失业率平均为25.63%，2003年第一季度达到31.20%的历史最高水平，并在2008年第四季度创下21.50%的历史新低。[⑤]

南非青年失业率从2018年第三季度的52.80%上升至2018年第四季度的54.70%。从2013年到2018年，南非青年失业率平均为52.15%，历史最高水平为55.90%。2017年第二季度和2014年第四季度的历史最低点为48.80%。目前，南非的青年和成人失业率仍居高不下；然而，根据非洲开发银行的数据，在2018年第一季度，15—34岁青年的失业率为38.2%，与非洲大陆其他地区的失业率相同。近三分之一的青年人失业。这意味着，在2018年第一季度，每三个青年中就有一个以上找不到工作。[⑥]

---

① 《中非合作北京行动计划论坛（2019—2021）》，外交部：https：//focacsummit，mfa. gov. cn/chn/hyqk/t1592247. html。

② 《南非总统在中非合作论坛峰会上的讲话引言》，新华网：http：//www. xinhuanet. com/english/2018 -09/04/c_ 137442038. htm。

③ 同上。

④ Trading Economics，South Africa Unemployment Rate，12 June 2019，https：//tradingeconomics. com/south-africa/unemployment-rate.

⑤ Ibid. .

⑥ Ibid. .

“我们希望为非洲的青年提供更多的培训和就业机会”，习近平主席指出，“中国决定在华设立中国—非洲经贸博览会；鼓励中国企业扩大对非投资”。[①] 中国将支持非洲到2030年实现粮食安全的目标，共同实施农业现代化合作。

2015年10月11日至18日，有52名南非青年通过国际关系与合作部（DIRCO）访问中国，并参加了首届中国青年领袖计划。该计划以中国和南非的5—10年战略合作计划为基础，其使命是促进双边青年文化交流。[②]

在共同反对帝国主义、殖民主义和种族主义的斗争中，中国和南非人民建立了深厚的友谊。两国领导人通过频繁的互访、会晤和其他交流方式，为两国关系提供了高层战略指导。中国已连续九年成为南非最大的贸易伙伴，南非已成为中国在非洲最大的贸易伙伴。

据IOL（独立在线）称，“中国对南非的直接投资增长了80多倍，累计超过102亿美元，为当地社区创造了数万个就业岗位，为南非经济提供了强大动力”。[③]

许多中国公司在南非的成功运作证明了我们共同发展的互利关系的必要性，南非公司在中国也取得了巨大成功。[④] 近年来，中国—南非年和高层民间交流机制的启动，使两国关系更加紧密，增进了两国的相互了解和友谊，尤其是促进了两国青年之间的相互了解和友谊。[⑤]

四　南非青年参与社会发展的新希望

《国家青年政策（2015—2020）》旨在制订青年发展计划，以应对

---

① 习近平：《携手共命运　同心促发展——在二〇一八年中非合作论坛北京峰会开幕式上的主旨讲话》，《光明日报》2018年9月4日第2版。

② 《中非合作北京行动计划论坛（2019—2021）》，外交部：https：//www. focac. org/eng/zfgx_ 4/zzjw/t1594399. htm。

③ IOL，South Africa's trade with China，July 2018，https：//www. iol. co. za/sunday-tribune/news/south-africas-trade-with-china-rockets-16177203.

④ Jyothi Laldas，“Concerns about Rising Teenage Pregnancies”，*News 24*，October 17，2018，https：//www. news24. com/SouthAfrica/Local/Stanger-Weekly/teen-pregnancy-a-rising-concern-20181010.

⑤ Ibid. .

南非青年面临的挑战，使青年有能力控制他们的未来。[①] 根据过去的青年政策和青年状况研究，《国家青年政策（2015—2020）》提出应优先考虑以下领域：经济参与程度、教育水平、爱国情怀等。[②]

为了提升青年经济参与度，《国家青年政策（2015—2020）》提出了如下措施：改善产业政策的干预以吸收劳动力，为青年提供在职经验，将年轻求职者与雇主联系起来，支持创业干预，改善公共就业计划。通过实施诸如土地改革等补救措施以及政府推动的激进经济转型议程，减少机会不平等现象。[③]

《国家青年政策（2015—2020）》建议应采取的改善教育和技能发展机会和质量的干预措施包括通过教师培训提高基础教育质量，引入课余托管计划，加强课程质量，逐步向贫困学生提供免费基础教育，直至本科阶段。应特别注意为非熟练和未受过教育的青年提供第二次机会。[④] 建议应采取的卫生干预措施包括鼓励青年改变行为，使青年人形成良好的自我形象，并利用法律、政策和娱乐设施来应对药物滥用和相关疾病带来的挑战，特别是青春疾病。《国家青年政策（2015—2020）》在实施过程中，将贯彻南非宪法的有关精神，塑造南非青年更加积极的社会身份和价值观，以促进社会凝聚力。[⑤] 青年发展机制也将进行优化，以有效实施和监测政策和战略。

为了确保实施该政策，南非青年署将制定一项实施战略，明确目标是与不同利益攸关方进行谈判，并在战略发布两年后进行实施评估，实施评估将显示政策是否按计划实施以及需要改进的地方。[⑥] 为了确保在2019年进行良好的评估研究，国家青年发展署将与规划、监测和评估

---

① National Youth Development Agency (NYDA), *National Youth Policy (NYP) 2015 - 2020*, April 2015.

② Ibid..

③ Ibid..

④ Ibid..

⑤ Ibid..

⑥ Ibid..

部门合作，确保在公报公布后立即绘制和收集数据。

在南非，青年和组织在社会、经济和政治领域充分发挥潜力，承担自身的责任，致力于为所有人创造更美好的生活。南非正在开启国家发展的新旅程。拉马福萨总统通过提出发展经济、创造就业机会、改善人民生活和促进社会转型的目标，将南非带入了一个充满希望和信心的新时代。中国热切希望与南非共同努力，争取更快、更好地发展两国的全面战略伙伴关系。

在“金砖国家在非洲：在第四次工业革命中共谋包容增长和共同繁荣”的主题下，中国将深化与南非和其他金砖国家的战略伙伴关系，加强金砖国家的团结与合作，促进金砖国家的相互联系。中国将与南非共同努力，开创中国与南非友谊的新纪元，青年则是两国关系发展的中坚力量。

第八章　南非青年参与社会发展的价值观

青年参与社会发展的价值观选择与意见的表达对社会的发展而言十分重要。南非是非洲大陆现代化发展的典型代表，透视南非青年在个人发展感受、国家发展期待与发展选择、个人发展态度三个维度上的价值观表现，可以给我们一个全新的视角去了解非洲社会发展现状。非洲青年的发展需求与相应的发展价值观，是我们观察非洲社会发展环境和状况的重要指向标。研究南非青年参与社会发展的价值观，将为使构建中非命运共同体成果惠及非洲青年，实现中非发展合作的精准对接提供理论与政策视角的参考。

“当今世界，现代化的推进特别是新科技不断产生，在推动经济社会发展的同时，也使人类社会进入现代‘风险社会’。现代风险不同于传统风险的最大特征就是不确定性和难以预测性，其迅速而广泛的传播可能造成大范围社会恐慌。比如，恐怖主义袭击带来的普遍社会紧张和社会不安；未知流行病和生态环境危机引发的社会恐慌；股灾、银行倒闭、债务危机等金融风险可能导致的大规模社会恐慌传导；等等。”① 在社会发展的过程中，技术革命、经济基础的变化，带来上层建筑形态的变化，二者之间的互动关系，不断推动着人类社会各个领域的发展

① 李培林：《用新思想指导新时代的社会治理创新》，《人民日报》2018 年 2 月 6 日第 7 版。

进程。

事实上，“经济发展水平并不是孤立的，而是与政治发展水平密切相关的，是相互影响、相互促进又相互制约的”[①]。近期，“在治安状况日益恶化的情况下，南非民众要求恢复死刑的呼声不断高涨”[②]。南非民众请愿要求恢复死刑的事实，再次表明死刑存废作为一种价值观的表现，其变化与目前南非社会发展环境有着密切的联系，而且打击犯罪也是南非青年强烈关注的价值观选项，这涉及生存与发展的环境。风险的无处不在和文化转型语境下的社会发展环境，使得价值观的变迁，特别是青年价值观的变迁及表现，成为国家的文化、经济与政治变迁的重要组成部分，更是一个观察社会发展是否良性、正向的指向标。一般而言，“一个国家多数人的需求层次结构是同这个国家经济发展水平、工业化程度以及人均受教育水平直接相关的。在那些不发达的国家里，生理上的需求和安全的需求是压倒性的”[③]。可以说，青年价值观“仅是更广泛的、从生存价值观到自我表现价值观的文化转型的一部分”[④]，而文化的转型又是广泛的社会发展的重要组成部分。可预见的是，作为文化转型，特别是政治文化转型的一个组成部分，价值观的变化，折射的是经济、社会、政治变迁的系统过程。宏观层面的社会发展、经济等方面的变化，折射到微观层面便是人们的看法、行为方式的变化，这些价值观的变化所带来的影响是深远的。

青年参与社会发展是一个动态的过程，价值观的变化与社会发展具

---

① ［美］罗纳德·英格尔哈特：《静悄悄的革命》，叶娟丽、韩瑞波等译，上海人民出版社 2016 年版，第 1 页。

② 《南非民众请愿要求恢复死刑》，新华网：http：//www. xinhuanet. com//world/2019 - 09/06/c_ 1124968527. htm，2019 年 9 月 6 日。

③ ［美］罗纳德·英格尔哈特：《现代化与后现代化 43 个国家的文化、经济与政治变迁》，严挺译，社会科学文献出版社 2013 年版，第 15 页。

④ 同上书，第 3 页。

有契合性。在青年人口居多的非洲大陆，关注非洲青年参与社会发展的状态，更深入地了解非洲社会发展的现状和需求，关注非洲青年参与社会发展的价值观表现，是一个严谨的指标和切入点。非洲是一块发展的热土，更具有发展的年轻力量。根据预测，“世界人口将继续增长，到2050年将达近百亿。尽管其他地区的人口增速将显著放缓，但到2050年，撒哈拉以南非洲地区人口预计将翻番，较之1960年增长近九倍，即从2.27亿增至22亿”[①]。人口的持续增长，特别是青年人口占比的提高，将为非洲的发展提供丰富的人力资源，为非洲大陆，特别是撒哈拉以南非洲实现现代化，提供可持续的发展动力。

从中非关系来看，推动中非青年携手构建中非命运共同体，离不开对非洲青年的了解，离不开对非洲青年价值观的理解。

一　南非青年参与社会发展的价值观取向

从在宏观层面关注整体的社会发展趋势，到在微观层面关注青年群体的发展，本部分将从两个层面研究南非青年参与社会发展的价值观表现。本文对南非整体经济社会发展环境和青年群体的人口、就业等分布情况的分析，主要使用世界银行的调查数据及在线分析系统（详见表8－1）；对南非青年价值观的表现及分析主要使用世界价值观调查的数据及在线分析系统（详见表8－2）。本文采用联合国的划定标准，根据联合国人口司2015年发布的人口报告，将青年定义为15岁至24岁的人口。[②]

① ［日］铃木惠美：《世界人口将继续增长到2050年将达近百亿》，世界银行，https：//blogs. worldbank. org/zh-hans/opendata/worlds-population-will-continue-grow-and-will-reach-nearly-10-billion-2050，2019－07－08.

② United Nations，*Population 2030：Demographic Challenges and Opportunities for Sustainable Development Planning*，https：//www. un. org/en/development/desa/population/publications/pd f/trends/Population2030. pdf，2015－12－19.

表 8－1　2000—2018 年南非青年（15—24 岁）失业情况对比①

时间（年）＼失业情况	青年总失业率（%）	男青年失业率（%）	女青年失业率（%）	年轻群体总失业人数
2000	53. 93	49. 598	59. 213	54. 435
2001	56. 274	52. 387	60. 871	56. 924
2002	60. 141	55. 05	66. 042	60. 721
2003	61. 437	56. 939	66. 624	62. 1
2004	56. 84	50. 536	64. 102	57. 446
2005	56. 408	49. 973	64. 131	56. 865
2006	54. 888	48. 664	62. 108	55. 376
2007	52. 732	46. 992	59. 848	53. 351
2008	45. 607	41. 723	50. 315	45. 178
2009	48. 353	45. 093	52. 353	47. 929
2010	51. 189	48. 101	55. 011	50. 789
2011	50. 279	46. 255	55. 05	49. 997
2012	51. 698	47. 636	56. 681	51. 499
2013	51. 43	47. 978	55. 546	51. 323
2014	51. 297	48. 022	55. 304	51. 269
2015	50. 143	46. 343	54. 89	50. 156
2016	53. 371	48. 618	59. 313	53. 412
2017	53. 29	48. 906	58. 606	53. 57
2018	53. 425	49. 176	58. 75	52. 853

数据来源：世界银行。

① 表 8－1 中数据来源于世界银行公开数据，数据更新以世界银行规定和网站信息为准，表中数据检索时间为 2019 年 7 月 1—20 日，具体来源：青年总失业率（Unemployment, youth total of total labor force ages 15 － 24, national estimate）数据来源：https://data. worldbank. org. cn/indicator/SL. UEM. 1524. NE. ZS? locations = ZA；男青年失业率（Unemployment, youth male of male labor force ages 15 － 24, national estimate）数据来源：https://data. worldbank. org. cn/indicator/SL. UEM. 1524. MA. NE. ZS? end = 2018&locations = ZA&start = 2000；女青年失业率（Unemployment, youth female of female labor force ages 15 －24, national estimate）数据来源：https://data. worldbank. org. cn/indicator/SL. UEM. 1524. FE. NE. ZS? end = 2018&locations = ZA&start = 2000；年轻群体总失业人数（Unemployment, youth total of total labor force ages 15 － 24, modeled ILO estimate）数据来源：https://data. worldbank. org/indicator/SL. UEM. 1524. ZS? locations = ZA。

从南非青年成长的宏观社会发展环境来看，20 世纪 60 年代以来，南非人口持续保持增长状态，21 世纪以来增速加快。截止到 2018 年，南非人口总数为 5777. 96 万人。[①] 在南非人口增长的同时，南非社会整体的经济发展水平与国民收入情况也发生了明显的变化，调查显示，自 1946 年到 2018 年，南非平均国内生产总值和平均国民收入经历了明显的起伏变化，自 1980 年以来，总体呈现下降趋势，具体变化情况如下：

1980 年南非平均国内生产总值为 25623 美元，达到七十多年来的最高点。1980 年到 2018 年，总趋势上处于持续的下降状态，但 2000 年到 2011 年处于一个上升区间，2011 达到进入 21 世纪以来的高点，为 23326 美元。2011 年达到高点后，进入下降趋势，2018 年为 22098 美元。

1974 年南非平均国民收入为 21230 美元，达到七十多年来的最高点。1974 年到 1980 年有所波动，出现一个 U 形的下降和反弹过程，1980 年达到 21074 美元，自 1980 年到 2018 年总趋势上处于持续的下降状态，中间个别年份区间略有反弹。2000—2011 年处于一个明显的上升区间，2011 年达到进入 21 世纪以来的高点，为 19721 美元。2011 年达到高点后开始下降，2018 年为 18565 美元。

从收入不平等的情况来看，自 1963 年到 2012 年，南非前 10% 的人口占税前国民收入的份额从 1963 年的 48. 9%，上升到 2012 年的 65. 1%，中间有年份略有下降，但总体处于上升状态，趋势较缓，但自 2000 年起，上升趋势明显加快。[②]

从以上数据可以看出，2011 年是进入 21 世纪以来南非经济社会发展的一个重要拐点。国际货币基金组织 2011 年 12 月的《金融与发展》刊

---

① 南非人口总数（Population, total, South Africa），数据来源：https：//data. worldbank. org/indicator/SP. POP. TOTL? end = 2018&lo cations = ZA&start = 1960&view = char。数据为世界银行公开数据，数据更新以世界银行规定和网站信息为准，此数据检索时间 2019 年 7 月 5 日。

② 南非平均国内生产总值（Average Gross Domestic Product, South Africa, 1946—2018）、南非平均国民收入（Average National Income, South Africa, 1946—2018）、1963—2012 年南非前 10% 税前国民收入的份额（Top 10% National Income Share, South Africa, 1963—2012）三项数据来源：世界财富与收入数据库（World Wealth & Income Database），网址：https：//wid. world/country/south-africa/，数据为世界财富与收入数据库公开数据，数据库按年度更新数据信息，文中数据检索时间为 2019 年 8 月 6 日。

发了题为“南非的困境”的报告，文中指出：“南非的私人部门投资和出口仍大大低于危机前的水平。更为糟糕的是，该国的工作岗位大为减少，数目之巨令人震惊——其失业状况与处于全球经济危机中心的国家的失业状况相仿。在经济衰退的两年之后，仅有少部分的工作岗位得以恢复。上述影响使得南非本已居高不下的失业和收入不平等状况更加恶化。”①

从与南非青年发展有关的年轻群体总失业人数和青年失业率两个指标来看，1991—2018 年，南非年轻群体总失业人数于 2003 年达到顶点 62.1% 后，2003—2008 年便开始处于持续、明显的下降状态，2008 年为 45.178%。2008—2018 年的十年，偶有波动，但是总体趋势处于上升状态，2018 年为 52.853%。从数据分析来看，南非 15—24 岁的年轻群体，目前没有工作但可以参加工作且正在寻求工作的劳动力数量始终占据较大的比例，基本占到 15—24 岁年龄段劳动力的一半，甚至有的年份超过一半。事实上，南非 15—24 岁的年轻群体无法有效、充分地实现就业。

从南非青年总失业率情况来看，15—24 岁的南非青年失业率与年轻群体总失业人数趋势大体保持一致。2000—2018 年之间，2003 年失业率达到最高点，为 61.437%，此后开始下降。2008 年失业率为 45.607%，失业率结束自 2003 年来的下降状态，开始上升。2018 年上升到 53.425%。自 2008 年到 2018 年的十年，南非青年总失业率上升幅度总体趋势平稳，没有大起大落。但是自进入 21 世纪以来，南非青年失业率没有低于 40% 的情况，始终处于高位运行，最低年份是 2008 年。南非 15—24 岁的青年处于就业难的状态。按性别来看，15—24 岁的南非女性青年失业率明显高于男性青年失业率，且高于青年总失业率。

从南非人口增长、南非平均国内生产总值、南非平均国民收入、收入不平等、青年失业率、年轻群体总失业人数等指标，可以分析出南非青年成长所处的社会发展环境的基本情况：（1）人口持续增长且

---

① ［埃塞俄比亚］奥比·艾默·塞拉西：《南非的困境》，国际货币基金组织：https：//www. imf. org/external/chinese/pubs/ft/fandd/2011/12/pdf/selassie. pdf，2011－12。

进入 21 世纪后增长加快；（2）收入增长放缓且处于下降状态；（3）收入不平等持续扩大，处于上升状态，前 10% 群体占比持续增加；（4）南非青年面临就业难，失业率长期处于高位，女性青年失业率高于男性，且 15—24 岁待业青年占比高。进入 21 世纪，特别是 2008 年前后，主要数据分化明显。从数据分析得出，南非青年参与社会发展的社会环境需要提高和改善，为青年提供充分的就业和共同富裕的发展环境。

青年参与社会发展的方式和途径在现实的社会条件下有很多，但主要途径是就业。就业是青年融入社会的关键一步，也是青年立足社会的前提和基础。就业体现机会公平，以就业为代表的公共政策的有效推进可以促进社会流动，帮助青年实现“梦想”。可以说，“青年不缺少梦想，不缺少理想，不缺少奋斗的精神，缺少的是人生出彩的舞台。这舞台是经济的增长，这舞台是安定的社会，这舞台是公平的环境，这舞台是良好的教育，这舞台是谋生的技能，这舞台是发展的希望”①。青年参与社会发展既受到大的宏观发展环境的影响，也受到微观个体适应性的影响，其价值观的形成和塑造也是个体与环境互动的结果，这一过程贯穿其社会化的全过程，直至形成稳定的对世界的看法和成熟的观点。

二　南非青年参与社会发展的价值观选择

在社会发展环境的基础上，南非青年参与社会发展的价值观表现值得观察。进入 21 世纪，南非社会发展出现重要拐点，下面将以“世界价值观调查”第四轮、第五轮和第六轮的数据，具体分析 21 世纪以来南非青年的价值观变化情况。

表 8 - 2 从个人发展感受、国家发展期待与发展选择、个人发展态

① 马峰：《携手青年构建更加紧密的中非命运共同体》，中国社会科学网：http://www.cssn.cn/zzx/yc_ zzx/201809/t20180906_ 4555627.shtml，2018 - 09 - 06。

表 8 - 2　**世界价值观调查：南非青年参与社会发展的价值观表现①**

分类	问题	选项	第四轮（1999—2004）2001	第五轮（2005—2009）2006	第六轮（2010—2014）2013	备注
个人发展感受	幸福感（Feeling of happiness）	非常高兴（Very happy）	38.70%	45.50%	41.60%	第四轮 V11，第五轮 V10，第六轮 V10
		开心（Quite happy）	39.40%	36.30%	37.00%	
		不是很开心（Not very happy）	19.30%	13.70%	16.90%	
		一点都不高兴（Not at all happy）	2.60%	4.40%	4.10%	
		不知道（Don't know）	*	0.10%	0.40%	
	健康状况（主观）[State of health (subjective)]	非常好（Very good）	53.90%	51.40%	51.10%	第四轮 V12，第五轮 V11，第六轮 V11
		好（Good）	28.00%	36.80%	41.50%	
		差不多（Fair）	16.20%	8.50%	6.30%	
		差（Poor）	1.90%	2.70%	1.10%	
		非常差（Very poor）	*	0.60%	*	
		不知道（Don't know）	*	*	*	

① 本部分数据为世界价值观调查数据，是美国学者罗纳德·英格尔哈特主持的一个跨度近四十年的世界范围内的价值观调查项目。本文所用关于南非青年的世界价值观调查数据均采自第四轮、第五轮和第六轮调查数据。第四轮调查时间跨度为 1999—2004 年，第五轮调查时间跨度为 2005—2009 年，第六轮调查时间跨度为 2010—2014 年，在南非的抽样调查具体时间分别是 2000 年、2006 年和 2013 年，涉及分析的问题主要选择与青年发展密切相关的个人发展感受、国家发展期待与发展选择、个人发展态度三个维度，围绕幸福感、健康、就业、经济增长、国家发展目标等方面，以探查南非青年的价值观表现。在涉及调查的问题中，同一问题在不同轮次的调查中位于问卷中的编号各有不同。在表 8 - 2 的备注部分，将每一轮对应的同一问题在不同调查轮次中的问题编号加以标注。同时，每一轮调查时间跨度平均为 4 年，具体在每一国家调查的时间不同，在表 8 - 2 中标注了在南非的具体调查年份。在分析过程中，年龄选择为最大到 29 岁（Up to 29），改变交叉变量（Change crossing variable）选项选择年龄（Age），添加第二交叉变量（Add a second crossing variable）选项选择年龄（age）。在数据显示（Display）部分，选择显示全部调查数据（Show total，all responses）选项，得到表 8 - 2 及后续部分调查数据。数据来源与分析网站为：World Values Survey，网址：http：//www.worldvaluessurvey.org/WVSOnline.jsp，检索时间为 2019 年 7 月 1 日—20 日，文中所用世界价值观调查数据均来源于此网站。关于本文涉及的数据分析中，世界价值观调查数据在线分析系统将年龄划分为 29 岁以下（含 29 岁），30—49 岁，50 岁（含 50 岁）及以上，为与联合国的标准保持一致性，重点采集和分析 29 岁以下（含 29 岁）年龄段的信息。表 8 - 2 及文中涉及世界价值观调查有关问题及选项内容采用中英文双标的形式，在中文翻译过程中，参考了世界价值观第六轮调查中文问卷的有关内容，网址：http：//www.worldvaluessurvey.org/WVSDocumentationWV6.jsp。

续表

分类	问题	选项	第四轮（1999—2004）2001	第五轮（2005—2009）2006	第六轮（2010—2014）2013	备注
国家发展期待与发展选择	最重要的选择：第一选择（Most important：first choice）	稳定的经济（A stable economy）	48. 20%	41. 10%	47. 40%	第四轮 V124，第五轮 V73，第六轮 V64
		向更以人为本的社会发展（Progress toward a less impersonal and more humane society）	6. 30%	7. 40%	20. 50%	
		由物质社会向后物质社会发展（Progress toward a society in which ideas count more than money）	6. 60%	9. 60%	8. 60%	
		打击犯罪（The fight against crime）	37. 70%	41. 40%	23. 50%	
		不清楚（No sabe）	1. 10%	60. 00%	*	
	国家目标：第一选择/下一个十年国家发展目标的第一选择（Aims of country：first choice/Aims of this country should be for the next 10 years）	快速经济增长（A high level of economic growth）	58. 80%	57. 30%	45. 90%	第四轮 V120，第五轮 V69，第六轮 V60
		强大的国防力量（Strong defence forces）	13. 60%	10. 70%	21. 70%	
		使人民拥有更多话语权（People have more say about how things are done）	21. 70%	23. 60%	23. 20%	
		努力是我们的城市和乡村更美丽（Trying to make our cities and countryside more beautiful）	4. 50%	8. 00%	9. 20%	
	保护环境 VS 经济增长（Protecting environment vs. Economic growth）	保护环境（Protecting environment）	30. 10%	23. 70%	38. 80%	第四轮 V36，第五轮 V104，第六轮 V81
		经济增长和创造就业（Economy growth and creating jobs）	59. 80%	66. 60%	59. 50%	
		其他答案（Other answer）	4. 40%	1. 30%	1. 70%	
		不知道（Don't know）	5. 70%	8. 40%	*	

续表

分类	问题	选项	第四轮（1999—2004）2001	第五轮（2005—2009）2006	第六轮（2010—2014）2013	备注
个人发展态度（工作）	对失去工作或找不到工作的担忧（Worries: Losing my job or not finding a job）	非常担心（Very much）	*	*	43.30%	仅有第六轮调查，V181
		担心（A great deal）	*	*	23.70%	
		不太担心（Not much）	*	*	9.20%	
		非常不担心（Not at all）	*	*	15.80%	
		不知道（Don't know）	*	*	8.10%	

数据来源：世界价值观调查。

度（工作）三个维度展示出29岁以下南非青年参与社会发展的价值观表现。

1. 个人发展感受维度

（1）幸福感（Feeling of happiness）的五个选项中非常高兴（Very happy）、开心（Quite happy）选项的占比高，主观幸福感表现积极。不是很开心（Not very happy）、一点都不高兴（Not at all happy）选项占比相对以上两个选项较低，但处于增长的趋势。非常高兴（Very happy）的选项第六轮比第五轮有所下降，可以明显看到选项数据的起伏，其中2006年调查的第五轮前后变化比较明显，非常高兴的指标在降低，不是很开心的选项在上升。经济因素的变化有一些影响，一点都不高兴的占比没有再下降到2000年第四轮调查的水平。总体上看，对幸福感的感知还是积极的，细节变化值得关注，在大趋势上与宏观环境变化具有一致性。

（2）健康状况（主观）［State of health（subjective）］选项中，认为非常好（Very good）的占到半数以上，这一趋势没有改变。认为好（Good）的选项也基本稳定，呈现上升趋势，变化比较明显。差不多（Fair）和差（Poor）占比较小，且呈现下降趋势，差不多的下降趋势明显。总体上看，南非青年主观上认为其健康状况是积极的，这一趋势具有稳定性。个别选项有波动，但总趋势较稳定。

综合数据得知，南非青年在个人发展感受度方面，幸福与健康维度表现积极。幸福与健康两个方面问题中的选项非常高兴和非常好呈现下降趋势，但是幅度微小。在幸福感的选项上，消极因素和感受有所增加。健康不代表幸福，但幸福一定需要身体健康。

2. 国家发展期待与发展选择维度

这一维度主要包括三个视角：①最重要的选择：第一选择（Most important：first choice）；②国家目标：第一选择/下一个十年国家发展目标的第一选择（Aims of country：first choice/Aims of this country should be for the next 10 years）；③保护环境VS经济增长（Protecting environment vs. Economic growth）。主要分析在南非青年心中国家最重要的发展任务与目标是什么，是考察个人与国家、个人与社会关系的重要参考。在每一个问题的选项设计上，几乎涵盖经济、国防、社会等领域，而“最重要的第一选择/下一个十年国家发展目标的第一选择”对于青年和国家而言是什么，其意义对社会发展是十分重要的。

三个问题涉及的有关经济方面的选项占比非常高。南非青年对经济增长的客观需求和关注的共识具有普遍性。无论是作为最重要选择的第一选择，还是十年后国家发展目标的第一选择，稳定的经济（a stable economy）和快速经济增长（a high level of economic growth）是青年的首要目标。在环境保护与经济增长方面，经济增长和创造就业（economy growth and creating jobs）的选项占比平均在60%左右，进一步说明南非青年首先关注的是经济的增长，环境保护可以放到第二选择上。

社会发展环境方面，南非青年对打击犯罪（the fight against crime）高度关注，这说明南非青年希望社会发展安定，营造良好的社会发展环境，实现经济增长、社会安定是南非青年的重要价值选择和对国家发展目标、选择的重要期待。对向更以人为本的社会发展（progress toward a less impersonal and more humane society）和使人民拥有更多话语权（people have more say about how things are done）的关注虽然位于两个不同的问题中，但是从所占比例关系可以看到，南非青年希望在社会发展的过程中，国家注重社会发展的公平、公正，国家要让社会发展更加以人为本，人民要有更多的话语权。向更以人为本的社会发展（progress toward a less impersonal and more humane society）选项从2001年的6.30%、2006年的7.40%大幅上升到2013年的20.50%，这折射出南非青年对建设一个更加以人为本的社会发展的强烈期待。

南非青年对强大的国防力量（strong defence forces）的关注度上升明显，强大的国防是对外部不安全的直观反映，这个与对经济增长和社会安定的期待具有一致性，经济的快速稳定增长和社会发展、打击犯罪需要强大的国防力量来维系，以维护国内环境和国际环境的稳定。

南非青年对国家发展期待与发展选择的态度具有高度一致性，经济增长、社会发展、国家安定、社会公平和公正、国防强大是南非青年表现出来的重要价值观特征。南非青年的这一价值观表现与南非青年所处的社会发展环境具有高度的一致性和契合性。

3. 个人发展态度（工作）维度

对失去工作或找不到工作的担忧（Worries：Losing my job or not finding a job）是世界价值观第六轮调查的新问题项。单就第六轮调查数据来看，南非青年对现实和未来个人发展最重要的问题——工作是非常担忧的。非常担心（very much）为 43.30%，担心（a great deal）为 23.70%，两者相加为 67%，这一数据揭示，大量青年担心自己失去工作或找不到工作，这也直接反映了南非社会发展的长期现实性问题，与社会发展的宏观环境具有高度的一致性，也间接呼应了国家发展期待与发展选择维度上南非青年对经济增长、社会安定的价值观选择。

通过对个人发展感受、国家发展期待与发展选择、个人发展态度（工作）三个维度探查南非青年在参与社会发展中的价值观表现，勾勒出南非青年群体的整体群像：这是一个幸福感高、乐观的群体，他们健康，对未来充满期待，希望国家经济增长、社会安定、社会发展更加公正与公平、国防稳固，对失去或找不到工作充满担忧。这些与他们成长的宏观社会环境的现实具有高度关联性。

三　南非青年参与社会发展的价值观分析

南非青年参与社会发展的价值观表现以及其成长所依赖的社会发展环境将南非青年群体参与社会发展的态度展示出来。需要透过现象看本质，从更深层次的维度分析这一价值观表现与社会发展环境之间的内在联系。

罗纳德·英格尔哈特根据世界价值观调查的长期研究，发现宏观经济社会发展与社会群体价值观形成和选择之间存在必然联系，并提出了著名的价值观代际转移理论，提炼出了物质主义与后物质主义的价值观概念。罗纳德·英格尔哈特的理论基于两个重要的假设：匮乏假设和社会化假设。

“匮乏假设是指：几乎所有人都渴求自由和自主，但是人们都倾向于赋予最紧迫的需求以最高的价值。物质必需品和人身安全直接与生存相关，一旦这些东西匮乏，人们就会将这些‘物质主义’目标放在首位。但是在富裕条件下，人们则更可能强调诸如归属感、尊重、审美和知识需求之类的‘后物质主义’目标。”①

“社会化假设是指：物质条件和优先价值观之间的关系不是能够即时调整的。在很大程度上，个人的基本价值观反映的是其未成年阶段的生活条件，并且价值观的转变主要是通过代际的人口更替实现的。”②

在后期的研究中，罗纳德·英格尔哈特也把物质主义价值观列为新的维度——生存价值观。③

通过匮乏假设的设定和构成条件，可以将现阶段南非青年价值观表现归纳为物质主义价值观，即生存价值观。南非青年将物质必需品和人身安全直接与生存相关的经济增长、社会安定、社会发展更加以人为本、公正、公平、国防稳固等列为价值观的优先关注项，对失去或找不到工作充满担忧。南非青年物质主义价值观（生存价值观）的表现与南非社会发展的宏观社会环境有着直接而密切的关系。形成物质主义价值观的基础是经济社会发展的“匮乏表现”。几乎所有人都渴求自由和自主，南非青年也不例外，但是在自由与自主存在的同时，其价值观的优先选项却随着经济社会的发展而有先后，这也可以理解为什么南非青年将经济安全列为首要国家目标，而将工作列为自身生存安全的重要关注项。

① ［美］罗纳德·英格尔哈特：《发达工业社会的文化转型》，张秀琴译，社会科学文献出版社 2013 年版，第 3 页。

② 同上。

③ 同上书，第 2 页。

在罗纳德·英格尔哈特的理论框架中，物质主义价值观与后物质价值观之间以生存安全与不安全为标准，所构成的价值观表现是不同的。在不安全的生存状态下，政治态度和经济态度明显偏向对生存的关注。①

表 8-2 中的选项“由物质社会向后物质社会发展”（Progress toward a society in which ideas count more than money）在第四轮、第五轮、第六轮所占比例分别为 6.60%、9.60%、8.60%，从 2000 年到 2013 年，长达 13 年的跨度，此一选项在南非青年的选择中始终没有超过 10%，而且在 2013 年还下降了 1%。从微数据视角来分析，在社会发展进程中，对于南非青年来说后物质的社会发展不是当前的必然需求，其优先需求是以经济建设为中心、物质优先发展的社会。从价值观维度上讲，重视精神、重视环境保护是后物质主义价值观的表现，而这两点在南非青年的价值观选择中不居于优先选项。优先选项是物质主义价值观，即生存价值观。

由上可见，南非青年参与社会发展的价值观表现与社会环境有着密切的联系，“参与到全球化中的青年，在发展的机遇面前需要技能的培训，在发展的挑战面前需要良好的教育，在发展的前途与人生的抉择面前需要梦想以支撑，在发展的爬坡中需要看到发展的前途，而这些与发展的同频共振是青年所需要的”②。

四　中国南非合作构筑青年发展新机遇

21 世纪第三个十年的历史关口正在向我们走来，世界发展面临百年未有之变局。2008 年国际金融危机的发生，给世界经济带来了深刻

---

① ［美］罗纳德·英格尔哈特：《现代化与后现代化 43 个国家的文化、经济与政治变迁》，严挺译，社会科学文献出版社 2013 年版，第 43 页。

② 马峰：《携手青年构建更加紧密的中非命运共同体》，中国社会科学网：http://www.cssn.cn/zzx/yc_zzx/201809/t20180906_4555627.shtml，2018-09-06。

的调整和更大的不确定。“当前，我们正处在一个挑战层出不穷、风险日益增多的时代”①，世界范围内的价值观优先选项的转移在青年一代身上正在发生，发展阶段的不同，让世界范围内不同国家和地区青年的反应形式有所不同，但是希望经济成长、社会稳定、社会发展公平、公正是这个时代青年的共同追求。然而，“人类社会在从工业社会向风险社会行进的过程中，科学、法律、民主、技术经济、政治制度等工业社会之理性基础将会受到质疑进而被冲破、被推翻了，而风险社会的理性基础还远没有形成，还需要讨论，需要重建”②。

因此，在青年最需要资源的时代，社会应辅助青年成长，为青年发展提供机会，防范社会风险，增加青年参与社会发展的机会与动力。联合国秘书长青年特使贾亚特玛·维克拉玛纳亚克指出：“根据联合国发布的《世界人口展望》报告，当今世界人口的中位年龄为30岁，也就是说，全世界一半人口的年龄在30岁以下。在非洲，一半人口的年龄在19岁以下，而政治人物的平均年龄在60岁以上。要弥合这道鸿沟，既需要加强制度设计，也需要青年从点滴小事做起，积极关注和参与社会治理。”③

南非青年在参与社会发展中的价值观表现及面对发展所表现出来的需求，与中非合作论坛北京峰会提出的“八大行动”倡议具有高度的契合性。“八大行动”倡议对接非洲发展，即：产业促进行动、设施联通行动、贸易便利行动、绿色发展行动、能力建设行动、健康卫生行动、人文交流行动、和平安全行动。“八大行动”倡议与非洲经济社会的发展需求、非洲青年的发展期待高度契合，为中非命运共同体提供了广阔的发展路径。

对于不同的国家和民族来说，青年都是国家和社会发展的未来和希

---

① 《习近平会见德国总理默克尔》，新华网：http：//www. xinhuanet. com/politics/leaders/2019 - 09/06/c_ 1124970182. htm，2019 - 09 - 06。

② ［德］乌尔里希·贝克：《从工业社会到风险社会（下篇）——关于人类生存、社会结构和生态启蒙等问题的思考》，《马克思主义与现实》2003年第5期。

③ ［斯里兰卡］贾亚特玛·维克拉玛纳亚克：《支持多边主义需要青年踊跃发声》，《青年参考》2019年7月19日。

望。中国与非洲——世界上最大的发展中国家与世界上发展中国家聚集最多的大陆之间的合作，将为双方青年的共同发展，缔造机遇与阳光、向上的价值观。习近平主席在2018年中非合作论坛北京峰会开幕式上指出："青年是中非关系的希望所在。我提出的中非'八大行动'倡议中，许多措施都着眼青年、培养青年、扶助青年，致力于为他们提供更多就业机会、更好发展空间。"[①] 新时代中非合作"八大行动"聚焦青年，致力于为青年提供更多就业机会和更好发展空间，同时也为新时代对非研究拓展了新的领域——聚焦青年发展。

让青年看到希望，社会才有希望，让青年拥有未来，社会才有前途。我们深刻思考社会发展与青年发展的互动关系，要坚持以人民为中心谋发展，不断满足青年群体对美好生活的向往，为青年成长提供和搭建人生出彩的舞台。南非青年参与社会发展的价值观表现，其启示是深刻的。从世界青年发展角度来看：一方面要关注影响青年发展的经济增长、社会流动、收入分配、社会安全等深层次社会发展问题；另一方面要关注青年在"四业"，即：就业、学业、置业、创业涉及个人未来发展方面的需求。社会发展环境与青年发展需求构成了一个整体的两个方面，既要不断解决影响青年发展的深层次社会发展问题，塑造良好的经济社会发展环境，又要引导青年融入社会发展、参与社会发展，让青年在参与分享中促进社会发展。

从我国青年发展的视角来看，我们要进一步做好青年工作：一方面，从宏观社会发展环境层面，要始终坚持以经济建设为中心，推动经济高质量发展。"提供全方位公共就业服务，促进高校毕业生等青年群体、农民工多渠道就业创业。破除妨碍劳动力、人才社会性流动的体制机制弊端，使人人都有通过辛勤劳动实现自身发展的机会。"[②] 而且，

① 习近平：《携手共命运 同心促发展——在二〇一八年中非合作论坛北京峰会开幕式上的主旨讲话》，《光明日报》2018年9月4日第2版。

② 习近平：《决胜全面建成小康社会夺取新时代中国特色社会主义伟大胜利——在中国共产党第十九次全国代表大会上的报告》，《光明日报》2017年10月28日第1版。

要始终坚持打击犯罪，维护社会稳定，为青年发展、成长，营造良好的社会发展环境。另一方面，从青年发展需求层面，要不断满足青年对美好生活的向往，为青年成长提供和搭建人生出彩的舞台，主动引导青年融入社会发展。

中国与南非同属发展中国家，在构建中非命运共同体的过程中发挥着重要引领作用。中国与南非青年对美好生活的向往是两国青年共同的价值观体现，中非合作“八大行动”倡议对接了南非青年的发展需求与期待，对接了非洲大陆追求现代化的期望。新时代中非携手构建人类命运共同体，离不开中非青年的心手相牵。

附　　录

一　新时代中非关系：中国—南非青年社会发展学术对话会综述

2018 年 8 月 27 日由中国社会科学院社会发展战略研究院、南非开普半岛科技大学共同主办，中国非洲研究院课题资助的纪念改革开放四十周年“新时代中非关系：中国—南非青年社会发展学术对话会”在京举行。

此次学术对话会上，中国和南非学者围绕南非青年参与社会发展的互动机制、青年文化变迁 30 年、非洲青年在中国、中国就业结构与青年就业问题、南非青年参与社会发展的互动机制、中国的城镇化与青年代际职业地位流动、新社会组织青年人才发展战略的目标及实现路径、第四次工业革命与青年发展等话题进行了广泛深入的探讨和交流。

南非开普半岛科技大学校长克里斯·恩释拉珀从南非青年的年龄结构及发展现实、南非青年发展的国家辅助政策及青年发展机构、南非开普半岛科技大学对学生参与社会发展、促进就业的机制等方面，阐述了南非青年参与社会发展的互动机制，分析了第四次工业革命中南非促进工业发展与促进青年就业之间的政策和机制。此外，克里斯·恩释拉珀认为，中南同为金砖国家，青年发展是双方社会发展中的共同话题，在促进青年参与社会发展方面，中国有很多的成功经验值得南非借鉴，特别是在促进青年就业方面。

中国社会科学院社会发展战略研究院马峰博士重点阐述了第四次工业革命对青年发展的重要影响。他认为，第四次工业革命既是青年发展的机遇，也是青年发展的生存之择。一方面，青年要积极参与到第四次工业革命带来的全球新旧动能转换的发展中来，在新动能的发展中实现技能的提升和命运的翻转，成为新技术革命中的主干力量；另一方面，要防止出现新技术革命发展中带来的“被遗忘的人和被边缘化的人”，重视人才资源的作用，特别是青年人才。

南非开普半岛科技大学教授颜炳文从南非青年发展战略、青年构成的年龄和性别结构、南非青年在人口增长中的结构、南非青年参与经济社会发展等方面，重点阐述了南非政府的青年发展政策。颜炳文认为，需要深入推进南非青年发展，实现南非青年 2020 年发展目标，让青年人掌握自己的未来。此外，要进一步降低青年失业率，在发展中促进青年融入社会，让青年成为社会发展的推动力量，共享发展的成果，重点解决影响青年发展的就业、贫困、收入不平等问题。

广东青年人才研究院院长谢素军认为，近年来，伴随“一带一路”的推进和延伸，非洲看似遥远实则就在身边，而非洲青年在其中扮演着“弄潮儿”的角色，他们进入中国并主要从事商贸活动，由此导致了中非关系逐渐呈现出“下移”的态势，中非民间交往成为中非交往的主力军。非洲青年在“言、行、食、情”方面所表现出的中国范儿，成为中非命运共同体的真实写照。可以秉持求同存异、兼收并蓄、尊重彼此生活习惯等原则促进非洲青年在中国发展，促进中非友好和青年交流。

中国青少年研究中心副研究员陈晨梳理了中国青年文化三十年的发展。陈晨认为，可以从四个角度理解青年文化变迁：第一，传媒技术的发展深刻影响了青年的个性和价值观；第二，新阶层新兴群体的崛起反映了青年多元的文化心态；第三，国内外形势的发展形塑了青年行为的环境；第四，对重大历史事件的记忆成为青年情感凝结和文化反思的载体。进入新时代以来，中国青年以更加积极向上的态度，融入时代的发展和新时代新青年文化的创造中，当代中国青年人在发展和实践中所表现出的更具个性化、创造性、自主性的特点，体现了与当代中国经济社会发展的同步性和文化发展的新特点。

中国社会科学院社会发展战略研究院副研究员孙兆阳对中国就业结构与青年就业问题进行了阐述。他认为，改革开放以来，中国就业结构转型呈现四个特征：一是第一产业向第二、第三产业转移；二是农村向城镇转移；三是以国有企业和集体企业为主向多种就业形式转移；四是从人口红利向老龄化社会转移。中国用改革开放 40 年的时间，走过了西方百年的现代化发展道路，取得了举世瞩目的历史性成就，但是在发展中还面临不平衡、不充分的矛盾，高质量的就业岗位还比较稀缺、就业结构性矛盾突出、青年就业面临新的发展瓶颈，需要进一步推进全面深化改革，破除妨碍劳动力、人才社会性流动的体制机制弊端，使人人都有通过辛勤劳动实现自身发展的机会”。

二　中国—南非青年发展学术研讨会综述

2019 年 5 月 22 日由中国社会科学院社会发展战略研究院主办，中国非洲研究院课题资助举办的“中国—南非青年发展学术研讨会”在京举行。学术研讨会围绕中国南非青年发展主题展开学术讨论，取得了丰硕的学术成果。

本次研讨会的召开，正值中国非洲研究院成立之际。研讨会围绕中国青年社会发展与社会参与、新时代扶贫立法与青年发展、影响南非青年发展的因素和一些重要的干预措施、青年与中国社会组织发展、青年与中国基层社会治理核心问题、社会创新与青年发展、新业态下大城市外来务工青年的就业状况及对策、改革开放以来就业结构转型等议题展开了学术讨论，形成了丰富的学术成果。通过学术交流，进一步丰富了国别研究的内涵，全景地展示了中华人民共和国成立七十年来中国青年发展事业的成就，南非青年发展的成绩。会议并就中国、南非助力青年融入社会发展的政策、措施及经验进行了深入交流，重点探讨了“八大行动”与南非、非洲青年发展对接，中非青年携手构建中非命运共同体，加强文明对话交流与合作。

中国社会科学院社会发展战略研究院副院长寇伟在开幕式上的致辞中指出，中国与非洲虽然相距遥远，但是中非人民“相知无远近，万里尚为邻”。这是第二次在中国社会科学院社会发展战略研究院举办中国非洲青年发展学术研讨会，研讨会的举办恰逢中国社会科学院中国非洲研究院成立之际，作为首批共同研究课题，希望双方团队精心协作、认真讨论，争取高质量完成研究工作，充分发挥学界与智库的智力支持作用，为共同构建中非命运共同体做出我们的贡献。

南非开普半岛科技大学颜炳文教授在致辞中指出：中国与非洲人民“志合者，不以山海为远”。非洲的中国热持续升温，习近平主席提出的“八大行动”计划，聚焦非洲青年发展和能力建设，为非洲现代化事业厚植发展力量。共同研究中国非洲青年发展，助力中非青年携手发展，对于中国青年了解非洲，非洲青年了解中国、学习中国发展经验具有重要意义。通过此次学术研讨会，我们可以更好地了解南非青年发展，了解中国青年发展，促进学术交流与合作。

中国社会科学院社会发展战略研究院副研究员余少祥在题为“新时代扶贫立法与青年发展”的演讲中指出，青年群体是扶贫的重要对象，在全面建成小康社会之际，进一步加强和完善扶贫立法，为青年发展提供人生出彩的舞台，满足青年群体对美好生活的向往具有十分重要的意义。一方面要用法治化的手段，秉持全面依法治国的原则，让扶贫事业有法可依，青年群体扶贫有规矩可循；另一方面，建立扶贫规范机制，总结扶贫经验，形成法治规范和法治惯例，系统总结扶贫立法的成功做法和经验，形成中国扶贫立法的中国经验和中国智慧，助力青年发展。

南非开普半岛科技大学教授颜炳文在题为“影响南非青年发展的因

素和一些重要的干预措施”演讲中重点阐述了南非青年发展促进机制及政策措施。颜炳文教授强调指出：在“八大行动”内容中，习近平主席非常重视青年发展，高度关注非洲青年发展问题。例如在实施产业促进行动方面，中国决定向非洲派遣500名高级农业专家，通过多种渠道帮助非洲培养一批青年农民致富带头人，开展本地化技术示范，推广中国农业生产技术和农村经济发展经验，带动当地农民增产增收。这将对青年农民自主创业和发家致富起到积极的指导作用。此外，南非总统西里尔·拉马福萨在中非合作论坛北京峰会上致开幕辞，赞扬中国取得的“卓越经济成就”，包括让数百万人摆脱贫困。

中国社会科学院社会发展战略研究院副研究员孙兆阳在题为“改革开放以来就业结构转型”的演讲中从中国就业结构转型的历史回顾、中国就业结构转型的主要特征、中国就业结构面临的主要挑战三个方面阐述了中国青年就业发展问题。分析了中国劳动力流动的四个阶段及特征，特征包括：从第一产业向第二、第三产业转移；人力资源要素重新配置带来生产率提升；在加快城镇化建设的同时，推动劳动力从农村向城市转移；在城镇地区，从国有企业向私营企业、个体就业为主的多种就业形式转移；从中西部地区向东南沿海转移。同时，中国就业面临结构性矛盾，促进青年就业和发展，要多措并举，创新宏观政策，将青年发展通过就业融入社会发展与国家进步大潮中。

中国社会科学院社会发展战略研究院副研究员马峰在题为“中国青年社会发展与社会参与”的演讲中重点阐述了中国青年的社会发展与社会参与。从中华人民共和国成立七十年青年发展事业的视角，展示了七十年来中国青年发展的成就。演讲从青年发展事业取得的历史性成就、青年发展事业与国家进步同频共振、青年发展事业在“追梦”与“圆梦”中不断前进、青年发展事业在新时代民族复兴中奋斗前行等方面解读了七十年来中国实现了由文盲大国向人力资源大国转变的历史进程，指出当代青年更具个性，更加自我，更强调参与性、主动性。同时，工作、家庭、婚恋、育儿、养老的因素，也让当代青年承受着事业上升和发展的压力，其人生观、世界观、价值观的波动也十分明显。“空巢青年”“蚁族”“留守青年”等词汇的出现，也折射出当今青年发展的多面性和多元性，以及青年群体内部的分化和结构构成。每一代青年都有每一代青年的奋斗群像，每一代青年都有每一代青年不同成长、发展的时代背景和时空背景。

中国社会科学院社会学研究所助理研究员林红在题为“青年发展与中国社会组织发展回顾、现状、展望”的演讲中重点阐述了中国青年发展与中国社会组织发展的历程、现状及未来。林红博士从中国社会组织发展回顾、中国社会组织的发展现状、中国社会组织的发展展望三个维度分析了中国社会组织发展进程中青年参与社会组织发展、社会发展的机制和路径。社会组织的发展从专业化道路、行业规范和制度化、第三部门参与公共事务制度化路径建构、从经验分享到参与全球环境治理的过程，为中国青年发展提供了广阔的空间。习近平总书记在纪念五四运动100周年大会上的讲话指出：“新时代中国青年，要有家国情怀，也要有人类关怀，发扬中华文化崇尚的四海一家、天下为公精神，为实现中华民族伟大复兴而奋斗，为推动共建‘一带一路’、推动构建人类命运共同体而努力。”

中国社会科学院社会发展战略研究院助理研究员戈艳霞在题为“特大城市外来青年人才的通勤压力、形成原因与治理对策”的演讲中，重点阐述了特大城市通勤压力给外来青年带来的深度社会发展参与的影响，并分析了其成因，提出了治理的对策。戈艳霞博士从北京外来人才的通勤压力现状、通勤压力的形成原因展开分析，采用定量分析的方法，分析了影响通勤原因的家庭和个人因素，并提出理论假设，进行了验证。分析发现，居住区位、家庭结构、职业因素和个人因素都对通勤时间有显著影响。在诸多影响因素中，居住区位和家庭人数结构对通勤压力的影响较大。总体来讲，当前导致外来人才通勤压力过大的主要原因还是就业区与居住区在空间上的过度分离，以及家庭成员随迁对住房空间和品质的刚性需求。要多措并举缓解外来人才的通勤压力，促进城市的健康持续发展。

中国社会科学院社会发展战略研究院助理研究员刘学在题为“社会创新与青年发展”的演讲中重点阐述了社会创新对于促进青年发展的重要意义和作用机制。刘学博士从现状与问题、新业态与社会发展、扶贫与人的发展机制、企业公益创新发展与青年发展等方面论述了新时代背景下，社会创新发展面临时代发展新的要求，需要聚焦创新的形式和内容，加大全面深化改革力度，打通青年参与社会创新发展的空间，合理界定企业利益边界、责任边界，促进企业公益创新发展，助力青年发展与社会治理现代化。

中国社会科学院社会发展战略研究院助理研究员张书琬在题为“新业态下大城市外来务工青年的就业状况及对策”的演讲中，重点阐述了新业态背景下大城市外来务工人员的就业状况，深度揭示了外来务工青年在社会参与和社会发展中的内在机制。通过对大城市中主要从事外卖配送行业工作人员的田野调查和问卷分析，建构了对新业态中就业青年群体群像的刻画，将显性群体的隐性发展问题进行了透镜式解析，提出了要从加强社会保障覆盖、健全流动的和群体的流动党组织建设、健全社会融入机制等举措，促进新业态健康发展以及外来务工青年健康成长。

本次中国—南非青年发展学术研讨会取得了丰硕的成果，达成广泛的学术共识。研讨会的学术讨论环节，学者们的讨论深入细致，学术交流精谨细腻。

与会学者认为，中国南非青年参与社会发展对于青年成长具有重要的意义，青年是人力资源的重要来源，青年发展是光明的，国家发展、世界发展是光明的，社会发展要为青年发展提供广阔的舞台和空间。

此外，在中非青年交流方面，要促进中国青年发展的中国经验、中国智慧与非洲青年发展的需求对接，落实“八大行动”计划，中非青年携手共同构建中非命运共同体，增进非洲青年了解中国、读懂中国，增进中国青年更广泛地参与非洲发展事业与“一带一路”建设事业。

与会学者认为，要促进中非文明交流互鉴。文明因精彩而不同，文明因多彩而多姿。中华文明与非洲文明的交流互鉴，美人之美、美美与共，将会更加有力地促进中非交流互鉴，构建更加紧密的中非命运共同体。

后　记

本书为中国非洲研究院首批资助课题“中国—南非青年参与社会发展机制及趋势研究”（CAI2017004）的研究成果。在撰写过程中，中国、南非双方课题组成员通力合作，完成了这一双方共同期待的研究成果。在完成过程中，作为课题组成员，姜宁宁博士，贡献了本书第一部分第二章《中国青年参与社会发展的社会组织机制及人才战略》的重要内容，分享了中国青年参与社会发展的社会组织机制研究成果。本书其余部分章节内容，根据研究计划分别由中国社会科学院社会发展战略研究院的马峰博士与南非开普半岛科技大学的颜炳文博士完成。

在此向所有支持、关心、参与本课题研究的学界同人致以诚挚的谢意。希望研究成果可以为促进中非友好，加强中非青年交流，助力中非青年携手发展，深化中非学界学术交流与合作贡献绵薄之力，起到“抛砖引玉”的作用。

课题组

2020 年 11 月于北京

Part I

Chinese Youth and Social Development

Chapter I Policies and Mechanisms for Chinese Youth's Participation in Social Development

Youth work has always been a key link and part of the work of the Party and the state. The state pays attention to the development and growth of young people. The great rejuvenation of the Chinese nation requires young people from generation to generation to take over the baton of history and succeed in a Long March of each young generation.

I Formulating medium-and long-term youth development plans and improving youth's participation in social development

The achievements of the five years since the 18th National Congress are destined to be included in the history of the Chinese nation's rejuvenation. In this process, with the development of the country as a whole and the promotion of theoretical and practical innovation, the theory and practice of youth development planning have also achieved new developments and new breakthroughs, with a focus of being more systematic, professional and comprehensive. The introduction of the *Medium-and Long-Term Youth Development Plan (2016 – 2025)* has realized the new development level of

China's theory and practice of youth development planning. From a higher overall level and vision, the Party and the state pay attention to youth development, care for youth progress, and promote youth development into a new historical stage of development.

Since the 18th National Congress of the Communist Party of China, General Secretary Xi Jinping has delivered a series of speeches on the issue of youth development and given scientific answers to the major issues which are valued by youth and concerning their needs for longing for a better life, including the ideals, beliefs, values, growth of young people, and building platforms for youth development. The focus is, from the view of theory and practice, in terms of the historical position of realizing "two centenary goals", the new development stage of socialism with Chinese characteristics, the new great journey requiring young people to take over the historical baton, to comprehensively plan work on youth development, and point out the direction for carrying out youth work in the new era and planning theory and practice innovation.

On May 4, 2013, General Secretary Xi Jinping delivered Speech *at the Symposium Outstanding Young Pelegates from All Walks of Life*, which systematically, comprehensively and scientifically answers questions about the ideals and beliefs of the youth, and closely links the individual dreams of the young people with the great ideal of realizing the Chinese Dream of national rejuvenation. "The Chinese Dream is a dream of our generation, but even more so, a dream of the younger generation. The Chinese Dream of national rejuvenation will be realized ultimately through the endeavors of young people, generation by generation. "① General Secretary pointed out, "Looking into the future, our young people will surely make great achievements. This is the

---

① Xi Jinping, "Speech at the Symposium with Outstanding Young Delegates from All Walks of Life", Xinhuanet, http: //www. xinhuanet. com/politics/2013 -05/04/c_ 115639203. htm.

historical law like ' in the Yangtze River the waves behind drive on those before', and the youth responsibility that ' each generation surpasses the preceding one'. The youth must bravely shoulder the heavy responsibilities given by the times, aim high, have your feet firmly on the ground, and fulfill youthful dreams in the course of realizing the Chinese Dream of national rejuvenation."① To encourage young people, he said, "Young friends, there is only one youth in a person's life. Now, youth is for struggle, and in the future, youth is memory".②

On May 4, 2014, General Secretary Xi Jinping once again walked among the young people and delivered a speech at the Peking University named *Youth Must Consciously Practice the Core Values of Socialism.* The speech of General Secretary focused on the major theoretical and practical issues influencing the development of youth, and young people's values. Values have an impact on a person's whole life. Values in youth are extremely important for understanding objective things and social development, and even have a life-time impact. General Secretary pointed out: "Why do I talk about the issue of socialist core values to the youth? It is because the value orientation of the youth determines the value orientation of the whole society in the future. Youth is in the period of formation and establishment of values. The development of values in this period is very important. Living one's life is like buttoning up one's jacket. If the first button is not fastened correctly, the rest will never find their rightful place. The buttons of life should be fastened well from the very beginning."③ General Secretary focuses on the issue of values that affect

---

① Xi Jinping, "Speech at the Symposium with Outstanding Young Delegates from All Walks of Life", Xinhuanet, http://www.xinhuanet.com/politics/2013-05/04/c_115639203.htm.

② Ibid..

③ Xi Jinping, "Young People Should Consciously Practice Core Socialist Values-Speech at the Symposium of Teachers and Students of Peking University", Xinhuanet, http://www.xinhuanet.com//politics/2014-05/05/c_1110528066.htm.

youth development, aiming at the long-term development of the country and society and the "two centenary goals". He attaches importance to the values of youth in the development of youth from the perspective of realizing the modernization of the country. This is the important feature and highlight of Xi Jinping Thought on youth in the new era. From the perspective of the important historical time node of national modernization, General Secretary pointed out: "Now the college students are all around 20 years old. When the well-off society is fully completed by 2020, many of you are less than 30 years old; by the middle of the century when the modernization is basically achieved, many of you are less than 60 years old. That is to say, you and thousands of other young people will participate in the whole process of achieving the 'two centenary goals'."① The research of youth values is the normal topic of youth development, but General Secretary gave a scientific answer by comprehensively analyzing the issue of youth values from the perspectives of cultivating the country's modernization cause and carrying out the great struggle of the new era.

On April 26, 2016, days before the International Labor Day on May 1st and the Youth Day on May 4th, General Secretary Xi Jinping delivered *Speech at the Symposium of Intellectuals, Model Workers and Youth Delegates*. This symposium was mainly for intellectuals, model workers and youth delegates. For the purpose of the symposium, General Secretary pointed out: "We have such an arrangement after consideration. China is a socialist country of people's democratic dictatorship under the leadership of the working class based on an alliance of workers and farmers. The intellectuals are part of the working class; the working people are the masters of the country; and the youth are the successors of the socialist cause with Chinese characteristics, the

① Xi Jinping, "Young People Should Consciously Practice Core Socialist Values-Speech at the Symposium of Teachers and Students of Peking University", *Guangming Daily*, May 5, 2014.

future of the country and the hope of the nation. "① In the speech, General Secretary put forward ardent expectations and demands for the intellectuals, the working masses, and the youth. When talking about youth development, General Secretary made requirements and gave a scientific exposition on the development of young people in the new era from the perspective that young people need to have capability. As for how to develop strong ability of the contemporary youth in different jobs and achieve synchronization of their own development and national development in the process of modernization, and to consciously dedicate their youth, General Secretary put forward a clear proposition. He pointed out: "The rural youth should show the new image of modern peasants in the development of modern agriculture and the construction of a new socialist countryside; the youth in enterprises should create more wealth in actively participating in production labor, product research and development, and management innovation; the youth in scientific research units should make more innovations in the in-depth study of the knowledge and the initiative to overcome problems, and the youth in government departments and public institutions should make contributions to better serving the society and the people. "②

The speech of General Secretary at the symposium on April 26th clearly outlines the development paths of contemporary youth in different jobs and the goals of youth in achieving the "two centenary goals". The speech makes important exposition and judgment on the ideals, beliefs and values of youth, and it is the important direction for the growth and progress of youth's personal career. The speech clarifies the goals and directions of youth struggle in the new era, and also points out the direction and goals of the research on youth

---

① Xi Jinping, "Speech at the Symposium of Intellectuals, Model Workers, and Youth Delegates", *Guangming Daily*, April 30, 2016.

② Ibid..

planning theory and practice.

The speeches of General Secretary on youth development focusing on completing the building of a moderately prosperous society in all respects, based on the strategic positioning of modernization, and facing the Chinese Dream of the "two centenary goals", clearly and comprehensively outline the thought on youth development from the macro, meso and micro perspectives in terms of the ideals, beliefs, values, development and dedication of the youth. They not only set the direction for the youth to define their own life planning and career planning, but also provide macro, meso and micro perspectives for youth development planning. The most important thing is to provide a research perspective, a practical perspective, and an innovative perspective for an era in which China is becoming stronger. Since the 18th National Congress of the Communist Party of China, General Secretary's series of important speeches on youth development are a scientific summary and judgment on the current and future career development, and have important guiding significance for succeeding in a Long March for youth development in the new era.

II Comprehensively promoting youth's participation in social development to achieve their self-worth

When talking about youth in the political report of the 19th National Congress of the Communist Party of China, General Secretary Xi Jinping clearly pointed out: "A nation will prosper only when its young people thrive; a country will be full of hope and have a great tomorrow only when its younger generations have ideals, ability, and a strong sense of responsibility. The Chinese Dream is a dream about history, the present, and the future. It is a dream of our generation, but even more so, a dream of the younger

generations. The Chinese Dream of national rejuvenation will be realized ultimately through the endeavors of young people, generation by generation. All of us in the Party should care about young people and set the stage for them to excel. To all our young people, you should have firm ideals and convictions, aim high, and have your feet firmly on the ground. You should ride the waves of your day; and in the course of realizing the Chinese Dream, fulfill your youthful dreams, and write a vivid chapter in your tireless endeavors to serve the interests of the people. "① In the specific work of planning theory and practice of youth development, we must firstly focus on the relationship between youth and the national destiny. The development of youth and the country has always been synchronized, and the youth are also the most sensitive to the changes of the times. Young people are always new, and so is youth development. The development of youth since the beginning of modern times, since the founding of the Party, since the founding of New China, and since the reform and opening up, has always been closely linked to the destiny of the country and the nation. "Only when the country and nation are well off can everybody be well off. "② "A nation will prosper only when its young people thrive. "③

Secondly, we must train and guide young people to "have ideals, ability, and a strong sense of responsibility" . Ideals determine beliefs, and ideals enable young people to have the spiritual strength to overcome difficulties, challenges,

---

① Xi Jinping, "Secure a Decisive Victory in Building a Moderately Prosperous Society in All Respects and Strive for the Great Success of Socialism with Chinese Characteristics for a New Era—Delivered at the 19th National Congress of the Communist Party", *Guangming Daily*, Oct. 28, 2017.

② Xi Jinping, "Build on Past Successes to Further Advance our Cause and Keep on Striving with Endless Energy toward the Great Goal of National Rejuvenation", Xinhuanet, http://www.xinhuanet.com//politics/2012-11/29/c_113852724.htm.

③ Xi Jinping, "Secure a Decisive Victory in Building a Moderately Prosperous Society in All Respects and Strive for the Great Success of Socialism with Chinese Characteristics for a New Era—Delivered at the 19th National Congress of the Communist Party", *Guangming Daily*, Oct. 28, 2017.

and setbacks, and to have lofty ambitions and sense of mission. Ability enables young people to have the power and means to practice ideals, serve the people and realize their own values and national values, so that they will do solid work rather than indulge in empty talk, work hard and not give in. Being responsible, you will have a sense of responsibility for the country and the people in a broad sense and for specific work and treating people in a limited sense. To cultivate young people, guide young people, and let contemporary youth become people with ideals, ability, and a strong sense of responsibility in the process of development and growth is fundamentally to let the youth take over the historical baton and "ultimately realize the Chinese Dream of national rejuvenation through the endeavors of young people, generation by generation."① Based on the Chinese Dream and youthful dreams, rooted in the new era and new background, we must do well in theory and practice of youth development planning.

Thirdly, we must do a good job in the theory and practice of youth development from the strategic perspective of "setting the stage for them to excel". Making young people excel is an important sign of a promising society. If young people cannot excel in their lives, they will lose hope for their future development. Young people are the most energetic and the most adept at accepting new things, and they have always been the main supporting force for social development and change. Moreover, it is necessary to pay attention to "setting a stage" for young people to excel. Without a stage, there is no way for the youth to excel. To set a stage is to provide a path for young people to exert their ability and to succeed. This requires us to do well in the research on the theory and practice of youth development, and comprehensively deepen reform, so as to do a good job in researching the system for the development of

① Xi Jinping, "Secure a Decisive Victory in Building a Moderately Prosperous Society in All Respects and Strive for the Great Success of Socialism with Chinese Characteristics for a New Era—Delivered at the 19th National Congress of the Communist Party", *Guangming Daily*, Oct. 28, 2017.

youth. We should also provide the theoretical and practical results for young people to realize their dreams and change their own fates. This is also the core of youth development planning. "It is important to enable young people to realize dreams and win dignity while enduring the enormous inertia of historical development and the pressure of survival in reality, in today's flashy society, where the fence of interests pattern is getting firmer. "①

The report of the 19th National Congress of the Communist Party of China puts forward new requirements and new propositions for the research on youth planning theory and practice in the new era. Xi Jinping Thought on Socialism with Chinese Characteristics for a New Era has provided a more comprehensive and pioneering historical vision and development realm from a more scientific and newer perspective to further improve the youth planning theory and practice in the new era. It is necessary to promote the theory and practice of contemporary youth development planning, so as to move toward an era in which China is becoming stronger.

From the report of the 19th National Congress on youth development, to do well in the theory and practice of youth development planning, we should learn three aspects, namely the relationship between youth and the state, guiding and training young people, and setting a stage for young people to excel. These three aspects are in line with the series of speeches by General Secretary Xi Jinping on youth development since the 18th National Congress of the Communist Party of China. The relationship between youth and the state is an issue of ideals and beliefs, guiding and training young people is one of the values, and setting a stage for young people to excel one of youth growth and success. Among them, setting a stage for young people to excel is the issue that

① Li Chunling, Ma Feng: " 'Young Empty Nesters': A Group Between 'Survival' and 'Dreams' ", *People's Forum*, No. 4, 2017.

young people care most about and pay most attention to. It directly echoes the sense of growth and accomplishment that young people need most in their youth, and responds closely to the issues that young people care most about and pay most attention to. This is to promote youth development and social participation in a timely reform responding to people's concern. With the only one word "stage", it points out a series of institutional issues involving youth development, and it is an important aspect of promoting vertical social mobility. "The weakening of vertical social mobility and the solidifying of social strata are major challenges for China's development. In a society with solidified social strata, people's social status is often determined by the factor of family background. People are constantly trying to change their destinies through their own efforts, but the channels are blocked, which leads to failure in spite of their efforts, thus creating a sense of frustration. The solidification of social strata will also lead to stratus disintegration, damage to fairness and justice, and the increase of social hostility."① The theoretical and practical research on youth development planning in this field is the most important aspect to care for the youth in the new era, give support to central work of the Party and the state, and provide decision-making references and recommendations. The most important thing is to approve the value of the hard work of people, especially the young people, and guide more young people to become rich and change their destiny through diligence, thus forming a social environment and public opinion atmosphere that is conducive to the upward flow of outstanding talents and forming diversified and multidimensional mechanisms for the upward mobility for youth and development mechanisms.

---

① *Learning Guidance for the Party's* 19*th National Congress Report*, Beijing: Party Building Books Publishing House, 2017, p. 143.

III Coordinating the overall design of mechanisms for youth's participation in social development

We should make the theory and practice of youth development planning more forward-looking from a strategic perspective. The research on the theory and practice of youth development planning should reflect the new look of the new era. The focus is to synchronize with the new era as socialism with Chinese characteristics has entered a new era. In accordance with the "two-step" development strategy, today's young people will participate in the whole process of China's move toward basic modernization and the establishment of a socialist modernization power. This process mainly involves three generations of "post-80s", "post-90s" and "post-00s", who are the main force of contemporary youth. The people involved include those working in rural areas, enterprises, research institutes, government departments and public institutions, and those who are employed in new business and new economic fields. For different youth employment groups and different generations, their different interests and development demands have become a new topic of youth development in the new era in the context of modernization process. We should focus on the synchronization of the youth in the new era and the development of the era. We should pay attention to the interest demands of different young people. We should put forward forward-looking theories and practical results of youth development planning from a macro perspective and from the strategic perspective of 2035 and 2050, with the focus of the macro orientation of ideals and beliefs of youth. From the macro level, we should connect the theoretical and practical development planning of young people's ideals and beliefs with the national strategic planning. Be clear that the basic realization of modernization is the important link between the ideals and beliefs of contemporary youth, especially the realization of their first individual development stage, and the synchronization of national development. Be clear that the stage of turning China into a modern socialist country is an important link between the realization of the individual dreams of youth and the realization of the great Chinese Dream. Young people's individual dream of success is closely linked to and is an important part of the Chinese Dream of national rejuvenation.

To do a good job in the theory and practice of youth development planning from the macro perspective, we must focus on cultivating successors of modernization cause. Today's youth are an important participating and driving force in realizing the Chinese Dream, which is the historical mission of this generation. To succeed in a Long March of the new generation, we must focus on talent training and successors in the new era. This is not an issue in one or two industries, but one needing holistic consideration. By 2050, the people born in the 1980s were all over 60 years old. Therefore, in the process from the 100th anniversary of the founding of the Party to the 100th anniversary of the founding of the People's Republic of China, young people are the backbone, and this process runs through the career of young people. Therefore, it is necessary to enhance the strategic urgency of research and it can not be separated from the youth, from the reality, or from the times.

We should study the needs of young people for a better life based on the principal contradictions in Chinese society in the new era. The youth group always has the strongest yearning for a better life. Young people are at the stage of struggle and growth. The yearning for a better life is the driving force for youth's growth, progress and struggle, and also young people's life goal of development and growth. Young people go to university, or do their jobs, or go away from home. They leave school and get into career, or move from rural to urban areas. They work in China or go abroad. They move from coastal to inland areas. They gradually become mature. During these periods, they hope to excel in life and have a good life, which is the common tint of young people of different ages. We need to meet the youth's yearning for a better life, to help young people grow and develop in the new era, to guide young people in the historical stage of China's development into a new historical position, to find the historical orientation of life, to link their own development orientation and national development orientation, and to make them "roll up sleeves to work harder"① together with all the people. This is the key to promoting youth's particpation in social development in this era.

The main direction for realizing the growth of young people and the need to develop a better life is to excel in life. It is the main driving force for young people to strive for a better life. It is also the important foundation for connecting their values of life and national development and correctly understanding social development. The key is to set a "stage" for young people to excel in the important period that affects the growth and development of youth. This stage is an opportunity and refers to comprehensively deepening of reform. It is necessary to break the barriers of solidification of interests with great political courage, so that young people can come out and make a difference. To promote fairness of opportunities is the most important thing for young people. "The key to preventing the solidification of the social strata is to deepen reform and promote fairness in opportunities."② The report of the 19th National Congress of the Communist Party of China pointed out: "We must remove institutional barriers that block the social mobility of labor and talent and ensure that every one of our people has the chance to pursue career

① "President Xi Jinping's 2017 New Year Address", Xinhuanet, http://www.xinhuanet.com//politics/2016-12/31/c_1120227034.htm.

② Ma Feng, "Deepen Reform to Stimulate Social Vitality and Correctly View Social Mobility", *People's Daily*, July 20, 2017.

through hard work."[①] This sentence profoundly tells us that promoting social mobility and removing institutional barriers that block the social mobility are of great significance to China's social stability and social development, especially to the youth's integration into social development. Every one of our people has the chance to pursue career through hard work. This is a huge institutional advantage of the socialist system with Chinese characteristics and a development achievement proved by the practice of the reform and opening up. "If we say that letting some people get rich first more than 30 years ago stimulated social vitality and promoted social mobility, then today we are using comprehensively deepening reform to stimulate social vitality and promote social mobility. In the process of comprehensively deepening reform, every one of our people has an opportunity to excel in life."[②]

The key to realizing the growth of young people and the need to develop a better life is employment. Employment is the basis of people's livelihood, and it is the foundation of the youth who have just stepped into the society. For some time to come, the biggest need for a better life of China's young people is employment. At the fifth press conference of the 19th National Congress of the Communist Party of China, Yin Weimin, Minister of Human Resources and Social Security, pointed out: "In the coming period, we are faced with two contradictions in employment. On the one hand, we still have great total pressure. In the three years to come, that is, in the process of finishing building a moderately prosperous society in all respects, more than 15 million people need to be employed in urban areas each year. The total pressure is very

---

① Xi Jinping, "Secure a Decisive Victory in Building a Moderately Prosperous Society in All Respects and Strive for the Great Success of Socialism with Chinese Characteristics for a New Era—Delivered at the 19th National Congress of the Communist Party", Xinhuanet, http://news.xinhuanet.com/politics/19cpcnc/2017-10/27/c_1121867529.htm.

② Ma Feng, "Deepen Reform to Stimulate Social Vitality and Correctly View Social Mobility", *People's Daily*, July 20, 2017.

high. Most of the 15 million people are young students. The number of college graduates will be more than 8 million next year, and this high level of more than 8 million will continue for a period of time. There are also about 5 million graduates of secondary vocational schools and technical schools, as well as some students who do not continue their studies after graduating from junior or senior high school. The total amount of employment required each year is very high."① Based on the transformation of China's economy from quantity-oriented to quality-oriented, we need to deeply research the employment issues affecting youth development and start from the structural contradictions in the job market. "The dilemma of 'difficult recruitment' and 'difficult employment' coexist in China's current labor market. There is a mismatch between industrial structure and employment structure. 'Doctors and masters have difficulty finding jobs, while senior technicians are hard to find.' There is a prominent issue of structural unemployment."② The demand for high-quality jobs for college graduates and young students is the main manifestation of the youth's yearning for a better life in this era, and it is also the embodiment of the change of the social principal contradiction in the youth group. On the one hand, China still has relatively large demand for labor, but on the other hand, high-quality jobs and positions that meet the needs of educated youth are still uneven and inadequate. Therefore, based on the reality of this new era, we should focus on the targeted and innovative research work of theory and practice for the development of youth. The change in the social principal contradiction has made the research on the development of youth in China more focused on the main contradiction, which is the key.

---

① Yin Weimin, "College Graduates to Exceed 8 Million Next Year", Xinhuanet, http://news.xinhuanet.com/politics/19cpcnc/2017-10/22/c_129724609.htm.

② *Learning Guidance for the Party's 19th National Congress Report*, Beijing: Party Building Books Publishing House, 2017, p. 141.

The foundation for achieving youth growth and developing a better life is education. Education is the fundamental measure to block the intergenerational transmission of poverty. The report of the 19th National Congress of the Communist Party of China pointed out: "We will strive to see that each and every child has fair access to good education." "We will improve the system of financial aid to students, and work to see that the vast majority of the new members of the urban and rural labor force have received senior secondary education, and that more and more of them receive higher education."① Making the vast majority of the new members of the urban and rural labor force receive senior secondary education, and that more and more of them receive higher education is a major strategy for national development, and its impact is far-reaching. If the vast majority of the new members of the urban and rural labor force can receive senior secondary education and higher education, this will greatly improve the quality structure of our population, providing a steady stream of talent dividends for upgrading the Chinese economy and the development of Chinese society, and laying a solid foundation for the youth to change their destinies, get rid of poverty, block intergenerational poverty transmission, and achieve fairness in starting points. This is a major move for young people in the new era who are currently at college or about to enter college. It can heighten their development platform for the realization of the modernized era and meet the quality requirements of the development of the new era. Education has always been an important aspect of the youth participation in social development. The education of youth should be synchronized with the era, and it should face the youth participation in social development which is at new stage.

① Xi Jinping, "Secure a Decisive Victory in Building a Moderately Prosperous Society in All Respects and Strive for the Great Success of Socialism with Chinese Characteristics for a New Era—Delivered at the 19th National Congress of the Communist Party", *Guangming Daily*, Oct. 28, 2017.

We should promote theoretical and practical research on governance planning on youth development based on the modernization of China's system and capacity for governance. "The overall goal of deepening reform in every field is to improve and develop the system of socialism with Chinese characteristics and modernize China's system and capacity for governance."① New breakthroughs have been made in the theory and practice of youth development planning since the 18th National Congress of the Communist Party of China, which has formed the system of theory and practice of youth development planning in the new era. Under the historical background of China becoming stronger, along with China's historical pursuit of modernization and the establishment of a socialist modernized power, the system of socialism with Chinese characteristics will be more mature and more stable, and China's system and capacity for governance will be more modernized. Youth governance is the ultimate goal of solving the problems in youth development. Realizing the modernization of youth governance and improving the system and capability for youth governance are fundamental to promoting the development of theory and practice of youth development planning. The foundation of the development of theory and practice of youth development planning is to realize the modernization of youth governance and serve youth governance. The key issues and important links involved in youth development, including macroscopic ideals and beliefs, mesoscopic values, and microscopic youth dedication and growth, are originally the issue of youth governance. To meet the youth's yearning for a better life, to achieve fair opportunities, to promote fairness in the starting point, and to set a stage for young people to excel rely on the improvement of the system and capacity for youth governance.

---

① Xi Jinping, "Secure a Decisive Victory in Building a Moderately Prosperous Society in All Respects and Strive for the Great Success of Socialism with Chinese Characteristics for a New Era—Delivered at the 19th National Congress of the Communist Party", *Guangming Daily*, Oct. 28, 2017.

To let young people have ideals and beliefs, establish correct values, and keep pace with the development of the times is to enable them to see the hope of development, share the fruits of development, and to have the channels and paths to grow into talents. This depends on the development of the country and the key is the improvement of the capacity for youth governance in development.

The youth are a precious asset of the Party and the state, and the future of the nation and the hope of the state. The development of the country to this day is the result of the struggle of young people from generation to generation, who take over the historical baton. In this process, the youth grow, progress and develop together with the country. Young people succeed from the development of the country, and in turn, promote the country's growth, progress and development. The two sides are always interactive.

The Party leads everything. The Party managing youth work is our greatest feature, and it is also the guarantee for the realization of the youth development planning. "The defining feature of socialism with Chinese characteristics is the leadership of the Communist Party of China; the greatest strength of the system of socialism with Chinese characteristics is the leadership of the Communist Party of China; the Party is the highest force for political leadership."① Based on youth growth, facing the realization of "two centenary goals", we must meet the youth's longing for a better life, set a stage for young people to excel, so as to realize a new realm of development theory and practice of youth development planning with Chinese characteristics in the new era and the modernization of youth governance.

---

① Xi Jinping, "Secure a Decisive Victory in Building a Moderately Prosperous Society in All Respects and Strive for the Great Success of Socialism with Chinese Characteristics for a New Era—Delivered at the 19th National Congress of the Communist Party", *Guangming Daily*, Oct. 28, 2017.

Chapter II Social Organization Mechanisms and Talent Strategy of Chinese Youth's Participation in Social Development*

Since the 18th National Congress of the Communist Party of China, both the central and local governments have stepped up efforts to cultivate and support social organizations, which have been flourishing ever since. By the end of 2017, there had been 762000 social organizations in China, up 8. 4% from the previous year; and employing a workforce of 8. 647 million from all walks of life, up 13. 2% on a year-on-year basis. ①Social organizations have been developing very well, ever-increasingly functioning as main players in social governance, and have become important providers of basic public services. The sufficient provision of human resources is indispensable for the prosperous development of any industry. Social governance is no exception.

---

* Dr. Jiang Ningning makes important contributions to the writing of this chapter. This is her brief introduction: Jiang Ningning, lecturer, Ph. D. in Public Management, postdoctoral in Sociology, Chinese Academy of Social Sciences, is now working in the Department of Administration, Grammar School, China University of Mining and Technology (Beijing). The main research fields are cooperative governance theory and cooperative organization. She has published papers in CSSCI journals such as China Administration, Nanjing Social Sciences and Administrative Forum, and has been responsible for and participated in three national projects.

① Ministry of Civil Affairs of the People's Republic of China, *2017 Statistical Bulletin on Social Service Development.*

Talent is the most valuable resources for social organizations, which will increasingly become important channels to attract outstanding talent. However, social organizations still face a series of shortcomings such as insufficient talent supply, lack of professionals and high mobility of talent, etc. The essay believes that the long-term existence of talent issues is due to the fact that talent environments at social organizations are insufficient to meet the needs for youth career development. It is an inherent requirement for the construction of a talent development mechanism suited to social organizations to carry out reforms and explore the needs for talent development at social organizations, build a suitable talent environment, and establish a large-scale talent team with a reasonable structure and high quality; and it is also a major measure for innovation in social governance.

I Participation mechanism of social organizations and talent development

The State Council has issued official documents for a number of times making arrangements and deployments of tasks on entrepreneurship and employment, especially stressing the role of social organizations as a social force. With the downward pressure on the economy, social organizations have become a new uncultivated land for absorbing employment. We can say that social organizations are facing a dilemma that they face urgent demand for talent but lack the environment for attracting talent. Although social organizations are an important choice for solving the issue of employment under the new normal in China, with the environment for the construction of talent teams being constantly optimized and the total quantity of talents on the rise year after year, they are still facing practical dilemmas in the following respects.

First, insufficient total quantity of talent and unreasonable talent structure in social organizations. Although the number of people employed in the society has been constantly increasing in recent years, the total quantity is still insufficient compared with the huge social demand. In terms of talent structure, there are such problems as insufficient professionals, imbalanced distribution of talent in different industries, and lack of support in professional titles. As a result, the demand for pushing ahead with innovation in social governance can't be effectively met. In the meanwhile, there are also such problems as limited room for promotion, relatively low salary and low identity on the side of employees, etc. According to statistics, over 60% of employees at national level social organizations think that their salary levels are lower or even far lower than the level of economic development, and only about 30% of such people believe that their current salary levels can mobilize their initiative at work①; and another survey indicates that only 2.26% of fresh graduates believe that social organizations are attractive employers②. All these factors have become major bottlenecks for the development of social organizations.

Second, relative lagging education related to social organizations and a prominent mismatch between talent cultivation and talent demand. In recent years, education related to social organizations has been developing rapidly. From higher vocational education to undergraduate education to graduate education, a talent education system for social organizations has been basically formed. But it is still lagging behind the requirement for the development of social organizations. The cultivation of talent for social organizations is not strong enough, training resources are insufficient, and

① Wang Aimin and Dong Zhichao, "Research on Remuneration Incentive Policy for Talent at Social Organizations", *TopHR*, No. 2, 2014.

② Zhan Chengfu, *Public Sentiment Report on the Development of Social Organizations in China (2014 - 2015)*, Beijing: China Social Press, 2016.

there are fewer training and educational organizations for talent cultivation for social organizations. Shortage of teachers has resulted in fewer opportunities of continuing education for employees at social organizations, and it has influenced their career development. In addition, there is a gap between current education for social organizations and practices, and the education modes at institutions of higher learning are rigid and closed. The divorce between theory and practice makes it difficult for talents to qualify themselves in knowledge and capability for related positions at social organizations.

Third, big difficulty in implementing policies on the construction of talent teams for social organizations. In recent years, government departments such as the Organization Department of the CPC Central Committee and the Ministry of Civil Affairs have released a series of guiding policy documents on the construction of personnel teams for social organizations, but no professional titles have been established, which makes it impossible for employees to participate in professional title appraisal at social organizations. Compared with personnel at Party and government departments, management personnel at enterprises as well as professional and technical personnel, those at social organizations still lag far behind in terms of policy implementation support.

To sum up, the personnel issue at social organizations actually reflects from different aspects the bottleneck that social organizations face in their development. To solve this issue, we must respect the features of such new organizations. It was from reconstructing interpersonal relationships when organizational structure went into a process of change. The power of globalization and post-industrialization places people in the increasingly interconnected and common environments. When facing common risks, people tend to have a wish to survive together and coexist. Referring to the management methods invented by human beings in industrial societies, both individual actors and group actors need to cope with new risks through cooperation; therefore, such a condition requires people to replace managerial organizations with new types of organization modes. "Cooperative organizations", a brand-new type of organization characterized by group actions, will manifest their advantages when coping with all kinds of crisis events thanks to their flexibility.

Just as President Xi Jinping pointed out, "Intellectuals at new economic organizations and new social organizations, such as professionals including lawyers, accountants, appraisers and tax accountants, etc., are rapidly growing social groups after China's reform and opening-up. At present, these people are mainly outside of the Party and the system and are highly mobile. They have active minds and common ways don't work much when trying to influence them. These people are understood to, more often than not, join various social organizations based on their professions or interests. We need to find out what's going on and carry out work through their organizations. For those typical people among them, we should cultivate them as key objects and guide them to play a positive role. Our Party has a good and long-standing method, namely, to organize people up. To organize people up under the new situation, we should pay attention to the Party and government organs, enterprises and institutions as well as mass organizations, and also to all kinds of new economic organizations and new social organizations."① It has become an important guarantee for further growth of social organizations in the new era to create the environment suited to the characteristics of young talents in the new domains like social organizations and work out talent development strategies meeting the needs of youth career development at social organizations.

---

① Xi Jinping, "Speech at the Session of United Front Work of the CPC Central Committee", *People. cn*, http://cpc.people.com.cn/xuexi/n1/2017/1122/c385476-29660701.html

II Environmental requirements of young talents for the social organization mechanism involved in social development

According to the talent problems at social organizations, we know that in the practices of social organizations, there are contradictions between the flow of young talent and the delayed establishment of posts, between the vertical promotion of talent and career systems, and between professional needs of young talent and relevant training and learning systems. The existence of such problems also reflects many deficiencies in the professional supply at social organizations, while these deficiencies are just the important indicators that young people consider when choosing their long-term careers. The occupational activities of people are very complex social activities. The selection of an industry and career or finally settling on a position are all determined by the overall development of the society, the supply of the industry and organizations, as well as the needs of individuals for survival and development. The social service industry is the one that focuses on repairing and expanding social relations or social capabilities of people. It requires person-to-person services. It is impossible for these professional activities to be replaced by mechanized managerial activities or emerging AI technologies. Therefore, the professional satisfaction or anxiety brought to people by this occupation is also non-existent in traditional production and manufacturing industries. For practitioners of social services, their choices can be explained by the "self-determination theory" (SDT)[①]. That's to say, job seekers pursue "self-consistency", requiring the consistency between the reasons for their pursuits and their interests and core

① E. Deci and R. Ryan eds., *Handbook of Self-determination Research*, NY: University of Rochester Press, 2002.

values. If the reason for personal pursuit is his or her intrinsic interest or ideal, it is very likely that he or she will attain his or her objective; even if they fail at last, they are still very happy, because the process of hardworking itself is full of fun. ①In addition, those who pursue targets in work for intrinsic reasons are more satisfied with their work. They believe that they are in better terms with the organization and can do even better. ②Therefore, through analyzing the expectations of young job applicants towards organizations and occupational environments by using SDT, we can draw some basic ideas about talent strategies for social organizations.

According to the survey of the social organizations industry and our knowledge about the basic situation of job application for social workers, we can conclude that young talents have basic requirements for occupational environments at social organizations in terms of standardization of organizational management and sustainability of industry's prospect.

First, job applicants with the intent to enter the social organizations industry are generally young people; what is more important is that they are social beings with specific ideals and values. They are committed to realizing some social goals, facilitating the solution to social issues and promoting the development of the society through their hard work. That is to say, the moral ideal and sense of social responsibility are the motive power for their job application. Of course, they are often the initiative and creative characteristic of young people, which explains the close relationship between talent strategies of social organizations and youth development.

"The initiative and creativity of people are by no means their abstract

---

① K. M. Sheldon, A. J. Elliot, and R. M. Ryan, "Self-concordance and Subjective Well-being in Four Cultures", *Journal of Cross-cultural Psychology 35*, No. 2, 2004.

② J. E. Bono and T. A. Judge, "Self-concordance at Work: Toward Understanding the Motivational Effects of Transformational Leaders", *Academy of Management Journal 46*, No. 5, 2003.

ability. They can't be attained simply through learning science, increasing knowledge or even professional training; instead, they are the manifestation of the intrinsic qualities of people and the realization of the essential qualities of managers as integral human beings in their career activities. Therefore, in the process of constructing a social governance system oriented towards the future, what we pursue is to construct a social governance platform through which the essential qualities of managers of the society can be realized. To this end, we need to convert social governance activities into helpful preconditions for the realization of the essential qualities of human beings. "① Therefore, the social and moral needs of human beings are the basis of talent strategies of social organizations that should be established first.

Second, job applicants have certain requirements for the development of organizations. When deciding to seek employment in the public welfare sector, job seekers are usually driven by some social ideals and have high requirements for the match between their interests, core values and career outlooks and the goals of organizations. Then, when selecting specific projects and organizations, they care about first such benefits as the remuneration provided by their employers as well as the construction of the social organization itself, its team structure, and the execution, cohesion and culture of the organization, etc. Although our expectations for remuneration in the public welfare sector is somewhat low, it becomes the biggest hidden danger of brain drain after job applicants are employed; in addition, human resource management at social organizations is weaker currently; as a result, nearly half of the staff leave some social organizations each year. Generally speaking, the incentive factors in the organization environment have become the most considered factors among young job applicants; they are also one of

① Zhang Kangzhi, *On Ethical Spirit*, Nanjing: Jiangsu People's Publishing Ltd., 2010, p. 96.

the basic needs of job applicants in their choice of posts and careers.

From the perspective of organizational management, there often exists the problem of imbalance between talent supply and demand and the mismatch between rights and responsibilities in current management practices of organizations. This is due to the "granulation" of posts within an organization through work analysis—that is, functions of an organization and roles of actors are broken down continuously so that the organization goes against its own actions and members. Such breakdown leads to the inability of the organization to form a kind of cohesion to cope with uncertainties and complexities of environments; and it also results in the fragmentation of the overall roles of individual actors as well as their rights and responsibilities. In complex environments, however, actors often need comprehensive abilities and composite roles to deal with complex problems; therefore, one of the important strategies for organizational change is to reconstruct human resource development and utilization modes—not only establishing posts with matched rights and responsibilities, but also mobilizing the initiative of people. In order to discover talent within an organization, the past management mode of choosing people for posts has to be changed to set up posts for people on the intermediate organizational level. The reason for this lies in the fact that an organization, as a collection of social man, is supposed to bring the cohesion of people into play; therefore, they should respect the social attributes and essential characteristics of people by making corresponding institutional arrangement and structural setting based on this to coordinate the initiative, otherness, personal pursuits, values and goals of individuals with the action objectives of the organization so as to construct an overall action framework. The management of organizational human resources under the principle of activism is essentially about the cultivation of individual collaborative abilities and guidance of action abilities. Therefore, within social organizations, individual members not only have the space for expressing and realizing their personal pursuits of social values but also their personal visions for long-term development including learning knowledge, transforming themselves and building social networks. It is possible that individual development and organizational actions can combine with each other. ①

Third, based on the particularity of the social service industry and the morality of job applicants, as well as the difference with other mature industries, job applicants also value such macro occupational factors as the overall development prospects of social organizations, the industry and their own careers, etc. , but all these factors are closely related to the development level of social organizations and social governance. In China, due to the complexity and richness of the macro occupational environment for social governance, the environment itself has become not only a basic requirement of young people for social governance careers but also a bottleneck of the social organization industry.

As we know, social organizations have experienced a battling process from gaining legal identity to becoming self-governors, which is also the process that the social governance structure experienced a major change. Therefore, regardless of the reform of management systems of the government for social organizations or the reform of internal governance structure of organizations, a new theoretical foundation and an action starting point should be established. This starting point is just the networking of organizational structures and the collaboration for organizational actions.

To sum up, the problem of talent is caused by dual dilemmas of social organizations themselves and the environment for social governance. Due to the bottlenecks in organizational management and industry development, young

① Jiang Ningning, Research on the Role of Social Organizations in the Transition of Social Governance Structure, Ph. D. dissertation, Renmin University of China, 2016.

people wouldn't stay, high quality talent wouldn't come and high-skilled talents can't be introduced. [1]Such a situation needs to be addressed on the strategic level and through multiple channels such as legislation, public policies, industry rules and organizational change, etc.

III Building a social organization mechanism and talent strategy that meet the needs of youth's participation in social development

The tertiary sector with social organizations as main players is a relatively new field, and social services are also an emerging industry. Generally speaking, the talent pool is weak in the field. Therefore, the talents at social organizations are mainly made up of young people who constantly flow in and out. Obviously, social organizations are making contributions to new employment and entrepreneurial modes. We should explore new organizational management modes and career development paths while respecting the temporality and mobility of organizational tasks to support the establishment of talent strategy for social organizations. "Young people are the most energetic and creative group in the society, so they should naturally be at the forefront of innovation and creation as enterprising and groundbreaking pioneers of the time."[2] Therefore, in order to best allocate young talent resources, inspire and encourage them to devote more wisdom and energy to national governance and social governance, the national macro policy departments and social organizations need to make the following explorations.

---

① Ma Shumei, "Analysis and Research of Talent Supply and Demand Indices and Professional Demand Trend for Social Organizations in China", http://www.chinanpo.gov.cn/700106/newswjindex.html.

② Xi Jinping, "Speech at the Symposium of Outstanding Young Delegates from All Walks of Life", *Guangming Daily*, May 5, 2013.

1 Opening up channels for young talent for social organizations and setting up talent pool

A steady flow of talent supply is indispensable for the development of an industry. Since the social governance field is complicated, it is the most fundamental measure to explore diversified talent channels and set up rich talent pools so as to strengthen the social services industry and promote the sustainable development of social organizations. For instance, seeking the talents who have pursued advanced studies in public health, international relations, medical treatment, social work, engineering, political science and media, etc.; cultivating professionals (social workers) holding related professional certificates and with high professional levels and training experiences; encouraging the groups who once worked in government departments or business circles and have higher reputation and influence to participate in social affairs; discovering the people who master multiple languages, have extensive travel experiences or study, living and working experiences abroad, or once worked in the region or environment where specific events happened and have a thorough knowledge of the event characteristics and impact and encourage them to participate in social services; cultivating the people who feature strong initiative and a sense of participation, frequently participate in voluntary activities or those who have the spirit of utter devotion towards certain groups served and related organizations to involve them in more professional social governance affairs.

On the basis of the preparatory work for talent pool, we should step up the support to talent statistics work at social organizations. The registration authorities of various levels should include talent statistics work at social organizations in the new *Outline of the National Medium and Long Term Talent Development Plan of Social Organizations* according to the statistical indicator

system for talent resources at social organizations, and establish a forecasting, tracking and monitoring system for talent resources at social organizations so as to master the basic data about talent at social organizations and improve the talent demand forecasting system.

2 Building a versatile talent system, and exploring a plan for cultivating young talent

The cultivation of professional talent for social organizations is a systematic project which requires not only traditional professional degree education but also rich and thorough vocational training as well as the establishment of a professional title system suited to the talent law of growth.

Degree education is characterized by a long period and strong systematicness, and plays a fundamental role in laying a solid knowledge foundation for talents of social organizations and in cultivating their professional qualities. Wang Ming proposed to establish a secondary specialty catalogue of "social organization management" under the first-level discipline of "public management" of "management" category in the specialty setup for undergraduate education at institutions of higher learning in China by revising and improving *the List of Disciplines for Degree Conferment and Talent Cultivation* formulated by the Academic Degrees Committee of the State Council and the Ministry of Education, and gradually establish a talent cultivation system covering higher vocational education and degree education including undergraduate and graduate education for social organization major. He also proposed to improve the project-based curriculum system integrating posts, courses and certificates that is based on ability training and professional teaching and highlights working process. ①

① Wang Ming, "Building and Perfecting a Talent Cultivation System for Social Organizations", a Proposal at the 2nd Session of the 12th National Committee of CPPCC, March 3, 2014.

On the basis of degree education, enriching vocational training is also an inevitable requirement of talent cultivation for social organizations. "As an important part of the national educational system and human resource development, vocational education is an important way for young people to succeed and shoulder the important responsibilities for training diversified talents, inheriting technical skills and promoting employment and entrepreneurship; therefore, we must attach great importance to it and accelerate its development."① Vocational training features a short period of time and strong timeliness and practicalness, so it can meet the needs of practitioners who have already entered social organizations. As a supplement to professional degree education, vocational training serves as an important way to transform theoretical knowledge into practical wisdom and also an important way to enhance the professional level and practical ability of talent at social organizations. In the system of vocational training, we should pay attention to the degree of communication and understanding between different institutions, different industries and different posts, and fundamentally enhance the comprehensive ability of professionals, including their theoretical ability and practical ability. "We should strictly adhere to the direction of school-running to serve development and promote employment, deepen the institutional mechanism reform, innovate all-type, all-level vocational education models, adhere to the principle of integration of industry and education, school-enterprise cooperation, as well as the combination of learning with working and the unity of knowledge and action, and guide all sectors of society, especially the industry enterprises, to actively support vocational education and strive to build a vocational education system with Chinese characteristics."②

---

① "Xi Jinping's Instructions on Accelerating the Development of Vocational Education", *People's Daily*, June 24, 2014.

② Ibid..

In addition, we should improve the professional qualification certification system for social organizations and promote such work as employment with certificates and professional title evaluation. We should also further standardize and define the post setting of full-time staff at social organizations, establish the vocational system for social organizations, improve the continuing education system for talents at social organizations, and realize the connection between professional training and vocational qualification. ①

All in all, by exploring the training mode of theory-practice combination, we should establish a system of young talent with comprehensive capabilities that meets the needs of complex social governance affairs. Only in this way can potential human resources be transformed into talents and the role of social governance brought into real play. Similarly, a good talent training system will also guarantee the development of young people and attract more young talents to join the social organization industry.

3 Exploring a cooperative mechanism among social organizations and establishing a career development platform in line with the law of talent flow

The affairs of social governance are complex and extensive, social organizations are consequently penetrating into various social fields, and the talent system of social organizations is more inclusive and more mobile. If the public sphere is a "market", then social organizations are its productive organizations whose resources, product demand and production costs all come from the society. The products are used for social consumption and the social capital from their "profits" is dedicated to social sectors to engage in reproduction. Within social organizations, certain industry systems and rules

① Wang Ming, "Building and Perfecting a Talent Cultivation System for Social Organizations", a Proposal at the 2nd Session of the 12th National Committee of CPPCC, March 3, 2014.

will be formed within different service areas. To establish a public welfare community, the support from different industries and a relatively mature state of social development are indispensable.

According to Michael Porter's value chain theory, all production activities of an enterprise, including design, production, sales and delivery, combine together to form a value chain. The competitiveness of an enterprise depends on the degree of perfection of the value chain within the organization. Therefore, the existence of value chain is meant to serve the efficiency and competitiveness of the business organization. But this implies another metaphor: the significance of the continuity of actions, ideas and values in an organizational action system actually embodies the concept of cooperation. The social service industry to which social organizations belong should also be a huge value chain, in which each organization and individual contributes to the final value output of the industry. Although there is competition among the same kind of players in the industry value chain, the industry chain provides supportive conditions for the development of organizations and individuals so that there is a good environment for organizations to concentrate on services, carry out benign competition and create social resources. For instance, in the public welfare sector, the public welfare value chain includes finance, industry, research and development, and consulting. If the value chain is unobstructed enough, the human resource of social organizations will be free from the difficulty of promotion.

Based on the value chain, when developing their talent strategies, social organizations should pay attention to the application of the platform, such as the establishment of industry communities, occupation communities and professional communities, etc., so as to explore the mechanisms for promoting talent exchange and mobility, promote the cultivation and introduction of inter-disciplinary, professional talent, and expand the space

for promotion. We should establish not only a talent flow mechanism within the organization, but also an inter-industry and cross-industry professional qualification certification and post mobility mechanism, perfect human resource mobility mechanism and so on. Once the flow of talents is realized, the flow of resources is realized accordingly. More specifically, it is necessary to achieve the horizontal flow of organization members with the same level of competence and the vertical flow of human resources as well. The ways of talent exchange adopted in the civil service system of China, such as secondment and taking a temporary post, may serve as a reference for the human resource flow system within and among social organizations.

IV Making social organizations a broad flowing platform for youth's participation in social development

In today's era, with the accelerated development of globalization and post-industrialization, a series of challenges like blurred industrial boundaries brought by transboundary confront various organizations with many constraints for their survival and development. Behind this difficulty, there is an essential problem, i. e., the performance of an organization is no longer determined by internal factors, but by external ones, such as environmental uncertainties, partners, transboundary rivals, and brand-new technologies, etc. It is especially the case with social organizations. As far as their increasingly important role in social governance, they need to have a better grasp of situational factors and integrate more resources. Of course, from the perspective of management, social organizations are a new type of cooperative organizations, and have the characteristics of being task-oriented, flat, flexible and cooperative. In the new organizational structure, an organization needs each of its members to break through their inherent advantages and behavioral habits, have an open learning mentality and take corresponding actions, and embrace information sharing, training and learning. Moreover, in a cooperative organization, the leader is a guide who creates a synergistic value environment of the large-scale organizational system and empowers every member of the organization with a mentality of "egolessness". Therefore, social organizations can become a platform for conglomeration of various social resources, and also have the natural endowment to establish a platform for talent flow. This requires researchers and practitioners to fully understand the characteristics of the new era, grasp the new attributes of social organizations, understand the occupational demand of young people in the new era, and by taking these factors into consideration, make a good plan for the development of the social organization industry, and develop a talent strategy for social organizations in line with the characteristics and needs of all parties concerned.

Chapter III Changes in the Trend of Chinese Youth's Participation in Social Development

I Synchronization of youth development, social development and national development

From the "poverty and blankness" in 1949 to China's GDP ranking the second in the world with 90 trillion yuan (By preliminary calculation, the annual GDP in 2018 was 900.309 billion yuan, an increase of 6.6% over the previous year.)[①], new achievements have continuously achieved in China's economic and social development. This has laid a solid material foundation and a prerequisite for China's youth development. The development of the youth cause synchronizes with the progress of the country, and with the continuous improvement of people's living conditions. People's material standard of living has changed from people's basic needs being met to their lives being generally decent. In 1949, the per capita cash income of urban households was less than 100 yuan, and the per capita net income of rural residents was only 44 yuan. In 1978, the per capita disposable income of urban residents reached 343 yuan, and the per capita net income of rural residents reached 134 yuan,

---

① National Bureau of Statistics, *Statistical Communique of the* 2018 *National Economic and Social Development of the People's Republic of China*, http://www.stats.gov.cn/tjsj/zxfb/201902/t20190228_1651265.html.

which was respectively 2. 4 times and 2. 0 times higher than those in 1949 by nominal growth, with an average annual growth rate of 4. 3% and 3. 9%. [①]In 2018, the per capita disposable income of urban residents was 39251 yuan, and the per capita disposable income of rural residents was 14617 yuan. [②]

Table 3 – 1 **Changes in Residents' Income at Major Time Nodes in the Seventy Years of China** unit/yuan

Year	Urban Residents	Rural Residents
1949	per capita cash income is less than 100 yuan	per capita net income is only 44 yuan
1978	per capita disposable income was 343 yuan	per capita net income was 134 yuan
2018	per capita disposable income was 39251 yuan	per capita disposable income was 14617 yuan

Source: National Bureau of Statistics of China.

With the increase of China's overall economic strength and the improvement of people's material living standards, the cause of youth development, especially the individual growth and development of young people and life planning, have made many impossibilities possible, making many youth development dreams seemingly impossible become development opportunities that many young people in ordinary families can enjoy. This has a close, direct and even fundamental relationship with the increase of residents' income and the country's openness and progress. For example, in terms of the situation of overseas students studying abroad and returning to China after

① National Bureau of Statistics of China, *New China in* 65 *Years*, Beijing: China Statistics Press, September 2014, p. 112.

② National Bureau of Statistics, *Statistical Communique of the* 2018 *National Economic and Social Development of the People's Republic of China*, http: //www. stats. gov. cn/tjsj/zxfb/201902/t20190228_ 1651265. html.

studying abroad, at the beginning of the founding of New China, there were 35 students studying abroad in 1950, in which year the statistics began. The number of students who returned to China after studying abroad was 16 in 1953. Before 1978, 1956 was the year with the largest number of students studying abroad, which was 2401. ①In the early development stage of the country's construction, government-sponsored overseas education was more common. At that time, the per capita income was very low, and even basic living needs couldn't be met, so it was unrealistic for hundreds of millions of Chinese youth to study abroad at their own expense. After the Third Plenary Session of the Eleventh Central Committee, with the development of the country and the improvement of people's living standards, especially since self-funded overseas education was approved, in addition to the means of the government-sponsored education, it has been possible for many ordinary young people to study abroad. Overseas education has become the possible means for young people to seek knowledge and chase their dreams. As of 2017, there were 608400 Chinese students studying overseas, and 480900 students returned to China after studying abroad, a record high. ②

Although the number of young people who are currently able to study abroad has reached a record high, we still need to realize that the total number of young people studying abroad is still small relative to China's huge youth group. There are many choices in life. To chase dreams, young people do not have to rely on studying abroad. The "dream-seekers" in the new era are progressing with the times, and developing with the country, which is becoming more and more open to the world. They should go global with a more confident attitude, and think about the role and significance of China in the tide of world

① National Bureau of Statistics of China, "New China in 65 Years", Beijing: China Statistics Press, September 2014, p. 292.

② *The 40th Anniversary of Reform and Opening Up*, Beijing: China Statistics Press, September 2018, p. 438.

Table 3 – 2 **Statistics on the Number of Students Studying Abroad Since the Reform and Opening Up**①

unit/person

Year	Students Studying Abroad	Students Who Returned to China after Studying Abroad
1978	860	248
1979	1777	231
1980	2124	162
1981	2922	1143
1982	2326	2116
1983	2633	2303
1984	3073	2290
1985	4888	1424
1986	4676	1388
1987	4703	1605
1988	3786	3000
1989	3329	1756
1990	2950	1593
1991	2900	2069
1992	6540	3611
1993	10742	5128
1994	19071	4230
1995	20381	5750
1996	20905	6570
1997	22410	7130
1998	17622	7379
1999	23749	7748
2000	38989	9121
2001	83973	12243
2002	125179	17945

① *The 40th Anniversary of Reform and Opening Up*, Beijing: China Statistics Press, September 2018, p. 438.

Continued

Year	Students Studying Abroad	Students Who Returned to China after Studying Abroad
2003	117307	20152
2004	114682	24726
2005	118515	34987
2006	134000	42000
2007	144000	44000
2008	179800	69300
2009	229300	108300
2010	284700	134800
2011	339700	186200
2012	399600	272900
2013	413900	353500
2014	459800	364800
2015	523700	409100
2016	544500	432500
2017	608400	480900

Source: National Bureau of Statistics of China.

development with more rational thinking. They should be brave surfers in the development tide of the times, and in the process of international exchanges. In recent years, the number of outbound tourists in China has continued to grow, and the youth are the main force. From 1995 to 2016, with the improvement of people's living standards, China's outbound tourism expenditures increased significantly. In 1995, China's outbound tourism expenditure ranked 25th in the world. In 2000, it rose to the eighth in the world. In 2013, it ranked second in the world and ranked first in the world in 2014 and 2015. In 2016, China's outbound tourism expenditure was US $261.1 billion, an increase of US $257.4 billion from the US $3.7 billion in 1995, an increase of 69.6 times. ①

Chinese youth go abroad with the progress of the country, and some experiences have become much-told stories of Chinese and foreign exchanges, and some have become the Chinese stories of Chinese and foreign exchanges, the story of Chinese youth. In 2013, President Xi Jinping visited Africa. In his speech entitled *Trustworthy Friends and Sincere Partners Forever* at the Julius Nyerere International Convention Centerin Tanzania, General Secretary Xi Jinping told a China-Africa story of young people: "Let me tell you a story of a young Chinese couple. When they were kids, both the boy and the girl got to know Africa from Chinese TV programs and have since been captivated by this continent. Later, they got married and decided to take Tanzania as their honeymoon destination. So on their first Valentine's Day after the wedding, they came here and backpacked across this country. They were overwhelmed by the hospitality and friendship of the local people and the magnificent savanna of Serengeti. After the couple went back to China, they posted what they saw and heard in Tanzania on their blog, which received tens of thousands of hits and several hundred comments. This is what they wrote in their blog, 'We have completely fallen in love with Africa and our hearts will always be with this fascinating land.' This story speaks to the natural feeling of kinship between the Chinese and African people. As long as we keep expanding people-to-people exchanges, friendship between our peoples will take deep roots and continue to flourish."②

The Chinese youth story told by General Secretary Xi Jinping reflects the true situation of the Chinese youth who are constantly writing in national development and international exchanges. Youth needs development and

---

① *The 40th Anniversary of Reform and Opening Up*, Beijing: China Statistics Press, September 2018, pp. 69 - 70.

② Xi Jinping, "Trustworthy Friends and Sincere Partners Forever at the Julius Nyerere International Convention Center in Tanzania", *Guangming Daily*, Mar. 26, 2013.

progress, but the premise is the development and progress of the country. Young people need skills training when facing opportunities for development. They need good education when facing development challenges. They need dreams when facing development prospects and life choices. They need to see the future of development when meeting with difficulties. The synchronization of these with development is what young people need. Young people do not lack dreams, ideals, or the spirit of struggle. What they lack is the stage to excel. This stage is economic growth, a stable society, a fair environment, a good education, a skill for making a living, or the hope of development. Youth development is the theme that cannot be circumvented in the current era. Injecting impetus for youth development and promoting youth employment are the basic premise for young people to establish themselves in society. Only if we make the youth know their life is promising, our society will be promising. Only if the youth master their future, our society will have a great future.

Strong youth lead to a strong country. If young people have the driving force for development, the society will have the vitality of development, the economy will have the energy to develop, and the country will move forward. In the 70 years since the founding of the People's Republic of China and over the past 40 years since reform and opening up, the development of China's cause of youth has synchronized with the development of the country. The infinite possibilities of the country's development have provided infinite possibilities for the development of Chinese youth and for national rejuvenation.

In the 2019 New Year's speech, General Secretary Xi Jinping said: "I noticed that this year, most of the people who went into college when enrollments first resumed in 1977 have retired. In their place, a large number of people born after the year 2000 have entered into university. "① From the then

① "President Xi Jinping's 2019 New Year Address", Xinhuanet, http: //www. xinhuanet. com/politics/2018 - 12/31/c_ 1123931806. htm.

young generation of meritorious medal winners of "atomic and hydrogen bombs and man-made satellite" to the most retired college students of the first batch of people who went into college when enrollments first resumed in 1977, and then to the large number of people born after the year 2000 who just entered into university, from generation to generation, young people in the 70 years of the People's Republic of China, have carried forward and developed the cause of socialism with Chinese characteristics. Socialism with Chinese characteristics has entered a new era, which has opened up a broader future for development for today's young people to struggle for their life and future. "China's history in modern times tells us that only socialism can save China and that only socialism with Chinese characteristics can develop China. Only with socialism can we realize the great rejuvenation of the Chinese nation. We must persist in developing socialism with Chinese characteristics and build China into a modernized socialist power. It is a long-term task that requires generations of people's continuous struggle. Just as what we have struggled all the way, our future needs young people to continue to struggle and continue to advance generation after generation."①

II Health: the basis and premise of youth's participation in social development

The report of the 19th National Congress of the Communist Party of China clearly stated the implementation of the Healthy China Strategy. "A healthy population is a key mark of a prosperous nation and a strong country."② The

---

① Xi Jinping, "Speech at the Symposium of Teachers and Students of Peking University", Xinhuanet, http://www.xinhuanet.com/politics/2018-05/03/c_1122774230.htm.

② Xi Jinping, "Secure a Decisive Victory in Building a Moderately Prosperous Society in All Respects and Strive for the Great Success of Socialism with Chinese Characteristics for a New Era—Delivered at the 19th National Congress of the Communist", Xinhuanet, http://www.xinhuanet.com//politics/19cpcnc/2017-10/27/c_1121867529.htm.

youth are the hope of the country and the future of the nation. Youth health is the fundamental premise and foundation for youth to grow and become talented. In the past 70 years since the founding of the People's Republic of China, along with the country's economic growth and progress, China's medical cause has made remarkable progress, and the people's health has improved markedly. A historic transformation has realized, which is from meeting basic living needs to living a happy and healthy life. The ideas of becoming moderately prosperous and keeping healthy is deeply rooted in the hearts of the people. The average life expectancy of Chinese residents was 35 years before 1949. In 1978, at the beginning of reform and opening up, it was 68. 2 years, and it was 76. 7 years in 2017, which was 41. 7 years higher than 1949. The infant mortality rate dropped from 200‰ before 1949, to 9. 5‰ in 2013 and to 6. 8‰ in 2017; the maternal mortality rate dropped from 150/100000 before 1949 to 94. 7/100000 in 1989, to 23. 2/100000 in 2010, and to 19. 6/100000 in 2017. ①The significant improvement of the youth's health level has provided important human resources for the country's economic and social development, and provided an important premise and foundation for the sustained development and release of the demographic dividend for the past 40 years since reform and opening up.

The development of medical care provides an important guarantee for the health and youth health of our people. In addition, the comprehensive health cause has also achieved historic development achievements, and the Healthy China Strategy has been further advanced. At present, there are more than 1 million sports venues in China, more than 240 times that of the early days after the founding of the People's Republic of China. In 2010, the proportion of

---

① National Bureau of Statistics of China, *New China in 65 Years*, Beijing: China Statistics Press, September 2014, p. 157; *The 40th Anniversary of Reform and Opening Up*, Beijing: China Statistics Press, September 2018, p. 250.

people meeting the level of "qualified" in the *National Standards for Physical Fitness was* 88.9%.[①]Moreover, in 2017, a total of 11.13 million people enjoyed the benefit of maternity insurance, which exceeded 10 million for the first time, an increase of 7.6 million compared with 2012, and an average annual increase of 25.8%. The per capita benefit level of maternity insurance in 2017 was 18126 yuan, an increase of 6839 yuan over 2012, with an average annual growth rate of 9.9%.[②]In terms of competitive sports, from 1949 to 2013, Chinese athletes won a total of 2902 world championships, of which 2876 were won from 1978 to 2013, accounting for 99.1% of the total since the founding of the People's Republic of China.[③]From 2014 to 2017, China won 438 world championships. From 1978 to 2017, China won a total of 3314 world championships.[④]The sports industry started from scratch, and has developed and grown stronger. Fruitful results have been achieved in the cause of youth sports. According to the *2018 National Time Use Survey Bulletin*, "The average time of fitness exercise for residents is 31 minutes, 41 minutes for urban residents and 16 minutes for rural residents. Residents grouped by 10 years, the average time residents aged 75 to 84 is the longest, 64 minutes; the time for residents aged 25 to 34 is the shortest, 14 minutes. The participation rate of residents' fitness exercise is 30.9%, 38.7% for urban residents and 18.7% for rural residents."[⑤]

From standing up to getting rich and to getting stronger, the youth

---

① National Bureau of Statistics of China, *New China in 65 Years*, Beijing: China Statistics Press, September 2014, p. 159.

② *The 40th Anniversary of Reform and Opening Up*, Beijing: China Statistics Press, September 2018, p. 288.

③ National Bureau of Statistics of China, *New China in 65 Years*, Beijing: China Statistics Press, September 2014, p. 159.

④ *The 40th Anniversary of Reform and Opening Up*, Beijing: China Statistics Press, September 2018, p. 444.

⑤ National Bureau of Statistics, *Bulletin of the 2018 National Time Use Survey*, http://www.stats.gov.cn/tjsj/zxfb/201901/t20190125_1646796.html.

development cause has been moving forward over the past years. The state pays attention to youth development and the family pays attention to the growth of children. In the past, people exercise to save the country. Now they exercise to realize the goal of getting overall well-off. The improvement of the health of the people reflects the historical changes in China's development orientation over the past 100 years. Young people from all walks of life are involved in the great journey of national construction and rejuvenation with healthy attitude, healthy posture, healthy life and healthy behavior. Today, the healthy Chinese youth, under the guarantee and promotion of the national health cause, not only arduously train themselves to win the world championships to win honor for the motherland, but also take root in the frontiers, mountain villages, or desert areas, and some even maintain world peace in areas of hardship and war. They interpret China's national image with a good image of Chinese youth. The sharp increase in life expectancy per capita and the significant reduction in maternal mortality are the best proof of the development of health in New China. Young people from generation to generation have taken over the baton of history and made great progress. In "health", they witnessed the healthy development of China's youth development.

III Education and employment: equity in starting point and opportunity for youth's participation in social development

Education and employment are important indicators for the cause of youth development, and they are an important prerequisite and path for young people to "chase dreams" and "fulfil dreams". Since the founding of the People's Republic of China, China's education and employment has made great achievements. In colorful youth, young people in the colorful China have woven colorful dreams that have pooled together into a youthful Chinese

Dream. General Secretary Xi Jinping pointed out: "Young people are both dream seekers and dream realizers. Chasing dreams requires passion and ideals, and realizing dreams require struggle and dedication. Young people should release youthful passion, pursue youthful ideals, and strive to contribute to national rejuvenation and the construction of our motherland."[①]

In the early days after the founding of the People's Republic of China, 80% of the country's population was illiterate. The illiteracy rate in rural areas was as high as 95%, and the enrollment rate of school-age children was less than 20%. Since the founding of the People's Republic of China, especially since the reform and opening up, China has transformed from a large illiterate country to a large human resource country. The educational level of the population has been rising. In 1982, the average period of the population being educated in China was 5.3 years, and the average period of getting education for the working-age population reached 9.3 years.[②] In 2016, the per capita period of getting education for China's working-age population reached 10.35 years. In 2017, the average period of getting education for new laborers reached 13.25 years, and the proportion of those who received higher education exceeded 45%.[③] By the end of 2018, the gross enrollment rate of senior high school in China was 88.8%.[④]

On the basis of the tremendous development achievements over the past 70 years since the founding of the People's Republic of China, we adhere to the people-centered development ideology. We believe the development is for

---

① Xi Jinping, "Speech at the Symposium of Teachers and Students of Peking University", Xinhuanet, http://www.xinhuanet.com/politics/2018-05/03/c_1122774230.htm.

② National Bureau of Statistics of China, *New China in 65 Years*, Beijing: China Statistics Press, September 2014, p. 131.

③ *The 40th Anniversary of Reform and Opening Up*, Beijing: China Statistics Press, September 2018, p. 274.

④ National Bureau of Statistics, *Statistical Communique of the 2018 National Economic and Social Development of the People's Republic of China*, http://www.stats.gov.cn/tjsj/zxfb/201902/t20190228_1651265.html.

the people, and the fruits of development are shared by the people. We aim at the long-term future of the youth development cause. The report for the 19th National Congress of the Communist Party of China shows: we will make senior secondary education universally available; we will improve the system of financial aid to students, and work to see that the vast majority of the new members of the urban and rural labor force have received senior secondary education, and that more and more of them receive higher education. ①The government work report made by Premier Li Keqiang at the Second Session of the 13th National People's Congress shows: the government will work hard to make senior secondary education universally available. ②

The development of education, especially of senior high school education, higher education and vocational education, has laid a solid foundation for the development of youth, and promoted the fairness of opportunities and of development. Education is the bottom line of social justice. Like the sun and the air, it is the most universal public product. It is the unshirkable duty of the government to provide this public product. *The Medium-and Long-Term Youth Development Plan (2016 - 2025)* clearly stipulates that by 2025, the right to education for young people will be better protected, the equalization of basic public education services will be gradually realized, and the fairness in education will be significantly improved. The average period of being educated for new laborers has reached 13.5 years, and the gross enrollment rate for

---

① Xi Jinping, "Secure a Decisive Victory in Building a Moderately Prosperous Society in All Respects and Strive for the Great Success of Socialism with Chinese Characteristics for a New Era—Delivered at the 19th National Congress of the Communist", Xinhuanet, http://www.xinhuanet.com//politics/19cpcnc/2017-10/27/c_1121867529.htm.

② Li Keqiang, "Report on the Work of the Government", delivered at the Second Session of the 13th National People's Congress of the People's Republic of China on March 5, 2019, Xinhuanet, http://www.xinhuanet.com/politics/2019lh/2019-03/16/c_1124242390.htm.

higher education has reached more than 50%.[①] This will certainly provide a more equitable development environment for the development of youth, a superior development foundation, and a more sustainable and stable supply of talent for the basic realization of modernization in 2035.

In terms of employment, diversification and personalization of employment are the most prominent features of the development of the times, and also indicate the tremendous progress in youth employment. From the founding of the People's Republic of China to the reform and opening up, China's urban employment experienced a rapid growth and then a stagnant state. At the end of 1949, the number of employed urban workers across China was 15.33 million, and the unemployed population was 4.742 million, with the unemployment rate of 23.6%. At the end of 1978, the employed population nationwide increased to 401.52 million, of which 95.14 million were employed in urban areas.[②] At the end of 2017, the total number of employed people reached 776.4 million, representing an increase of 329.48 million compared with 1978, an increase of 346%, and an average annual increase of 8.45 million.[③] By the end of 2018, there were 775.86 million employed people nationwide, including 434.19 million urban employees.[④]

Employment is the basis of people's livelihood. Promoting employment has always been the top priority of the work of the Party Central Committee and the State Council. Youth employment is placed in an important position. "We

---

① *Medium-and Long-Term Youth Development Plan (2016 - 2025)*, http://www.gov.cn/zhengce/2017-04/13/content_5185555.htm#1.

② National Bureau of Statistics of China, *New China in 65 Years*, Beijing: China Statistics Press, September 2014, p. 107.

③ *The 40th Anniversary of Reform and Opening Up*, Beijing: China Statistics Press, September 2018, p. 200.

④ National Bureau of Statistics, *Statistical Communique of the 2018 National Economic and Social Development of the People's Republic of China*, http://www.stats.gov.cn/tjsj/zxfb/201902/t20190228_1651265.html.

have nearly 900 million labor resources, more than 700 million employed people, 170 million high-quality talents with higher education and vocational education, and more than 8 million college graduates each year. "① These provide reliable guarantee for long-term development of China.

In addition, education and youth employment have achieved joint development, which has greatly improved the structure and quality of the employed population, especially the youth groups, and provided a large number of high-quality talents and labor for the development of the labor market in China. The return of a large number of overseas students has also further improved the quality and structure of employed population. From 1982 to 2017, the proportion of those with a college education or above increased from 0.9% to 19.5%; the proportion of those with a primary school education or below fell from 62.6% to 19.2%. From 1978 to 2017, 3.132 million overseas students chose to return to China, accounting for 83.73% of the overseas students who completed study abroad. ②

In the process of moving from a high-speed growth phase to a high-quality growth phase, we have always placed employment as a prior development strategy, implemented a positive employment policy, and listed employment as a macro policy together with monetary policy and fiscal policy. Under the pressure of economic downturn, it can better "keep employment stable". In January and February of 2019, the national urban unemployment rate was 5.1% and 5.3%, respectively, lower than the expected target of 5.5%. According to the Ministry of Human Resources and Social Security, the number

---

① The State Council Information Office Held the 2018 National Economic Operation Conference, http://www.scio.gov.cn/xwfbh/xwbfbh/wqfbh/39595/39709/index.htm.

② National Bureau of Statistics, *The State Continuous Growth in Total Employment & Adjustment and Optimization of Employment Structure-14th of the Series of Reports on Economic and Social Development Achievements in the 40 Years of Reform and Opening-up*, http://www.stats.gov.cn/ztjc/ztfx/ggkf40n/201809/t20180912_1622409.html.

of new jobs in urban areas in January and February was 1.74 million.[①] At present, the employment situation in China is generally stable and the quality of employment has steadily increased. However, China's employment still faces structural contradictions. The structural contradiction of having difficulty in both finding jobs and recruiting workers are more prominent. Some college graduates face difficulties in finding jobs. On the other hand, the shortage of technical talents urgently needed by enterprises is serious. Both in the coastal areas and in the central and western regions, some enterprises have experienced shortages of skilled workers and new-type talents. According to the Ministry of Human Resources and Social Security, in recent years, the job vacancies-to-seekers ratio for skilled workers has been above 1.5, and this ratio for senior technicians has even exceeded 2.0 or more.[②] This requires us to intensify policy adjustments, aim at the staged characteristics and long-term strategic goals of economic development, and push forward the policy for "keeping employment stable". We need to make youth employment, especially the structural problems in youth employment, an important priority in policy making, expand the linkage between employment policies and education policies, and promote supply-side structural reform of employment.

More than 70 years since the founding of the People's Republic of China and more than 40 years of reform and opening up have laid solid material development foundation for promoting the supply-side structural reform of employment, expanding the linkage between employment and education, giving full play to education and training to boost employment, and improving the quality and skills of employed people. In 2019, the improvement campaign of vocational skills kicked off, using 100 billion yuan from the balance of the

---

① Li Xiru, "Overall Employment Situation is Stable & Structural Contradictions Need Attention", National Bureau of Statistics, http://www.stats.gov.cn/tjsj/sjjd/201903/t20190314_1653894.html.

② Ibid..

unemployment insurance fund for skills upgrading and job transfer training for jobs with more than 15 million people. At the same time, we reform and improve the examination methods for higher vocational colleges, encouraging more senior high school graduates, retired military personnel, laid-off workers, migrant workers to take entrance examinations for higher vocational colleges, with a large-scale expansion of enrollment of 1 million people. "Through major reforms and the development of modern vocational education, we will move faster to train the different types of technicians and skilled workers urgently needed in China's development, enabling more young people to gain professional skills and realize their potential and producing a vast range of talent ready to shine bright. "①

From a "big illiterate country" to a big country of human resources, from employment for solving the problem of food and clothing to high-quality employment, to the joint development of education and employment, to solving the structural contradictions of employment, during the past more than seventy years, youth education and employment have always accompanied and developed stably in "dream chasing" and "dream fulfillment" . The report of the 19th National Congress of the Communist Party of China pointed out: "We will provide extensive public employment services to open more channels for college graduates and other young people as well as migrant rural workers to find jobs and start their own businesses. We must remove institutional barriers that block the social mobility of labor and talent and ensure that every one of our people has the chance to pursue career through hard work. "②

---

① Li Keqiang, "Report on the Work of the Government", delivered at the Second Session of the 13th National People's Congress of the People's Republic of China, March 5, 2019, Xinhuanet, http: //www. xinhuanet. com/politics/2019lh/2019 – 03/16/c_ 1124242390. htm.

② Xi Jinping, "Secure a Decisive Victory in Building a Moderately Prosperous Society in All Respects and Strive for the Great Success of Socialism with Chinese Characteristics for a New Era—Delivered at the 19th National Congress of the Communist", *Guangming Daily*, Oct. 28, 2017.

Education and employment are important forms and paths to guide young people to participate in social development, and they are also important stages for socialization of young people. Promoting the development of education is fundamentally storing the most essential inexhaustible motive force for the long-term development of the nation. To promote the development of employment, continuously improve the employment environment, and provide ladders for the development of youth is fundamentally accumulating boundless power for the country's long-term development. Through continuous exertion of demographic dividends and continuous accumulation of talent dividend, the quality structure of our youth has undergone a historic change. Further promoting comprehensively deepening reform and removing institutional barriers that block the social mobility of labor and talent in accordance with the strategic deployment made by the party's 19th National Congress, will surely open up a new future for the development of youth in the new era, and let the youth constantly "fulfill dreams" in "seeking dreams" and continue to create new miracles of China's development in "fulfilling dreams". Chasing and fulfilling the dream of life development, in the final analysis, is to chase and fulfill the dream of national rejuvenation. "A mobile China is full of vitality. We are all running very hard. We are all dream chasers."①

① "President Xi Jinping's 2019 New Year Address", *Guangming Daily*, Jan. 1, 2019.

Chapter IV Changes in History: The Spirit of the May Fourth Movement Inspires Youth to Strive for Their Dreams in the National Rejuvenation in the New Era

I The youth is the future of the country and hope of the nation

General Secretary Xi Jinping pointed out in the report of the 19th National Congress of the Communist Party of China: "A nation will prosper only when its young people thrive; a country will be full of hope and have a great tomorrow only when its younger generations have ideals, ability, and a strong sense of responsibility. The Chinese Dream is a dream about history, the present, and the future. It is a dream of our generation, but even more so, a dream of the younger generations." ①

The youth are the future of the country and the nation. In the past 100 years, Chinese youth have been integrated into the tide of historical

① Xi Jinping, "Secure a Decisive Victory in Building a Moderately Prosperous Society in All Respects and Strive for the Great Success of Socialism with Chinese Characteristics for a New Era—Delivered at the 19th National Congress of the Communist", *Guangming Daily*, Oct. 28, 2017.

development, integrated into the destiny of the country and the hope of national development. In the course of a hundred years of development, Chinese youth have devoted themselves to the people's cause and national cause led by the Party, devoted themselves to every historical stage, such as national liberation, resisting foreign humiliation, struggle for "atomic and hydrogen bombs and man-made satellite", and the endeavor in reform and opening up, writing each historical moment of the youthful struggle of China. For the next 30 years, basic modernization will be achieved by 2035, and a socialist modernized power will be built by 2050. Young people in the new era will have to take over the historical baton of national rejuvenation and race to create a good future.

We are witnessing major changes unfolding in our world, something unseen in a century. The history of the past 100 years is like a drop in the ocean. However, the great struggle of the Chinese youth for the country, the nation and the people in the past 100 years has taken an important position in the historical development of the Chinese nation in 5000 years. The May Fourth Movement is the beginning of the great awakening of Chinese youth, Chinese society and the Chinese people. The May Fourth Movement was lively and the youth who struggled for it were also lively. This has never changed in the past 100 years and will not change. That's because to seek the people's happiness and the rejuvenation of the nation is the unchanged original aspiration of generations of Chinese youth and the youthful tint without regret.

A hundred years ago, throwing themselves to national rejuvenation and saving the nation from peril were the only choices of Chinese youth in their life. "Studying for a prosperous and rising China" has inspired a generation of young people to struggle during the period of "standing up"; "Unite to revitalize China" has become the most profound brand of the youth development the times during the period of "getting rich", inspiring a

generation of young people to strive to be "the new generation in the 1980s"; "We are all dream chasers" is the most real tint for the youth development in the era of "getting strong". It encourages this generation of youth people to take over the historical baton and bravely struggle on the road of chasing dreams. Whether it was a hundred years ago or a hundred years later, the leadership of the Party, and synchronizing with the times, the people, and the nation, are the unchanging tint of the Chinese youth struggle, the most beautiful color of youth.

General Secretary Xi Jinping pointed out: "In the new era, Chinese youth must, as brave pioneers and contributors in the forefront of the times, fearlessly face all difficulties and obstacles, advance in waves, open up the world in thorns, and create achievements in the difficult situation, and use youth and sweat to create new miracles that amaze the whole world!"①

II Struggle is the brightest tint of youth

Youth would be meaningless without struggle! The synonym of youth is struggle. Youth without struggle is incomplete. General Secretary Xi Jinping pointed out: "Today, our living conditions are better, but the spirit of struggle cannot be less. The good tradition of Chinese youth's permanent struggle cannot be lost at all."②

The development of the times is different, and the pursuit and values of the youth are also undergoing tremendous changes. However, the struggling youth is the constant background color of the Chinese youth, and is the brightest color of China. From the revolutionary war years, to the socialist

① Xi Jinping, "Speech at a Ceremony to Mark the Centenary of the May Fourth Movement", *Guangming Daily*, May 1, 2019.

② Ibid..

revolution and construction period, to the new historical period of reform and opening up, young people have been struggling for national rejuvenation. The majority of young people have responded to the party's call and devoted themselves to all walks of life and all aspects of the construction of the motherland, and takeactions to practice the strong voice of the times of uniting and rejuvenating China.

From the then young generation of meritorious medal winners of "atomic and hydrogen bombs and man-made satellite" to the most retired college students of the first batch of people who went into college when enrollments first resumed in 1977, and then to the large number of people born after the year 2000 who just entered into university, from generation to generation, young people in the 70 years of new China, have carried forward and developed the cause of socialism with Chinese characteristics. Socialism with Chinese characteristics has entered a new era, which has opened up a broader future for development for today's young people to struggle for their life and future.

Having more individuality and more emphasis on participation and initiative becomes the distinctive features of youth development in this era. At the same time, the pressure of work, family, marriage, child-rearing and old-age care also puts contemporary young people under the pressure when they pursue career development. Therefore, there is obvious volatility in their outlook on life, world outlook and values. Each generation of youth has their own image of struggle. Each generation of youth has a different time and space background to grow and develop. The Chinese youth's image of struggle means positivity, sunniness, dedication and friendliness, which are like the brightest stars in the night sky, always dazzling.

When the mission of national rejuvenation is passed to the shoulders of the "post-80s", "post-90s" and "post-00s", they do not escape the responsibility given by the times and history. Instead, they try to realize their own values as

shoulder the national responsibility in the struggle of youth. Some even sacrificed their youthful lives for the cause of the Party and the people. In the Muli forest fire in Sichuan in 2019, 27 of the firefighters lost their lives. Most of them were "post-90s" or even "post-95s", and two were "post-00s" . Their deeds would be forever remembered from the 70th anniversary of the People's Republic. The people of the whole country feel sorry and sorrowful for their deaths. They proved that the young people of the present are reliable and can be trusted with their own practical actions. On behalf of the Party Central Committee and the State Council, the State Councilor Wang Yong pointed out at the memorial activity for the martyrs in the Muli forest fire: "In the face of the test of blood and fire, life and death, all the combatants regarded the fire as an order, and took it as their mission to defend the forest and maintain ecological security. They have practiced with blood and life their oath of contributing everything fearlessly to the maintenance of people's lives and property as well as social stability. The heroes who sacrificed are typical representatives among them. They are the model in the new era! The heroic deeds of the martyrs will always be recorded in the history of the People's Republic!"① These young people who have lost their lives for the people and the country are the loveliest people in the new era.

In the future, the development tasks will be even more arduous, and it is still necessary to maintain a hard-working style on the way forward. "In the new journey of realizing the great rejuvenation of the Chinese nation, there will inevitably be arduous tasks. There will inevitably be difficulties, obstacles and even storms, which particularly needs us to carry forward the spirit of hard struggle. Struggle is not just a loud slogan, but the spirit in accomplishing every task and fulfilling every duty." The development of the country cannot be achieved without the participation of the youth. The revival of the nation

① "Sichuan Held the Memorial Activity for Martyrs in the Muli Forest Fire", http://www.gov.cn/xinwen/2019-04/05/content_5379813.htm.

cannot be realized without the struggle of the youth. In the era of thousands of vessels on rivers competing for the advancement, the contemporary youth who struggle in the journey of national rejuvenation, are meeting the challenges and working hard, and will brighten the tint of youth more shining.

III　Doing a good job in youth work in the new era

The Party Central Committee with Comrade Xi Jinping as the core attaches great importance to the cause of youth development and cares for the youth. General Secretary Xi Jinping has repeatedly delivered important speeches on the cause of youth development, which constitute a guide to the cause of youth development in the new era. In the new era, the Party's youth work focuses on the historical mission and responsibility of basically realizing modernization, building a socialist modernized power, and cultivating qualified successors for the cause of the Party and the people. General Secretary Xi Jinping pointed out: "Since the founding of the Communist Party of China, the youth work has always been regarded as an extremely important task of the Party."① "In order to pursue the great cause of the Chinese nation, the Communist Party of China must always represent, win over and rely on its young people, do its youth work with great strength, ensure that the Party's cause is passed on from generation to generation, and ensure the sustainable development of the Chinese nation."②

To promote the cause of youth development in the new era, we must take The Thought on Socialism with Chinese Characteristics for a New Era as the guide, implement the series of important expositions of General Secretary on

① Xi Jinping, "Speech at a Ceremony to Mark the Centenary of the May Fourth Movement", Xinhuanet, http://www.xinhuanet.com/politics/leaders/2019-04/30/c_1124440193.htm.

② Ibid..

youth development, carry forward the youth culture, establish ourselves in the youth reality, solve the youth problems, constantly create stages for young people to excel, and train qualified builders and successors for the cause of the Party and the people, so that the new youth of the new era can take the Long March that belongs to this generation. General Secretary Xi Jinping sent a message to contemporary youth, pointing out: "Young friends, there is only one youth in a person's life. Now, youth is for struggle, and in the future, youth is memory." "Only the youth with passionate struggle and with dedication to the people will leave a youthful memory that is full, warm, lasting and regret-free."①

The youth stage is the initial stage of life and the stage of struggle in life. Happiness comes from struggle, and only happiness in struggle is true happiness, happiness of the people, and happiness in the process of national rejuvenation. General Secretary stressed: "Young people have different life goals and different career choices. But only by integrating yourself into the motherland and the people, keeping pace with the times and sharing the same future of the people, can you realize the value of life."② To face the cause of youth development in the new era, we must implement the national medium-and long-term youth development plan, focus on a series of realistic issues such as youth employment, education, housing, and platform; strengthen guidance on their outlook on life and world view, let them realize their own values by integrating their youth into national development and social progress, and realize their own values; focus on social issues that affect the long-term healthy development of young people, and create a sound economic environment,

① Xi Jinping, "Speech at the Symposium of Outstanding Young Delegates from All walks of Life", *Guangming Daily*, May 5, 2013.

② Xi Jinping, "Speech at a Ceremony to Mark the Centenary of the May Fourth Movement", *Guangming Daily*, May 1, 2019.

social environment and virtual world environment for youth development; focus on the cultivation of young people's sustainable development capabilities, enhance vocational education, help young people get rid of poverty, and support youth entrepreneurship through youth support programs.

The youth are the future of the new era and of the nation. The successful practice of the cause of socialism with Chinese characteristics in the new era is in the youth. The history of youth development tells us that the new era is the best development era in the past 100 years, but also an era close to the national rejuvenation. Achieving national rejuvenation will be no walk in the park; it will take more than drum beating and gong clanging to get there. After the 100 years in modern times, 70 years of New China, and 40 years of reform and opening up, today's happy life and development are the results of continuous struggle and bloodshed of generations of people with lofty ideals. Looking back at the path we have traveled, looking ahead at the path in distance, and comparing the paths of others, we have found that only the path of socialism with Chinese characteristics can be the fundamental path for the development of Chinese youth. Further promoting comprehensively deepening reform and removing institutional barriers that block the social mobility of labor and talent in accordance with the strategic deployment made by the party's 19th National Congress, will surely open up a new future for the development of youth in the new era, and let the youth constantly "fulfill dreams" in "seeking dreams" and continue to create new miracles of China's development and in "fulfilling dreams". Chasing and fulfilling the dream of life development, in the final analysis, is to chase and fulfill the dream of national rejuvenation. "A mobile China is full of vitality. We are all running very hard. We are all dream chasers."①

① "President Xi Jinping's 2019 New Year Address", *Guangming Daily*, Jan. 1, 2019.

IV Chinese youth in the new era should not only care about their family and country, but also have concerns for humanity

China in the new era has undergone a fundamental transformation in its international status and development environment. As the world's second largest economy and a permanent member of the UN Security Council, China's international role in the global governance system and capacity building as well as in participating in and leading globalization has undergone an important transformation. China has become one important "latus" in the development of multilateralism. The promotion of the Belt and Road Initiative has won wide support from the international community. The youth's Belt and Road Initiative and the youth's community with a shared future for mankind have allowed the world's peaceful development cause to continue. The youth are of a country and a nation, but also of the world. Young Chinese peacekeepers participate in actions to maintain regional and world peace; young Chinese builders participate in infrastructure construction and development in countries along the Belt and Road Initiative; young Chinese medical staff and medical teams participate in the medical career of the African people; young Chinese scholars participate in the knowledge exchange with foreign young people to promote cultural exchanges between China and countries along the Belt and Road.

General Secretary Xi Jinping pointed out that "the young people of the new era should not only care about their family and country, but also have concerns for humanity, carry forward the spirit of taking the whole world as one community in the Chinese culture, struggle for the great rejuvenation of the Chinese nation, and work hard to promote the joint construction of the Belt and Road Initiative and the building of a community with a shared future for mankind. "①

Caring about our family and country is the most shining value left by the May Fourth spirit to Chinese youth. The core spirit of the May Fourth Movement is patriotism. This is the inheritance of the spiritual values of the Chinese nation for thousands of years. It is noble and holy, and it is inherited from the soul and blood of every Chinese. Patriotism is the natural feeling of every Chinese. General Secretary Xi Jinping profoundly summed up: "A person who is not patriotic, even deceives the motherland or betrays the motherland, is very shameful in his own country and in the world, and has no place to stand. For every Chinese person, patriotism is the duty and responsibility. It is natural flow of our feelings. For the young people of the new era, patriotism is the foundation of their development and success. "②

Having concerns for humanity is the new spiritual connotation of the struggle and development of Chinese youth in the new era. This is closely linked to the development of the country and the pulse of the times. China's development cannot be separated from the world, and the development of the world requires China's full support. Concern for humanity of the young people in the new era is the inheritance of the Chinese people's spirit of "planning and worrying ahead of the people" since ancient times. It is the embodiment of the spirit of the Chinese communists who are committed to promoting the cause of human development. The developing world requires the youth of all countries to work together and assume more responsibilities for the development of human society. Is the development of human society at the crossroads is moving forward or retreating? To answer this question, we cannot neglect the attention

---

① Xi Jinping, "Speech at a Ceremony to Mark the Centenary of the May Fourth Movement", *Guangming Daily*, May 1, 2019.

② Ibid. .

to the needs of young people, or the perception of the wishes of young people. The youth are the future. The hope of the development of human society lies wherever the youth are. The concern of Chinese youth for humanity closely combines the pursuit of the development of the Chinese people with the pursuit of promoting the development of the cause of all mankind. Let the youthful China light up the future of the world youth to build a community with a shared future for mankind.

Avoiding the distractions of unsubstantial ideas and superficial fame, the Chinese youth in the new era have taken over the baton of the May Fourth spirit and will struggle to chase their dreams in the new era. "We are all dreamer chasers." This is the group image of Chinese youth of this era!

Part II

South African Youth and Social Development

Chapter V Policies and Mechanisms for South African Youth's Participation in Social Development

I Overview of South African youth groups

In general, there is no universal definition of the youth population. From the perspective of traditional meaning, "youth" is traditionally defined as the transition period from childhood to adulthood. [①]Obviously, this is expressed in various ways according to different organizational perspectives. In the *African Youth Report 2009* (hereafter, the AYR), "youth" are defined as people between 15 and 39 years of age. [②]However, some African countries have different definitions of the youth population. For example, Ghana, Tanzania and South Africa define the youth population as the population between the ages of 15 and 35; Nigeria and Swaziland define it as between 12 and 30 years; Botswana and Mauritius define it as 14 to 25 years. [③]These different definitions of the youth population make it difficult for us to effectively discuss the general problems

---

① United Nations Economic Commission for Africa (UNECA), *African Youth Report (AYR): Expanding opportunities for and with Young people in Africa*, June 2009, https://www.uneca.org/sites/default/files/PublicationFiles/africanyouthreport_09.pdf.

② Ibid..

③ Ibid..

affecting African youth and to compare the youth information across countries.

According to Population 2030 by the Department of Economic and Social Affairs of United Nations, youth is defined as the population between 15 and 24 years. Based on the mandate of the National Youth Commission Act (1996) and the National Youth Development Policy Framework (2002), the NYP 2015 – 2020 defines the youth in South Africa as the population between 15 and 35 years. According to the National Youth Commission (NYC) 1996 Act: "The essence is that among the many older youth, most of them are disadvantaged by the struggle against apartheid and need to be included in the Youth Development Initiative."① As a result, the bill has largely incorporated many older people into the realm of youth.

However, although the situation of youth has changed a lot since the advent of democracy in 1994, the motivation for the 35-year-old age limit has not changed, as the country's historical imbalance has not yet been fully resolved. ②This is also in line with the definition of youth as documented in the *African Youth Charter* (which also defines youth as a youth between the ages of 15 and 35). The NYP, recognising that young people are not a homogenous group, has adopted a differentiated approach, targeting its interventions according to age cohorts and specific groups within its broad definition of "youth" to address their specific situations and needs. ③

This differentiated approach makes it possible for the NYP to take into account other definitions set out in relevant legislation and policies, such as the National Youth Development Policy Framework, the definition of children under the age of 18 in the Children's Act (2005), and the criminal justice

---

① National Youth Commission Act (1996).

② National Youth Development Agency (NYDA), *National Youth Policy (NYP) 2015 – 2020*, April 2015.

③ Ibid..

system refer to young offenders between the ages of 14 and 25, and their differences between children and "adult youth". [①]The latter is not considered a specialised group in need of special rehabilitative programmes.

II Youth development and national future: policies for South African youth's participation in social development

1 Youth development policy and background

South Africa is one of the few countries in Africa that has developed and attempted to implement a comprehensive youth policy in the past few decades.

Due to South Africa's unique history, youth policy has become an integral part of its policy of providing social justice and equitable development. During the post-apartheid period, South Africa adopted a series of youth policies, including the National Youth Policy (NYP) in 2000, the National Youth Development Framework (NYDF) in 2002 - 2007, and the NYP in 2009 - 2014. [②]In addition, the South African government passed the National Youth Commission (NYC) Act of 1996 and it has established such a commission. NYP (2009 - 2014) focuses on four areas of intervention: education, health and well-being, economic participation and social cohesion. [③]Youth groups with special attention include young women, youth with disabilities, unemployed youth, out-of-school youth, rural youth and youth at risk; policy tools provide specific interventions with measurable benchmarks for each goal. The implementation of this policy will involve the government, the private sector and

---

① National Youth Development Agency (NYDA), *National Youth Policy (NYP) 2015 - 2020*, April 2015.

② Presidency of South Africa, *National Youth Policy 2009 - 2014*, Presidency, Pretoria, http://www.thepresidency.gov.za/download/file/fid/122.

③ Ibid..

non-governmental organizations. NYP (2009 – 2014) calls for the establishment of youth units or management committees in each government ministry or department. There is also a need to establish a mechanism for impact assessment of South Africa's youth programmers. Given the high youth unemployment rate, NYP (2009 – 2014) attaches great importance to providing employment opportunities for youth. ①In order to achieve better implementation results, any policy needs to be carefully designed and strategically planned, taking into account all the factors in the environment.

Since 1994, the South African government has conceptualized, tested and implemented various strategies and programs to promote youth development in South Africa. Although a lot of efforts have been made and some progress has been made in youth development research, some of the factors influencing youth development still hinder the development of South African youth. These factors include unemployment, dropout rates, inadequate skills development, lack of sports and cultural opportunities, social cohesion and volunteerism, and inadequate youth work frameworks. ②

In response to these influencing factors, the South African government has developed the *2015 – 2020 National Youth Policy*. The policy was developed for all youth in South Africa, with a focus on meeting the specific challenges of youth in the country and addressing the urgent needs of youth. It has improved and renewed its previous policies by addressing the new challenges facing young South Africans, while acknowledging that much remains to be done to address the challenges identified in the first National Youth Policy. ③The *National Youth Policy 2015 – 2020* aims to create an

---

① Presidency of South Africa, *National Youth Policy 2009 – 2014*, Presidency, Pretoria, http: //www. thepresidency. gov. za/download/file/fid/122.

② Ibid. .

③ National Youth Development Agency (NYDA), *National Youth Policy (NYP) 2015 – 2020*, April 2015.

environment in which youth in South Africa can reach their full potential as much as possible. The policy outlines interventions to promote the optimal development of youth, both as individuals and as members of South African society, enabling them to become new capabilities for economic development and national governance.

The policy refers to the South African Constitution, the United Nations World Program of Action for Youth to the Year 2000 and Beyond (1995), the African Youth Charter (2006), the National Development Plan (NDP) (2012) and various other policies. By 2030, the program aims to build an inclusive society and build its active citizenship. *National Youth Policy 2015 – 2020* endorses this vision and is based on ensuring that South Africa has the potential and capacity to eradicate poverty and reduce inequality over the next two decades. This requires a new approach, that is, a transition from a passive civil society to economically inclusive society in which people are active champions of their own development, supported by an effective government. ①

Youth are the main human resources for any country and their impacts on social and economic development and innovation are considerable. Their mindset, principles, energy and visions are critical to the constant development of society. *National Youth Policy 2015 – 2020* aims to recognize the important role youth play in building South Africa, to ensure that there are processes and opportunities, and to enable youth to develop and realize their potential. This policy avoids quick solutions and shifts attention to complex institutional and system issues that need to be addressed. ②It is imperative for South Africa to offer and develop long-term solution capacity and this will provide opportunities

① National Youth Development Agency (NYDA), *National Youth Policy (NYP) 2015 – 2020*, April 2015.

② Ibid..

for youth to participate and take advantage of the opportunities.

2 Youth development and Prospect

Before we discuss the youth population and population prospects, it is necessary to analyse the population groups and gender categories across South Africa. Table 5 – 1 shows the mid-year population estimates by population group and gender. The mid-year population is estimated at 57.73 million, where the black population of Africa is the majority (46.68 million), accounting for about 81% of the total population of South Africa, and the white population is estimated at 4.52 million, the coloured population is 5.07 million, and the Indian/Asian population is 0.145 million.[①] The male population accounts for 49% of the total population (28.18 million), and the female population is just over 51% (29.55 million).[②]

Figure 5 – 1 below shows that the growth rate of the South African population has increased between 2002 and 2018. The estimated overall growth rate increased from approximately 1.04% for the period 2002 – 2003 to 1.55% for the period 2017 – 2018.[③] The proportion of elderly people in South Africa is on the increase, indicating that the estimated growth rate has increased from 1.21% in the period 2002 – 2003 to 3.21% in the 2017 – 2018 period.[④] In view of fluctuations in fertility over time, between 2002 and 2012, the growth rate of children aged 0 – 14 increased and with a stall in the period 2013 – 2018.

Stats SA estimates that the mid-year population is 57.73 million (estimated in July 2018).[⑤] However, there is currently no detailed demographic data showing the demographic structure associated with youth

① Statistics South Africa (Stats SA), *Mid – 2018 Population Estimates*, 2018, Pretoria.

② Ibid..

③ Ibid..

④ Ibid..

⑤ Ibid..

employment in 2018. Therefore, the 2017 figures are used here. In 2017, Stats SA estimated that the population in the middle of the year was 56.52 million. ①

Table 5 - 1　**Mid-year population estimates by population group and sex (2018)**

Population group	Male		Female		Total	
	Number	% of total male population	Number	% of total female population	Number	% of total population
Black African	22786200	80, 9	23896700	80, 9	46682900	80, 9
Coloured	2459500	8, 7	2614800	8, 9	5074300	8, 8
Indian/Asian	740200	2, 6	708100	2, 4	1448300	2, 5
White	2194200	7, 8	2325900	7, 9	4520100	7, 8
Total	28180100	100.0	29545500	100.1	57725600	100.0

Source: Stats SA, 2018.

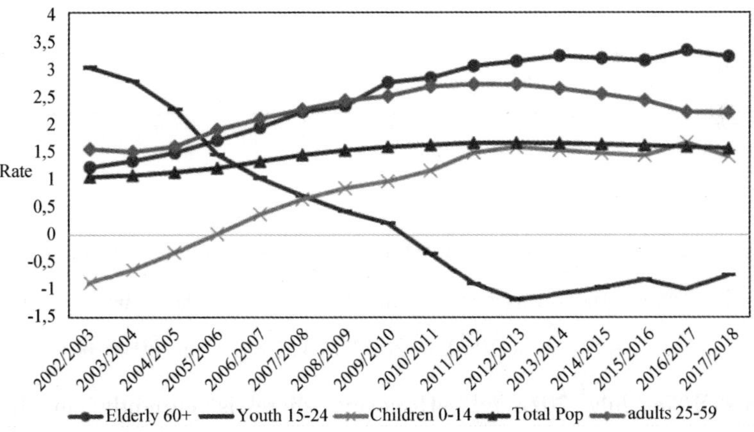

Figure 5 - 1　Population growth rates by selected age groups over time (2002 - 2018)

Source: Stats SA, 2018.

① Statistics South Africa (Stats SA), *Mid - 2017 Population Estimates*, Pretoria.

According to Table 5 – 2, it shows that the total youth population (15 – 35 years old) (20. 4 million) in 2017 accounted for approximately 36. 08% of its total population. ①This in itself is a unique aspect of youth development policy. This means that youth development in South Africa is not only a priority for the youth sector, but it should be a national priority if growth and development are to be achieved.

Table 5 – 2 **South African youth population (15 – 35 years of age)**

Age	Black African			Coloured			Indian/Asian			White		
	Male	Female	Total	Male	Female	Total	Male	Female	Total	Male	Female	Total
15 – 19	1911064	1934788	3845852	205394	203685	409079	44979	42742	87712	126279	123069	249348
20 – 24	2100859	2128984	4229843	215112	214307	429418	54761	50943	105704	133602	132703	266305
25 – 29	2326453	2350758	4677212	217062	217516	434577	66283	57990	124273	141495	140748	282243
30 – 34	2208498	2202074	4410572	198595	201063	399659	74584	62150	136734	153579	306769	460348
Total	8546874	8616604	17163479	836163	836571	1672733	240607	213825	454432	554955	549709	1104664

Source: Stats SA, 2017.

Table 5 – 3 below shows the implied growth rate of the South African population from 2002 to 2017. The estimated overall growth rate increased from approximately 1. 17% from 2002 to 2003 to 1. 61% from 2016 to 2017. ②

The youth population continues to grow at a higher rate than the general population, even though overall South African population growth rate has declined over the past 20 years. The fertility rate is also significantly lower than the countries in the region. Analysis of fertility rates by population groups in

① Statistics South Africa (Stats SA), *Mid – 2017 Population Estimates*, Pretoria.

② Ibid. .

South Africa also demonstrates higher fertility rate amongst black Africans, who constitutes over 80% of the fertility rate amongst Whites. [①]Figure 5 - 2 below depicts graphically the structure of the South African population, clearly showing the significant bulge around the youth ages. [②]

Table 5 - 3 **Estimated annual population growth rates (2002 - 2017)**

Year	Child 0—14	Youth 15—34	Middle-Aged and elderly people 60 +	Total
2002—2003	-0. 85	2. 48	1. 34	1. 17
2003—2004	-0. 50	2. 35	1. 45	1. 20
2004—2005	-0. 16	2. 18	1. 60	1. 23
2005—2006	0. 21	1. 96	1. 74	1. 26
2006—2007	0. 45	1. 73	1. 87	1. 29
2007—2008	0. 58	1. 61	2. 11	1. 32
2008—2009	0. 74	1. 49	2. 30	1. 35
2009—2010	0. 84	1. 36	2. 46	1. 38
2010—2011	0. 94	1. 24	2. 59	1. 41
2011—2012	1. 23	1. 02	2. 69	1. 45
2012—2013	1. 39	0. 87	2. 75	1. 48
2013—2014	1. 46	0. 78	2. 90	1. 51
2014—2015	1. 44	0. 68	2. 95	1. 54
2015—2016	1. 54	0. 32	2. 98	1. 58
2016—2017	1. 56	0. 18	2. 99	1. 61

Source: Stats SA, 2017.

A careful study of the situation in South Africa will reveal that the current prevailing situation is slightly different from the normal state, and the degree of dependence is not as low as expected, so the transfer of resources will not be so automatic. In addition, although economic growth has remained stable over the past few years and has been relatively economically invested, youth continue to

① Statistics South Africa (Stats SA), *Mid - 2017 Population Estimates*, Pretoria.

② Ibid..

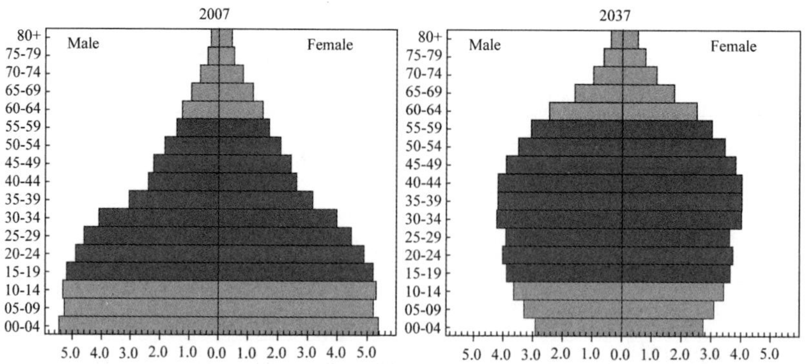

Figure 5 – 2 Age and Sex Structure of the Population of South Africa (2007 – 2037)

Source: Stats SA, 2017.

be unemployed and economically independent. Based on the projected demographic structure shown in Figure 5 – 2, in 2037, South Africa's policies need to first address the innovation plans and strategies of the current youth challenge, and then take advantage of the demographic dividend. ①

According to the statistics of the Stats SA in 2018, about 29.5% of the population is younger than 15 years old, and about 8.5% (4.89 billion) is 60 years old or older. ②A similar proportion of people under the age of 15 live in Gauteng (21.1%) and KwaZulu-Natal (21.0%) and among the elderly aged 60 and over, the highest percentage is 24.0% (1.18 million) living in Gauteng. ③As living conditions improve, the proportion of older people in the 60-year-old age group and above is increasing over time.

Looking back over the past 20 years, overall, the economic participation of South African youth is not optimistic, and the unemployment rate is high and the level of entrepreneurship is low. As of 2011, South Africa's

① Statistics South Africa (Stats SA), *Mid – 2017 Population Estimates*, Pretoria.

② Statistics South Africa (Stats SA), *Mid – 2018 Population Estimates*, 2018, Pretoria.

③ Ibid..

unemployment rate was 25%, and about 70% of the unemployed were young (14 – 35 years old). [①]The youth unemployment rate is higher in the 15 to 24 age group. [②]This unemployment pattern has remained unchanged for many years, and African indigenous and colored youth are the most affected.

Unemployment can be said to depend not only on the ability of the economy to absorb labor, but also on the education level and work experience of youth. The marginalization of youth is mainly reflected in the high youth unemployment rate. It is urgent for the government to introduce interventions targeting youth to make South African youth actively participate in social and economic activities. In an environment where work is scarce, finding jobs is especially difficult for young people. This is not just a local issue.

In 2013, according to the International Labor Organization (ILO) estimates, on a global scale, 73.4 million young people who want to work and are actively looking for work cannot work properly; one in every two youth (52.9%) is unemployed or frustrated, not in an educational institution.[③] According to the ILO's same report, the world is facing a deteriorating youth employment crisis, and youth are three times more likely to be unemployed than adults. South Africa is not immune to this global trend.[④]

According to South Africa's June 2014 Labour Force Survey, 36.1% of youth between the ages of 15 and 35 are unemployed, which is almost twice the 15.6% of those unemployed between the ages of 35 and 64. [⑤]The labor

① South Africa's Ministry of Finance, Facing Youth Unemployment: South Africa's Policy Choices, 2011.

② Ibid..

③ Assaad, R. & Levison, D., Employment for Youth-A growing Challenge for the Global Economy, Commissioned Paper for the High-Level Panel on Post-2015 UN MDG Development Agenda Employment and Economic Growth, University of Minnesota, 2013, http://citeseerx.ist.psu.edu/viewdoc/download?doi=10.1.1.366.1460&rep=rep1&type=pdf.

④ Ibid..

⑤ Statistics South Africa, *Labor Force Survey*, Season 2, 2014, Pretoria.

absorption rate of adults is 57. 8% , which is almost twice that of youth, which is 30. 8% ; young women face higher unemployment rates – 34. 5% of young women have neither employment nor school, including continuing and higher education, compared with 29. 9% for young men. ①Although youth are less likely to be employed than older people, they usually have more years of schooling. From this view point, young people with university degrees will have better employment opportunities.

According to Statistics South Africa (2014), young people constitute 37% of the country's population. ②This presents a powerful resource for the country, provided the youth are supported and able to become active members of society. The NDP states that: "Having a relatively young population can be advantageous; provided the majority of working-age individuals are gainfully employed…The challenge is to convert this into a demographic dividend. ③This will only be possible if the number of working age individuals can be employed in productive activities" . Yet social norms continue to side-line young South Africans, treating political and economic participation as the prerogative of older people, which is why there is a continued need for policies and implementation frameworks that pay deliberate attention to youth concerns.

According to the Quarterly Labor Force Survey released by the Stats SA (2018), South Africa's unemployment rate decreased by 0. 4% to 27. 1% in the 4th quarter of 2018 compared to the 3rd quarter of 2018. ④The working-age population increased by 149000 or 0. 4% in the 4th quarter of 2018 compared to the third quarter of the same year; compared to the 4th quarter of 2017, the percentage of young persons aged 15 – 34 years who were not in

① Statistics South Africa, *Labor Force Survey*, Season 2, 2014, Pretoria.

② Statistics South Africa, Mid-year Population Estimates for 2014, Pretoria.

③ National Youth Development Agency (NYDA), *National Youth Policy (NYP) 2015 – 2020*, April 2015.

④ Statistics South Africa, *Quarterly Labour Force Survey 2018*, Quarter 4, 2018, Pretoria.

employment, education or training (NEET) increased by 0.5% from 38.4% to 38.9% in the 4th quarter of 2018 (Stats SA, 2018). [①]

Based on the above, South Africa urgently needs to develop a specific youth policy for young people to prevent unemployment from negatively affecting personal and social impacts. It is very difficult for some youth who cannot leave their parents' homes to make a living. [②]They are often marginalized by the community and cannot find meaningful ways to reach out to society. Youth are usually not eligible for the Unemployment Insurance Fund because it only covers those who have previously worked. This forced a considerable number of young people to become the burden of the family and became the "neet group".

Many young people are actively promoting community and corresponding youth development initiatives, and are committed to improving the lives of others. However, youth are both victims of crime and perpetrators. Research by the Institute of Security Studies (2003) shows that the 12 to 21 age group has the largest number of offenders and victims compared to other age groups in South Africa; the dangerous behaviour of youth leads to high morbidity and mortality. They face the highest rates of HIV/AIDS infection and HIV prevalence peaks among women aged 30 to 34 (36.8%). [③]In 2013, 2515 out of 5698 transport-related deaths in South Africa were young, and similarly, 69% of beatings and 59% of intentional self-injuries occurred between the ages of 15 and 34. [④]

The *National Youth Policy 2015 - 2020* further clarifies the specific recommendations of the National Development Policy for youth based on some

① Statistics South Africa, *Quarterly Labour Force Survey 2018*, Quarter 4, 2018, Pretoria.

② National Youth Development Agency (NYDA), *National Youth Policy (NYP) 2015 - 2020*, April 2015.

③ Ibid..

④ Ibid..

successful implementation of previous youth policies. The policy strengthens existing interventions, introduces new interventions, and discards measures that have not yet worked, and it aims to improve the quality of the services provided, expand coverage and increase impact, and try to address gaps and stubborn challenges through new approaches. *National Youth Policy 2009 - 2014* has played an important role in guiding the government's thinking on youth development. ①This policy provides a compass for state agencies to guide their planning and contributions in this important area. It also created a coordination platform for the National Youth Development Agency (NYDA) and promoted coordinating bodies, such as the Interdepartmental Committee on Youth Development, to promote the participation of national institutions. ②

In general, the social and economic conditions of youth have improved over the past five years. While these improvements may not necessarily be attributed to the *National Youth Policy 2009 - 2014*, the policy provides a framework and space for other policies that contribute to youth development. ③Despite these advances, much remains to be done. Access to education and skills development has improved, but quality of education and educational outcomes remain a challenge. There are still a large number of young people in the country who are not educated, employed or trained. ④Although some progresses have been made in involving national institutions in youth development, limited work has been done to involve the private sector. This may be partly due to the demise of the Youth Development Forum, which coordinates the involvement of the private sector in this area. Incorporating and mainstreaming youth development into national

① National Youth Development Agency (NYDA), *National Youth Policy (NYP) 2015 - 2020*, April 2015.

② Ibid. .

③ Ibid. .

④ Ibid. .

institutions and the private sector is not optimal. Civil society has also played a limited role in youth development, mainly due to lack of funding and the loss of leadership in government and paying sectors. ①

Youth economic participation (through entrepreneurship and participation in the labour market) is an area that still requires serious attention. The various interventions taken to improve youth's opportunities and skills have little impact. Adolescent pregnancy, youth mortality and access to health facilities improve youth health and well-being, but more needs to be done to reduce HIV infection and infection rates, drug abuse, violence and risk behaviour, as well as improve nutrition and encourage health life. ②

In terms of social cohesion, youth are participating in sports and community organizations. However, youth involvement in efforts to improve ethnic relations and citizen participation (such as voting) requires attention. The National Youth Service is the main programme for youth development and has achieved positive results, but it is limited by the current coordination mechanism. There is no special funding for the program, which means that its implementation depends on the goodwill of the implementer. In addition, the structural capacity for coordination is limited. ③

One of the factors that led to the poor impact of NYP 2009 – 2014 was the "Integrated Strategy for Youth Development". ④The strategy aims to provide a blueprint for the public sector, civil society and the private sector to implement youth development plans to address NYP's goals. There is also limited work of lobbying and advocating for programs that respond to policy goals.

---

① National Youth Development Agency (NYDA), *National Youth Policy (NYP) 2015 – 2020*, April 2015.

② Ibid..

③ Ibid..

④ Ibid..

According to the Article 75 of the National Youth Development Agency Act (2008), it does not affect the provinces. [①]This limits the ability of organizations and departments to effectively lobby and coordinate the development of provincial youth. The lack of a youth work regulatory framework has played an important role in limiting policy implementation.

National Youth Policy 2015 – 2020 proposed strategic policy interventions to fill gaps and shortcomings of previous policies and meet the needs of youth, which will identify new interventions; consolidate youth development in mainstreaming projects by key role players, especially government role actors; map the progress of the implementation of the assessment policy; identify accountability and monitoring mechanisms for continuous improvement of interventions. [②]

The concept of youth development in South Africa is influenced by the historical conditions that shape the country and its democratic goals. It is based on the principles of social and economic justice, human rights, empowerment, participation, active citizenship, the promotion of the public interest, and the values of distribution and freedom. [③]Youth development determines the future of South Africa and it should be at the heart of its development schedule.

The policy responds to the social and economic forces that influence global and regional development in the 21st century, especially the consequences of the international financial crisis. It aims to align youth development with the government's approach to tackling poverty and underdevelopment, as the NDP has diagnosed. [④]Weak youth must be empowered through effective institutions

---

① National Youth Development Agency (NYDA), *National Youth Policy (NYP) 2015 – 2020*, April 2015.

② Ibid..

③ Ibid..

④ Ibid..

and policies to overcome the disadvantages that are unfavourable to them. Similarly, marginalized youth and those who are already separated from education, social and economic mainstreams must reintegrate into society through second chance measures and other supportive actions. ①This will require a multi-sectoral approach involving the public sector, civil society and private sector stakeholders, to make every one work together to promote youth development and serve the youth.

The vision of *National Youth Policy 2015 – 2020* is consistent with the vision of the National Youth Development Policy Framework. According to the *National Youth Policy 2015 – 2020*, the South African youth development vision is integrated, holistic and sustainable youth development; aware of historical imbalances and current imbalances and realities; establishing a non-sexist, non-racial in a democratic South Africa. Youth and their organizations not only have full potential in the social, economic and political spheres, but also recognize and develop their responsibilities to create a better life for all. ②

The *National Youth Policy 2015 – 2020* approach is to consolidate youth initiatives and empower youth to change their economies and societies. ③This will be achieved by meeting their needs, promoting positive outcomes, opportunities, choices and relationships, and working to develop all youth, especially for youth outside the social, political and economic mainstream.

According to the *National Youth Policy 2015 – 2020*, the goals of youth development in South Africa are consolidating the mainstreaming of youth development into government policies, plans and national budgets;

---

① National Youth Development Agency (NYDA), *National Youth Policy (NYP) 2015 – 2020*, April 2015.

② Ibid. .

③ Ibid. .

strengthening the capacity of key youth development agencies to ensure integration and coordination in the provision of youth services; building the capacity of youth to control their well-being by building assets and harnessing their potential; strengthening the patriotic civic culture of youth and help them become responsible adults who care for families and communities; cultivating national cohesion while recognizing the diversity of the country and instilling a spirit of patriotism by encouraging distinct and active participation in different youth initiatives, projects and nation-building activities.

The *National Youth Policy 2015 – 2020* is part of a rich legislative and policy framework defined by the South African Constitution (1996) and is guided by an internationally informed approach to rights-based growth and development. The NYP 2020 informs and cooperates with numerous legislation and policies in an integrated manner. The Constitution of the Republic of South Africa establishes the specific rights, responsibilities and principles that all South Africans must uphold; it lays the foundation for youth economic empowerment and stipulates the rights of people (including youth) in the Bill of Rights and recognizes the values of human dignity, equality and freedom. ①

The National Development Plan provides an ideal vision for South Africa in 2030 and puts forward the following recommendations: providing nutrition interventions for pregnant women and young children to ensure universal access to early childhood development and improving the school system, including increasing the number of students with literacy and math scores of more than 50%, increasing learner retention to 90% and strengthening teacher training; strengthening youth service programs and launching new community programs to provide youth with life skills training, entrepreneurship training and

① National Youth Development Agency (NYDA), *National Youth Policy (NYP) 2015 – 2020*, April 2015.

opportunities to participate in community development programs; strengthening and expanding the number of continuing education and training (FET) colleges, increasing the participation rate to 25%, increasing the FET college graduation rate to 75%, providing full funding for students from poor families, and developing community safety centers to prevent crime; developing tax incentives for employers to reduce the initial cost of hiring young labor market entrants, subsidizing resettlement departments, identifying, preparing and arranging for college graduates to enter jobs; expanding learning capabilities and providing training vouchers directly to job seekers; introducing formal graduate recruitment programs for public services to attract highly skilled personnel and expanding the role of state-owned enterprises in training artisans and technical professionals; accommodating school and community sports and recreation, and encouraging healthy and active lifestyles. ①

The New Growth Path (2011) emphasises the need for the state to create jobs through direct employment schemes, targeted subsidies and an expansionary macro-economic package; support labour-absorbing activities, particularly in agriculture, light manufacturing and services, to generate large-scale employment, while creating a set of incentives and support mechanisms to encourage the private sector to invest in new ventures and extend existing operations and concentrating resources in areas that yield the most jobs, which will make the greatest impact. ②The main indicators of success are employment (the quantity and quality of job creation), growth (growth, labor intensity and composition of economic growth), equity (low income inequality and poverty) and environmental outcomes. ③

---

① National Youth Development Agency (NYDA), *National Youth Policy (NYP) 2015 – 2020*, April 2015.

② Ibid..

③ Ibid..

The Department of Trade and Industry's Industrial Policy Action Plan identifies priority sectors in which industrial and infrastructural development opportunities can be exploited.

Both the Industrial Policy Action Plan and the New Growth Path acknowledge the importance of prioritising youth in job creation and strengthening entrepreneurship. [①]A new marketplace is needed—one in which innovative and profitable business models are developed and incubated to become major industrial and manufacturing players and employers of the future. This will create supply chains that provide further employment opportunities for the previously disadvantaged and procurement opportunities for micro and small businesses. [②]

The Youth Employment Agreement (2013) and the Skills Agreement (2011) signed by businesses, governments, labor, civil society and non-governmental organizations (NGOs) aim to improve the equipment and placement of youth at work, and the economy is often sensitive to the employment needs of youth. [③]The NYDA Act (2008) requires NYDA to develop an integrated youth development strategy for South Africa and to initiate, design, coordinate, evaluate and monitor all programs designed to integrate youth into the economy and society. [④]The act instructs the agency to promote a uniform approach to youth development by all organs of state, the private sector and NGOs.

The Broad-Based Black Economic Empowerment Act (2003) mandates all spheres of government and the private sector to promote the constitutional right to equality, increase broad-based and effective participation of black people in

---

① National Youth Development Agency (NYDA), *National Youth Policy (NYP) 2015 – 2020*, April 2015.

② Ibid..

③ Ibid..

④ Ibid..

the economy, increase employment and promote more equitable income distribution. It also mandates the establishment of a national policy on broad-based black economic empowerment (BBBEE) to promote the economic unity of the nation, protect the common market, and promote equal opportunity and equal access to government services. ①The revised codes is published in the Government Gazette (Notice 800, 2012) for public comment. ②

The African Youth Charter (2006) is a political and legal document that serves as a strategic framework for the direction of empowerment and development of youth at the continental, regional and national levels. The charter was adopted in May 2006 and was endorsed by the African Union Head of State in July 2006, including South Africa. ③It identifies the following priorities: education, skills and capacity development, employment and sustainable livelihoods, youth leadership and participation, health and well-being, peace and security, environmental protection, and cultural and ethical values. The African Youth Charter is in line with the South African Constitution, and almost all of its provisions are consistent with the country's current and envisaged socio-economic programmes. ④The *National Youth Policy 2015 – 2020* shares the Charter's goal of fully developing youth by supporting actions and processes that bring youth into the mainstream of the economy and society; it is also known through the following Millennium Development Goals (MDGs): eliminating poverty and hunger (MDG 1); achieving universal primary education (MDG 2); reducing child mortality (MDG 4); improving maternal health (MDG 5). ⑤

---

① National Youth Development Agency (NYDA), *National Youth Policy (NYP) 2015 – 2020*, April 2015.

② Ibid..

③ African Union, *African Youth Charter Addis Ababa: African Union*, 2006.

④ National Youth Development Agency (NYDA), *National Youth Policy (NYP) 2015 – 2020*, April 2015.

⑤ Ibid..

The *National Youth Policy 2015 - 2020* is located in the United Nations World Programme of Action for Youth in 2000 and Beyond (United Nations Department of Public Information, 1997) and the United Nations Annual Programme of Action for Youth (United Nations Public Information 2005). ① The United Nations has identified more than 10 priorities to address the challenges facing youth, including education, employment, hunger and poverty, health, the environment, drug abuse, juvenile delinquency, leisure, participation of girls and young women, globalization, information and communication technologies, HIV/AIDS, youth and conflict, and intergenerational relationships. ②All these important areas is based on key matters, detailed purposes and activities to be implemented by the parties to accomplish them.

---

① National Youth Development Agency (NYDA), *National Youth Policy* (*NYP*) *2015 - 2020*, April 2015.

② Ibid..

Chapter VI Influencing Factors and Problems of South African Youth's Participation in Social Development

I Employment

The youth unemployment rate in South Africa is approximately double that of the general adult unemployment rate and the general unemployment rate is also extremely high from a global comparative perspective. ①Moreover, these unemployment levels have been a chronic feature of the South African economy since the transition to democracy in 1994, and unemployment rates were probably also very high for a substantial period before 1994, but the lack of suitable data from that period makes precise measurement of the unemployment rates for that era quite impossible. ②

By 2013, one in three South Africans received a social grant. It is estimated that more than 16 million people will remain dependent on grants in the near future. ③Youth unemployment not only puts pressure on government

---

① "Social grants reach almost one third of South Africans", June 19, 2014, http://www.southafrica.info/about/social/grants-190614.htm#.VlWwdXYrLDc.

② Mlatsheni, C and Ranchhod, V, *Youth Labor Market Dynamics in South Africa: Evidence from NIDS 1-2-3*, REDI3x3 working paper 39, July 2017.

③ National Youth Development Agency (NYDA), *National Youth Policy (NYP) 2015-2020*, April 2015.

resources, it also arouses people's concerns about social stabitity. ①

In 1996, the ILO conducted a review of the South African labor market, and its report puts forward that most analysts agree that unemployment rose sharply in the 1970s and that this rise continued through the 1980s and 1990s. ②

As shown in Figure 6 – 1, youth unemployment rates are high, both in narrow and broad definitions of unemployment, and persist even in the context of national economic growth. ③

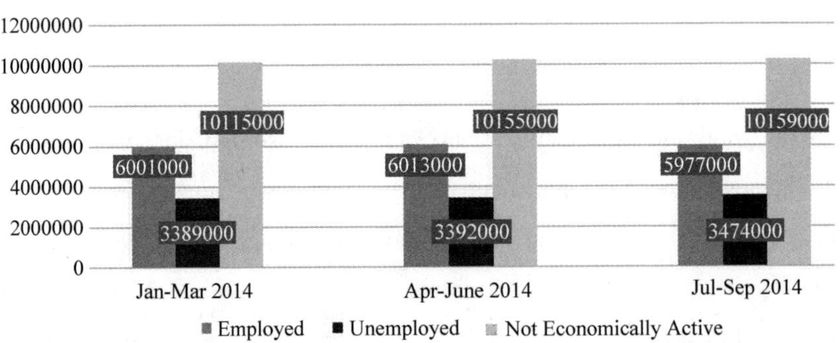

Figure 6 – 1 Employed, unemployed, not economically active

Source: Stats SA Labour Force Surveys, 2014.

According to Stats SA Labor Force Survey, the youth unemployment rate in South Africa increased from 52.80% in the third quarter of 2018 to 54.70% in the fourth quarter of 2018. The youth unemployment rate in South Africa averaged 52.15% from 2013 to 2018, reaching an all-time high of 55.90%. The record low of the second quarter of 2017 and the fourth quarter

① Mlatsheni, C and Ranchhod, V, *Youth Labor Market Dynamics in South Africa: Evidence from NIDS 1 – 2 – 3*, REDI3x3 working paper 39, July 2017.

② National Youth Development Agency (NYDA), *National Youth Policy (NYP) 2015 – 2020*, April 2015.

③ Statistics South Africa, *Labor Force Survey*, Season 2, 2014, Pretoria.

of 2014 was 48. 80%. ①

According to the survey, the main challenges that hinder youth from meaningfully participating in the mainstream economy are unemployment, poverty and inequality. ②If left unresolved, the socio-economic impact of this situation will be terrible, including the increase of crime, poor economic performance, extreme unemployment and poverty, and an increased likelihood of political instability. In this context, *National Youth Policy 2015 – 2020* places employment creation at the centre of all youth development interventions. ③

Youth unemployment is sitting at a staggering 36. 1%, compared to 16. 3% amongst the adult population, with absorption rates of 30. 7% and 57. 6%, respectively. ④To say these figures are disappointing would be an understatement. These high unemployment number amongst the youth have been described as "toxic" and a "ticking time bomb". ⑤

According to Stats SA Statistical release (see Figure 6 – 2), after an increase of 127000 in the number of unemployed persons in the third quarter of 2018, the number of unemployed persons declined by 70000 in the fourth quarter of 2018. ⑥Notable from the figure 6 – 2 is that the number of unemployed persons showed declines in every fourth quarter of each year since 2013; the largest decline was recorded in the fourth quarter of 2017 (down by 330000) followed by the fourth quarter of 2014 (down by 242000) and the

① Statistics South Africa, *Labor Force Survey*, Season 2, 2014, Pretoria.

② National Youth Development Agency (NYDA), *National Youth Policy (NYP) 2015 – 2020*, April 2015.

③ Ibid..

④ Mtwesi, A., "An Overview of Youth Policy", *Helen Suzman Foundation Magazine*, Iss. 74, November 2014.

⑤ Ibid..

⑥ Statistics South Africa, *Quarterly Labour Force Survey 2018*, Quarter 4, 2018, Pretoria.

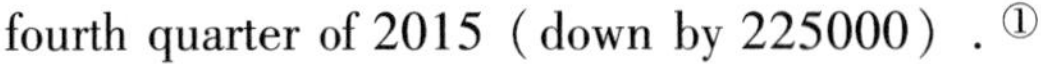

fourth quarter of 2015 (down by 225000). ①

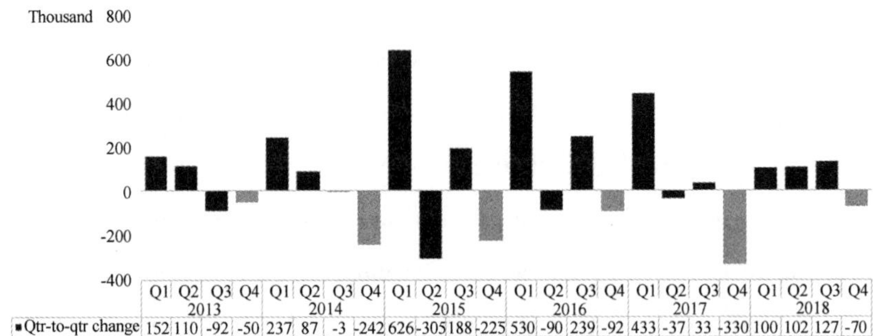

Figure 6 – 2 Quarter-to-quarter changes in unemployment, Q1: 2013 to Q4: 2018

Source: Stats SA, 2018.

II Education

The low quality of education at all levels of the system offsets the increase in the participation rate of school education. The skills pipeline is riddled with obstacles that undermine equitable access to opportunities in the labour market. ②

Literacy and numeracy skills at primary school level are well below the international average. Low uptake and pass rates for mathematics and science at Grade 12 level inhibit growth in higher education, particularly in engineering, science and technology. About 47% of 22 to 25 years old in the country have completed Grade 12, compared to 70% in most developing countries.

Large numbers of learners are dropping out of secondary schools without getting a National Senior Certificate or Grade 12, or an Further Education and Training (FET) or adult basic education and training qualification. About 1

① Statistics South Africa, *Quarterly Labour Force Survey 2018*, Quarter 4, 2018, Pretoria.

② National Youth Development Agency (NYDA), *National Youth Policy (NYP) 2015 – 2020*, April 2015.

million young people exit the schooling system annually, of whom 65% leave without achieving a Grade 12 certificate.

While participation rates in FET institutions have grown significantly, they are still insufficient in number and quality to meet the skill needs of the economy. Only a small number of those who leave the schooling system enrol in technical vocational education and training (TVET) colleges or have access to any post-school training. In 2011, only 115000 people enrolled in general vocational programmes at FET colleges. ①

The low throughput of higher education affects the supply of high-level, skilled graduates. School graduates have limited access to pre-school education and training, and because of the poor quality of education and training offered, those who have access to these opportunities are often not adequately prepared for the workplace. The challenge for preschool education is how to find ways to help the majority of academic graduates who are not eligible to enter higher education or employment directly. ②

III Skills training

Improving the skills of youth will increase their chances of gaining employment opportunities. The main reason for the high youth unemployment rate in South Africa is the shortage of skills of the youth. In 2011, only 31% of youth completed their Grade 12 education. ③The 2013 General Household Survey estimated that 983698 students enrolled in higher education institutions in 2013; nearly 66.4% of these students are black, 22.3% are white;

① National Youth Development Agency (NYDA), *National Youth Policy (NYP) 2015 - 2020*, April 2015.

② Ibid..

③ Ibid..

6.7% are colored, and 4.7% are Indian or Asian. ①

Although most students are black, the students participation rate of this group is still relatively low compared to the Indian, Asian and white groups. In 2013, about 4.3% of people aged 18 to 29 were enrolled in higher education institutions in the country, an increase from 4% in 2002. ②It is estimated that whites in this age group account for 18.7%, and India or Asians account for 9.2%. The number of people registered in higher education institutions is 3.1% and 3.2% of the population of the colored and black, respectively. ③ The proportion of individuals without any school education fell from 10.6% in 2002 to 5.6% in 2013. ④This suggests that opportunities for schooling are increasing, but there are not enough youth in preschool age to participate in the different skills training required.

A large number of youth withdraw from the education system too early, without professional or technical skills, making them effectively unemployed. About 60% of unemployed youth under the age of 35 have never worked. ⑤If there is no targeted intervention, they will continue to be excluded from the economy. A multifaceted method is essential for reinforcing basic education and reducing the dropout rate of existing students. It must create a viable path for graduates to gain post-learning opportunities while directly addressing the lack of skills and work experience of out-of-school youth.

It is widely believed that existing youth development agencies have more room for improvement. This perception is based on the high youth unemployment rate and the low employment rate of graduates, the persistence

---

① National Youth Development Agency (NYDA), *National Youth Policy (NYP) 2015 – 2020*, April 2015.

② Ibid..

③ Ibid..

④ Ibid..

⑤ Ibid..

of HIV/AIDS among youth, the persistent high dropout rates in schools and higher education institutions, and the high rate of violence. ①

Reasons for this lacklustre performance among youth development institutions include lack of clear mandates and fragmentation, resulting in duplicated responsibilities and focus areas, and there appears to be considerable overlap between the mandates of the National Youth Council and the Youth Directorate in the Presidency; lack of coherent coordination of existing programmes and the implications of this for accountability, monitoring, evaluation and assessment of implemented programmes; lack of capacity. The NYDA was set up to be the main driver of youth programmes, but it does not have enough capacity. ②

In summary, improving the skills of youth will increase their chances of gaining a paid career.

IV Youth work framework

Youth work is a field of practice that focuses on the holistic development of a young person. In South Africa, the process of professionalising youth work started in the late 1980s, the Youth Practitioners Advocacy Group which became the South African Youth Workers Association in 2008 produced the "Hunter Rest Declaration" and a draft youth-work policy, which was presented to the inter-ministerial committee on youth at risk. ③The South African Youth Workers Association consulted and collaborated with the Professional Development of Youth Work Consortium to facilitate the

① National Youth Development Agency (NYDA), *National Youth Policy (NYP) 2015 – 2020*, April 2015.

② Ibid..

③ Ibid..

professionalization process.

The *National Youth Policy 2015 – 2020* puts forward that for youth work to thrive, the following needs to be in place: establishing a legislative framework on youth work and a database of young workers, etc. ①

The NYDA and the South African Youth Workers Association developed a draft code of ethics for youth workers which were adopted during a national summit in 2013. ②One of the summit's major resolutions was that South Africa should legislate the professionalization of young workers, hence the NYDA developed the draft bill for Youth Work Profession, and it will continue this work in line with the development of the NYP 2015 – 2020. ③

V Youth health

According to the *National Youth Policy 2015 – 2020*, South Africa's health challenges are not just medical risks, and unhealthy lifestyles also play an important role in physical condition. Although chronic diseases, especially those associated with unhealthy lifestyles, are relatively uncommon among youth, young people have many unhealthy behaviours during adolescence, making these diseases show up their risks for some of the youth in their later years. ④

One of the biggest challenges facing youth in South Africa is sexual and reproductive health. The third juvenile risk behaviour monitoring in 2011 and 2012 was conducted by the Medical Research Council in collaboration with various departments for health and education. In this study, a sample of 8th, 9th, 10th, and 11th grade learners selected from nine public schools found

---

① National Youth Development Agency (NYDA), *National Youth Policy (NYP) 2015 – 2020*, April 2015.

② Ibid. .

③ Ibid. .

④ Ibid. .

that 36% of students reported having sex and 12% reported their age of sexual behavior is under 14 years old. ①Among learners who have had sexual intercourse, 47% have two or more sexual partners in their lifetime, 18% have sex after drinking, and 13% have sex after taking drugs; 33% use condom, 18% are pregnant; one in seven learners reported having received HIV/AIDS education in schools. ②

Lack of quality sanitation leads to high maternal mortality rates and high fertility rates (especially teenage pregnancies). The "Save the Mother Report" (the National Committee on Confidential Enquiries into Maternal Deaths, 2011 - 2013) shows that the five main causes of maternal mortality are: non-pregnancy-related infections, mainly AIDS (34.7%); complications of obstetric hemorrhage and hypertension (30.4%); obstetric hemorrhage (prenatal and postpartum hemorrhage) (12.4%); pregnancy-related sepsis (9.0%); pre-existing maternal diseases (11.4%). ③

The same report stated that 60% of these deaths can be avoided. ④This is due to poor quality of care during prenatal, intrapartum and postpartum periods. Some of the identified weaknesses included poor clinical evaluation, delayed referrals, failure to follow standard protocols, and no response to abnormalities during patient monitoring. The lack of properly trained doctors and nurses resulted in 15.6% and 8.8% of maternal deaths, respectively. The prevalence of pregnancy increases with age, from 0.7% for 14-year-old children to 12.1% for 19-year-old children. ⑤

According to News 24, there are concerns about rising teenage

---

① National Youth Development Agency (NYDA), *National Youth Policy (NYP) 2015 - 2020*, April 2015.

② Ibid..

③ Ibid..

④ Ibid..

⑤ Ibid..

pregnancies. Girls between the ages of 15 and 19 account for 11% of the world's birth population. Of these 11%, almost all newborns (95%) are in low-and middle-income countries, including South Africa. [①]The World Health Organization claims that teenage pregnancy remains the leading cause of maternal and child mortality, in addition to feeding ill health and poverty. Adolescent pregnancy is still a major problem, despite the continued awareness and deterrence of government and non-governmental organizations. About 16 million girls between the ages of 15 and 19 are pregnant each year, and about 1 million girls under the age of 15 give birth. According to the fact sheet, 3 million girls receive unsafe abortions every year. [②]

According to the latest statistics of the Stats SA in 2018, the HIV infection rate of the South African population is estimated to be about 13. 1%. In 2018, the total number of people living with HIV was about 75. 2 million. For adults aged 15 – 49, an estimated 19% of the population is infected with HIV. [③]

Drug abuse has become a serious health problem in South Africa. [④]In particular, the high level of violence caused by alcohol abuse is directly related to motor vehicle accidents. In South Africa, the Western Cape has the highest proportion of alcohol consumers, 46. 15%, followed by Northern Cape Province with 37. 3%, Gauteng with 34%, Eastern Cape with 24. 1% and Free State with 20. 8%. [⑤]In particular, more and more youth are trying drugs and alcohol. The 2011 – 2012 Youth Risk Behavior Monitoring Study found that 33% of the learners surveyed reported that in the past month, they

① News 24. Concerns about rising teenage pregnancies. By Jyothi Laldas, October 17, 2018.

② Ibid. .

③ Statistics South Africa (Stats SA), *Mid – 2018 Population Estimates*, 2018, Pretoria.

④ National Youth Development Agency (NYDA), *National Youth Policy (NYP) 2015 – 2020*, April 2015.

⑤ Ibid. .

had been driven by an alcoholic person and 13% reported they used to be drunk on the streets; about 28% of students reported having smoked; among learners who have never smoked cigarettes, 43% had been exposed to passive smoking in the past week, and 20% had parents or guardians who smoked; about 32% of respondents said they had excessive drinking during the month before the survey, and 25% had alcohol abuse in the past month; 13% of learners have used dagga (a dangerous drug in Africa), 12% have used inhalers, 5% have used cocaine, 6% have used crystallization, and 5% have used Mandrax. ①

In summary, South Africa has many characteristics that expose youth to risks of mental health issues such as prevalent poverty, family destruction, high levels of criminal activities and family deaths caused by HIV/AIDS. Alcohol abuse, smoking and drugs can also impact on mental health negatively among young people.

The South African Department of Sports and Recreation (SRSA) oversees the development and management of sports and entertainment in South Africa. The department is committed to increasing the accessibility of sports and recreational facilities, increasing nation-building contributing to national development, social cohesion and healthy national lifestyle goals, as well as diversification with common national identity. The department plans to encourage sports and recreational activities at all levels to promote the transformation of sports and entertainment, and to support talented and high-level athletes to succeed in the international sports arena. ②

SRSA offers public participation in sports and entertainment through a variety of activities and events, such as the National Youth Camp, Big Walk

① National Youth Development Agency (NYDA), *National Youth Policy (NYP) 2015 - 2020*, April 2015.

② Ibid..

(partnership with loveLife to encourage active lifestyle choices), and indigenous games and school sports. [①]It will continue to use resources for targeted vulnerable groups and individuals to promote participation and increase the use of sports and recreational facilities. The department will assist 60 national federations in the medium term to support school sports programs and improve the use of sports facilities to promote the development of black athletes. [②]Youth will have the opportunity to demonstrate their skills in activities such as the National School Championships, thus giving the National Federation and talent scouts a broader exposure to South African sports talent.

Sports and cultural activities can create healthy and active citizens, foster national pride, and promote social and economic change. Priority needs to be shifted to maximize benefits from existing and planned sports and recreation as well as arts and cultural programs and initiatives. Both sectors are likely to contribute to South Africa's economic growth and are particularly attractive to South African youth. As a result, these sectors have the potential to develop skills, provide employment and entrepreneurial opportunities, and contribute to the nation-building of the country. [③]

VI Youth development, social cohesion and volunteer service

According to the 2014 Human Sciences Research Council (HSRC) Voter Participation Survey, most South Africans are patriotic. 86% prefer to be South African citizens, not any other country. [④]The public clearly recognizes the

---

① National Youth Development Agency (NYDA), *National Youth Policy (NYP) 2015 - 2020*, April 2015.

② Ibid..

③ Ibid..

④ Ibid..

importance of a range of core democratic principles, including free and fair elections, the right to assemble and demonstrate, deliberative democracy, electoral accountability, freedom of speech and political tolerance. Free and fair elections remain the highest-rated democratic ideal. ①However, youth feel they are excluded because of high unemployment and lack of economic participation.

Corruption is a public concern, with 25% mentioned in 2013 and only 9% in 2003. ②Service delivery has also become an urgent issue, with a focus on 24% in 2013, compared to 12% in 2003.

Trust in the political system continues to decline. The national government's trust fell from 61% in 2009 to 44% in 2013. Only 44% trust their provincial government, and less than one-third (34%) trust their local government, while less than a quarter trust political parties or politicians. ③The trust of the Independent Electoral Commission improved slightly from 2012 to 2013 (from 60% to 63%). ④Nearly three-quarters (73%) of people do not know that South Africans can register to vote when they are 16 years old. ⑤Although people between the ages of 16 and 19 are more likely to know this than ordinary people, most people in this age group are still unaware of the age of registration. ⑥This is a potential focus area for the future electoral education of the Independent Electoral Commission. Two-thirds (68%) of those aged 16 and over agree to keep the minimum voting age at 18 years; less than one-fifth (17%) believe that the voting age should be lowered, while only 11% advocate raising the eligibility criteria. ⑦

---

① National Youth Development Agency (NYDA), *National Youth Policy (NYP) 2015 – 2020*, April 2015.

② Ibid..

③ Ibid..

④ Ibid..

⑤ Ibid..

⑥ Ibid..

⑦ Ibid..

Approximately 7.5% of the South African population (2870130) suffer from a disability, with the prevalence of disability among the youngest (aged between 15 - 34) (see Figure 6 - 3). [①]

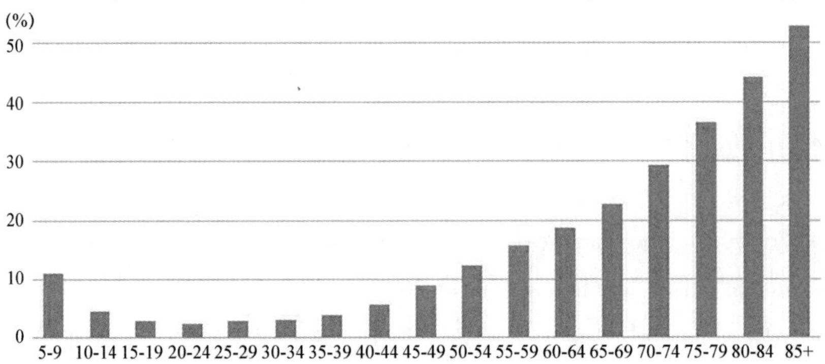

Figure 6 - 3 Disability prevalence by age group

Source: Stats SA 2014, Census 2011.

According to the South African Treasury (2011) study, there is a large gap between youth productivity and entry-level wages. Skill mismatches lead to this gap between real wages and productivity, making education and skills development a long-term priority for the government and a necessary condition for alleviating youth unemployment. [②]Interventions are essential for improving the quality of basic and higher education, re-engaging in the education system and providing an environment that not only develops academic skills but also develops technical and vocational skills. Educational interventions that correct these skill problems need to take time to implement and produce results, especially considering the number of young South Africans who start but do not

① Statistics South Africa, *Census 2011: Profiles of persons with disabilities in South Africa*, 2014, Pretoria.

② National Treasury, *Confronting youth unemployment: Policy options for South Africa*, 2011, Pretoria.

complete secondary education. ①

If labor demand is weak, school leavers will continue to struggle to integrate into the labor market, since employers cannot adequately judge youth productivity and job adaptability. The mission of the Growth Committee is to provide the best understanding of basic policies and strategies for rapid and sustained economic growth and poverty alleviation, recognizing the importance of education and upgrading skills for job growth, and highlighting the enormous benefits of increased labor demand. ②

South Africa's current labour market policy focuses on skills development and direct public employment initiatives supported through expanded public works programs. The private sector has little involvement. However, the vast majority of young workers are employed in the private sector. This is especially true for low-skilled and semi-skilled workers. ③

The severity of the youth employment challenge and the urgent need to stimulate labor demand mean that the private sector plays a key role in accelerating employment growth. This makes incentives for job creation in the private sector a necessary pillar of government employment policy. ④The focus of youth employment subsidies is to stimulate labor demand while using basic work experience and on-the-job training to provide employment prospects. This can be done in isolation, but there are some interventions that can supplement employment subsidies and may increase their effectiveness. For example, an assessment of employment subsidy programs emphasizes that these subsidies tend to be more effective when combined with training.

---

① National Youth Development Agency (NYDA), *National Youth Policy (NYP) 2015 – 2020*, April 2015.

② National Treasury, *Confronting youth unemployment: Policy options for South Africa*, 2011, Pretoria.

③ Ibid. .

④ Ibid. .

The *National Youth Policy 2015 – 2020* focuses on the challenges that particularly affect youth. Analysis of the situation suggests that the policy should promote economic participation and transformation, develop skills, promote lower risk behaviors, improve health, and enhance trust between different races and classes. Meanwhile, it is necessary to establish long-term contracts needed to address the root causes of inequality and exclusion. [①]Therefore, the ultimate focus of this policy is national construction and social cohesion.

① National Youth Development Agency (NYDA), *National Youth Policy (NYP) 2015 – 2020*, April 2015.

Chapter VII Formulating and Forming More Active Policies and Mechanisms for South African Youth's Participation in Social Development

I Promoting the transformation of policies and mechanisms for youth's participation in social development

1 Transformation of socio-economic development and youth participation

Reducing the high unemployment rate in South Africa requires the economy to embark on a growth path that absorbs labor. This depends on the successful repositioning of the economy to increase labor demand and a corresponding improvement in supply. Re-industrialization and economic divergence are also needed for job creation. These factors are at the heart of the New Democracy Party, the new growth path (employment drivers) and industrial policy action plans (sectoral strategies and other programs that support economic transformation). ①

Measures taken by the public sector, such as infrastructure investment,

① National Youth Development Agency (NYDA), *National Youth Policy (NYP) 2015 - 2020*, April 2015.

have promoted youth employment in the construction industry, and the expanded public works program has expanded the enrolment and participation of youth. The recently introduced employment tax incentives should encourage the private sector to hire new people into the labor market. Income from higher education and continuing education has particularly improved. ①

In the past few years, there have been many South African literature focusing on assessing legislation, especially the structure that the government has developed to address the country's youth challenges.

Some scholars studying NYDA are concerned with the specific plan for empowering the structure for youth, ② and the NYDA grant program focuses on creating young entrepreneurs. Therefore, it is related to this research as it attempts to empower youth economically, and empowering youth politically or economically is an important step towards participation. Industrial development companies and small business financing institutions have pledged to invest 2. 7 billion rand to fund young businesses. NYDA also supports a range of youth companies and cooperatives. ③Many youth-owned businesses have benefited from national and private sector procurement and corporate development programs.

The Youth Employment Agreement signed in 2013 is a significant landmark. The agreement sets a framework for cooperation among social partners to address youth unemployment and support youth-owned businesses. ④ The Youth

---

① National Youth Development Agency (NYDA), *National Youth Policy (NYP) 2015 – 2020*, April 2015.

② Fatoki, O. and Chindoga, L., "An Investigation into the Obstacles to Youth Entrepreneurship in South Africa", *International Business Research*, Vol. 4, No. 2, 2011, pp. 161 – 169; Hartley, S. and Johnson, H., Learning to co-operate: "Youth Engagement with the Co-operative Revival in Africa", *The European Journal of Development Research*, Vol. 26, No. 1, 2014, pp. 55 – 70; Malebana, M. J., "The Effect of Knowledge of Entrepreneurial Support on Entrepreneurial Intention", *Mediterranean Journal of Social Sciences*, Vol. 5, No. 20, 2014, p. 1020.

③ National Youth Development Agency (NYDA), *National Youth Policy (NYP) 2015 – 2020*, April 2015.

④ Ibid..

Employment Agreement aims to improve the education and skills of youth and help them find jobs or start their own businesses. As part of the agreement, the government is committed to increasing employment in the public sector, while some industries have set youth development goals. All parties, governments at all levels, organized labor, organized businesses, communities and youth organizations have agreed to implement a coordinated youth employment strategy. ①

2 Social policies to support youth participation in social development

(1) Active employment

The intervention programme should be implemented in two phases to support youth employment. In the short term, decisive intervention will provide income, community services and opportunities for unemployed and poor youth. In the medium to long term, economic measures will be used to promote the growth of sustainable employment for youth. ②Thus, it is important for the government to implement public employment programs effectively to offer better possibilities than the existing programs. The National Youth Development Agency will work with the National Youth Service Centre to involve at least 1 million youth within two years.

Furthermore, it needs to increase income by providing temporary, socially useful jobs for the unemployed, which will ensure that most opportunities flow to youth and mobilize youth to help the community while earning income and gaining valuable work experience. ③

(2) Training young entrepreneurs

The community work projects should be offered for youth, which provide

---

① National Youth Development Agency (NYDA), *National Youth Policy (NYP) 2015 – 2020*, April 2015.

② Ibid..

③ Ibid..

two days of employment per week and public participation in the selection and shaping of projects to gain more information about existing opportunities. It should also encourage youth to proactively determine priorities, provide methods and determine which youth can be targeted. The National Youth Service should be reconfigured to incorporate the revised youth goals into the community work programme to highlight the contribution of programmes such as the Community Health Workers Programme to the absorption of more youth and to develop a national youth volunteer programme that focuses on participation. Youth who are out of school participate in volunteer service. ①

The Ministry of Economic Development should cooperate with enterprises to effectively implement the agreement. This process should be understood through the implementation of lessons learned from the Youth Employment Agreement. Companies should be required to create jobs for youth. Trade and industry, economic development, public works, cooperative governance and traditional affairs, energy and national finance departments should develop measures to achieve youth employment goals. ②

While this will have an impact in the medium to long term, it is important to identify the sectors with the greatest potential for absorbing youth in the employment-driven drivers, industrial policy action plans and agricultural policy action plans for the overall new growth path. Measures to support job creation and monitoring and evaluation frameworks must be developed. In addition, the economic sector should work with the energy and environmental sectors to develop strategies for youth participation in the green economy. Youth in the Information and Communication Technology (ICT) strategy must be developed by the economic sector led by the Ministry of Telecommunications and Posts. ③

---

① National Youth Development Agency (NYDA), *National Youth Policy (NYP) 2015 – 2020*, April 2015.

② Ibid..

③ Ibid..

Moreover, the Ministry of Economic Development should develop strategies for youth participation in creative industries, tourism, sports and entertainment. It is important to determine the skills that learners need to prepare for the world of work. In addition, the education and economic development departments need to be prepared to work with companies on how to train youth in the workplace. ①

(3) Active skills training

Lack of work experience limits youth to work. There are many public and private sector initiatives that match job seekers to jobs, including the Department of Labor and NYDA. ②

It is also suggested that employers, especially small businesses, are reluctant to work hard to create new jobs; SMEs do face some constraints, but with appropriate support and favorable economic conditions, they can make a significant contribution to job creation. ③In this regard, the Ministry of Higher Education needs to develop strategies to support these small companies in training and hiring youth. Pre-employment services minimize the transaction costs of hiring new employees for the company and prepare them for potential employees in the workplace. ④

(4) Supporting youth enterprises and cooperatives

Many youth have already started their own businesses or cooperatives in South Africa. However, due to poor reporting, the number of businesses owned and controlled by young South Africans is not known. ⑤Because ownership is not broken down by age or gender in the procurement or supply

---

① National Youth Development Agency (NYDA), *National Youth Policy (NYP) 2015 – 2020*, April 2015.

② Ibid. .

③ Ibid. .

④ Ibid. .

⑤ Ibid. .

chain process. Initiatives are being implemented to support youth companies in the financial, business and market linkages of the public and private sectors. According to NYP 2015 – 2020, no matter what challenges are encountered, refusal to participate in the technological revolution is not an option. To promote technological advancement, developing countries should invest in quality education for youth and provide ongoing skills training for workers and managers, and ensure that knowledge is shared as widely as possible throughout society. ①

The Ministry of Trade and Industry and the Small Business Development Department launched a youth enterprise development strategy to promote the development of large-scale youth enterprises, such as providing mortgage grants to youth companies. NYDA has implemented programs to support youth corporate finance, training and market linkages, and many government agencies and municipalities implement corporate development programs in their own space. ②

(5) Promoting rural development and youth land reform

Since 1994, the main challenge for rural development has been the marginalization of the poor. Addressing this requires changing access to resources (land, water, education and skills) and improving rural infrastructure and other government services. The traditional approach to rural development and increased agricultural income in poor countries is to help farmers move upstream in the value chain by supporting agro-processing. ③ However, in South Africa, corn, wheat, sugar, sunflower oil, tea, flour, peanut butter, cigarettes, beer, juice and canned foods have been highly

---

① National Youth Development Agency (NYDA), *National Youth Policy (NYP) 2015 – 2020*, April 2015.

② Ibid..

③ Ibid..

concentrated, vertically integrated agricultural processing sectors.

Rural development is often inextricably linked to land reform. Rural development strategies that increase agricultural production can provide basic services by increasing employment rates in rural areas, supporting small farmers, expanding land ownership, and investing in water, transportation, and other network infrastructures. A well-implemented agricultural output strategy can create 1 million jobs by 2030. ①

Youth living in rural areas are often difficult to participate in the economy due to lack of land or land supply and weak economic and social infrastructure. They also face dualism in the rural economy. ②Therefore, rural development strategies also need to take into account the lack of homogeneity in rural areas across the country. ③

(6) Vocational training for youth

Education should allow youth to build their abilities and reach their potential. The NDP outlines South Africa's educational vision that South Africans should receive the highest possible quality of education and training by 2030, significantly improving learning outcomes. South African learners should behave in an international standardized test with the performance of learners in countries with similar levels of development.

The NYP 2015 – 2020 suggests that the education system should cater to different groups and cultivate highly skilled personnel. Graduates of South African universities and colleges should have the skills and knowledge to meet the country's current and future needs. Innovation is critical to addressing the pressing challenges of South Africa, bringing new products to market and

---

① National Planning Commission (NPC), *National Development Plan 2030 (NDP 2030): Our Future-Let It Work.*

② National Youth Development Agency (NYDA), *National Youth Policy (NYP) 2015 – 2020*, April 2015.

③ Ibid..

producing products and services more efficiently. Research and development should be greatly expanded to support innovation and competitiveness.

The education system will play a greater role in building an inclusive society, providing equal opportunities and nurturing all South Africans to realize their full potential, especially those who were previously disadvantaged by apartheid policies, namely blacks, women and people with disabilities. The goals set for this vision include the vocational and technical education and training sector, which covers approximately 25% of age-related youth, which means that it will increase from the current 300000 to 1.25 million by 2030.

South Africa needs a skilled workforce to increase economic growth. These skills include engineers and health professionals in different occupational categories to provide quality healthcare. Researchers and innovators play a key role in creating new products and new ways to produce existing products cheaply and more efficiently, including Public Service. To achieve these goals, the preschool education and training department should improve the quality of access and the quality of results. ①

(7) Promoting youth health programs

South Africa's health system is based on the principles of primary health care and regional health systems, thus, establishing a national health insurance system is an important goal. ②There are four prerequisites for its success: improving the quality of public health care, reducing the relative cost of private care, recruiting more professionals in the public and private sectors, and establishing a health information system across public and private health service providers. ③Long-term health results are influenced by factors

① National Youth Development Agency (NYDA), *National Youth Policy (NYP) 2015 – 2020*, April 2015.

② Ibid..

③ National Planning Commission (NPC), *National Development Plan 2030 (NDP 2030): Our Future-Let It Work.*

beyond the health system. These include lifestyle, diet and nutrition levels, education, sex, sports, traffic accidents and levels of violence. To ensure universal access to quality health care, the government will establish a publicly funded and managed National Health Insurance (NHI) fund to facilitate the launch of the NHI program. [①]NHI-funded model will achieve three key principles of NHI: universal access to quality health care, social solidarity through cross-subsidization, and equity. [②]To achieve this goal, the government will pass the NHI Act over the next five years to finalize the funding model for NHI funds (including budgetary redistribution of regional primary health care and personal health services) and create the fund by 2016 to 2017, and the fund is designed to ensure that facilities are clean, safe and reliable, and that patients are respected and their rights are upheld. [③]

By 2030, the health system should provide quality care to all, free of charge at the point of service, or through public or privately funded insurance. Hospitals should be effective and efficient, providing quality secondary and tertiary care to those in need, and there should be more health professionals, especially in poor communities. [④]

II State and society: building a developmental and cohesive youth's participation in social development

The South African government provides basic services and invests in the skills of personnel to build capacity. The development of a competency approach

---

① National Youth Development Agency (NYDA), *National Youth Policy (NYP) 2015 – 2020*, April 2015.

② Ibid..

③ Ibid..

④ National Planning Commission (NPC), *National Development Plan 2030 (NDP 2030): Our Future-Let It Work.*

that focuses on what people can do, including the ability of people to help monitor the government, is critical to expanding opportunities, which is an essential element of the nation-building process. [①]Ensuring that South Africans can interact across races and classes will contribute to social cohesion. [②]

The *National Youth Policy 2015 – 2020* aims to narrow the identified gaps, address challenges and propose new measures to improve and accelerate the implementation of youth policies, including the following four areas: education, health and well-being, economic participation and social cohesion. The NDP predicts that by 2030, South Africans will live in a more cohesive society that crosses the differences of race, gender, space and class and accepts the multiple identities of people. [③]Youth must take the lead in realizing a constitutional dream of a unified, non-gender, non-racial, democratic, prosperous and equal society.

South Africa's own history and experience in other countries have shown that solidarity and social cohesion are necessary to achieve social and economic goals. If South Africa makes progress in reducing ownership and economic control without reducing poverty and inequality, then the transition will be superficial. Similarly, if poverty and inequality are reduced without a significant change in the ownership model, progress will be volatile and fragile. [④]

At least in the next decade, employment equity should focus primarily on providing opportunities for youth in historically disadvantaged communities. More specifically, race and gender should continue to be the main determinants of choice. This will ensure that society can harness the full human resources of the country and contribute to social cohesion. In this regard, building a stronger

① National Youth Development Agency (NYDA), *National Youth Policy* (*NYP*) *2015 – 2020*, April 2015.

② Ibid. .

③ Ibid. .

④ Ibid. .

and more effective monitoring and enforcement system is essential. ①

Safety and security are directly related to socio-economic development and equality. A safe and secure country encourages economic growth and transformation by providing an environment conducive to job creation, improved education, health outcomes, and enhanced social cohesion. ②

The Constitution is the starting point for building unity. The values included are dignity, non-sexism, non-racism and the rule of law. These values have laid the foundation for a new identity in South Africa, in which South Africa can overcome its history and build a society based on equality, freedom and dignity. National symbols such as national flags, badges and national flowers help to provide a common identity and should therefore be known to youth. "National symbols usually represent not only the general concept of the state, but they also condense knowledge, values, history and memory associated with a country." ③

III China-Africa cooperation: focusing on African youth development

President Xi Jinping pointed out at the Opening Ceremony of the Beijing Summit of the Forum on China-Africa Cooperation that the "Eight Major Initiativess" draw a blueprint for the development of China-Africa relations in the new era and opened a grand chapter in China-Africa cooperation in the new era. ④ The "Eight Major Initiatives", based on the construction of a new type

① National Youth Development Agency (NYDA), *National Youth Policy (NYP) 2015 - 2020*, April 2015.

② Ibid..

③ Butz, D., "The national symbol was the promoter of psychological and social change", *Political psychology*, Vol. 30, No. 5, 2009.

④ Ibid..

of international relations and the community of human destiny, uphold the true concept of sincerity and correct view of interests, and broadly and deeply seek the basis of opinions and suggestions from all walks of life in China and Africa. The initiatives, closely follow the theme of "Win-Win Cooperation, Join Hands to Build a Closer Community of China-Africa Destiny", and jointly build the Belt and Road, promote "the UN 2030 Agenda for Sustainable Development", the AU "2063 Agenda" and the development of African countries. ①The strategy is docked to focus on helping Africa foster endogenous growth capacity, innovating the concept of cooperation and promoting China-Africa cooperation to a higher level.

According to United Nations statistics, the current population of Africa is 1.3 billion, of which 40% is under 15 years old and 70% under 30 years old. Africa is in the period of demographic dividend potential. ②There is an urgent need to improve youth labor skills, increase effective employment, convert potential demographic dividends into real-life development momentum, and promote social stability and economic development in African countries. The AU's "2063 Agenda" clearly states that supporting youth to be the driving force for African revival requires 70% of youth to have the skills to train thousands of young African leaders by 2025. ③For a long time, China has actively assisted African countries in cultivating various talents, strengthening human resources development cooperation, providing a large number of government scholarships and training places, and playing a positive role in enhancing the independent development capabilities of African countries. In view of this, China will focus on cooperation with Africa under

---

① Butz, D., "The national symbol was the promoter of psychological and social change", *Political psychology*, Vol. 30, No. 5, 2009.

② United Nations, Department of Economic and Social Affairs, Population Division, *Population 2030: Demographic challenges and opportunities for sustainable development planning*, 2015.

③ Ibid..

the capacity building action, and focus on cultivating various talents and supporting innovation and entrepreneurship.

According to the Ministry of Foreign Affairs and the Forum on China-Africa Cooperation Beijing Action Plan (2019-2021), in cultivating various talents, China will coordinate all resources to further deepen cooperation with African countries in the field of human resources development, focusing on African countries to train government officials, political party cadres, experts and scholars, technicians and other industries and sectors. ①In 2019 - 2021, China will provide 50000 training palces and 50000 Chinese government scholarships to African countries. ②The Chinese side will also invite 2000 African youths to come to China for discussion and exchanges, continue to send young volunteers to African countries, strengthen the friendship between youth in China and Africa, and enhance mutual understanding. ③

South African President Cyril Ramaphosa delivered a speech at the opening ceremony of the 2018 Beijing Summit of the Forum on China-Africa Cooperation (FOCAC) on September 3, 2018. President Ramaphosa praised China's "excellent economic achievements", including lifting millions of people out of poverty. ④He emphasized that "Africa can learn many valuable lessons from China's impressive growth model, especially using its capabilities and natural resources as a catalyst for growth". ⑤

Trading Economics shows that the unemployment rate in South Africa fell from 27.5% in the previous period to 27.1% in the fourth quarter of 2018. The number

---

① Ministry of Foreign Affairs, Forum on China-Africa Cooperation Beijing Action Plan (2019 - 2021), 8 September 2019, https://www.focac.org/eng/zfgx_4/zzjw/t1594399.htm.

② Ministry of Foreign Affairs, Forum on China-Africa Cooperation Beijing Action Plan (2019 - 2021).

③ Ibid..

④ Quotes from South African president's speech at FOCAC summit, Xinhua Net, September 4, 2018, http://www.xinhuanet.com/english/2018-09/04/c_137442038.htm.

⑤ Ibid..

of unemployed people decreased by 70000 to 6.14 million, and the number of employed people increased by 149000 to 16.53 million.[①] Unemployment rates usually fall in the last quarter of one year due to increased work activities during the holiday. From 2000 to 2018, South Africa's unemployment rate averaged 25.63%, reaching an all-time high of 31.20% in the first quarter of 2003 and a record low of 21.50% in the fourth quarter of 2008.[②]

The youth unemployment rate in South Africa increased from 52.80% in the third quarter of 2018 to 54.70% in the fourth quarter of 2018. The youth unemployment rate in South Africa averaged 52.15% from 2013 to 2018, reaching an all-time high of 55.90%. The record low of the second quarter of 2017 and the fourth quarter of 2014 was 48.80%. At present, youth and adult unemployment rates in South Africa are still high. However, according to the African Development Bank, in the first quarter of 2018, the unemployment rate for youth aged 15 – 34 was 38.2%, the same in other parts of the African continent. Nearly one-third of the age group is unemployed. This means that more than one in every three youth in the workforce did not find a job in the first quarter of 2018.[③]

"We hope to provide more training and employment opportunities for youth in Africa," said President Xi.[④] "We decided to open a China-Africa trade fair in China to encourage Chinese companies to increase their investment in Africa. China will support Africa's goal of achieving general food security by 2030 and work together to implement agricultural modernization cooperation."[⑤]

---

① Trading Economics, South Africa Unemployment Rate, 12 June 2019, https://tradingeconomics.com/south-africa/unemployment-rate.

② Ibid..

③ Ibid.

④ Xi Jinping, "A keynote speech at the opening ceremony of the 2018 Beijing Summit of the Forum on China-Africa Cooperation (FOCAC)", Xinhua, 3 September 2018.

⑤ News 24. Concerns about rising teenage pregnancies. By Jyothi Laldas, October 17, 2018, https://www.news24.com/SouthAfrica/Local/Stanger-Weekly/teen-pregnancy-a-rising-concern-20181010.

From October 11 to 18, 2015, 52 South African youths visited China through the Department of International Relations and Cooperation (DIRCO) and participated in the first China Youth Leadership Program. The mission of the program is to promote bilateral youth cultural exchanges. The plan is based on the 5 – 10 year strategic cooperation plan between China and the Republic of South Africa. ①

In the common struggle against imperialism, colonialism and racism, the people of China and South Africa have established a profound friendship. The leaders of the two countries have provided high-level strategic guidance for bilateral relations through frequent exchanges of visits, meetings and other exchanges. China has become South Africa's largest trading partner for nine consecutive years, and South Africa has become China's largest trading partner in Africa. ②

According to IOL (Independent Online), "Preliminary statistics show that China's direct investment in South Africa has grown more than 80 times, accumulating more than $10.2 billion, creating tens of thousands of jobs for local communities and providing a strong impetus to the South African economy." ③

The successful operation of many Chinese companies in South Africa is a testament to the mutually beneficial relationship of our common development. South African companies have also achieved great success in China. ④In recent years, the China/South Africa Year and the launch of high-level non-

---

① Ministry of Foreign Affairs, Forum on China-Africa Cooperation Beijing Action Plan (2019 – 2021), 8 September 2019, https://www.focac.org/eng/zfgx_4/zzjw/t1594399.htm.

② News 24. Concerns about rising teenage pregnancies. By Jyothi Laldas, October 17, 2018.

③ IOL. South Africa's trade with China. TRIBUNE REPORTERS. NEWS, 22 JULY 2018, https://www.iol.co.za/sunday-tribune/news/south-africas-trade-with-china-rockets-16177203.

④ News 24. Concerns about rising teenage pregnancies. By Jyothi Laldas, October 17, 2018, https://www.news24.com/SouthAfrica/Local/Stanger-Weekly/teen-pregnancy-a-rising-concern-20181010.

governmental exchange mechanisms have brought the two countries closer together and enhanced mutual understanding and friendship, especially among the youths of the two countries. ①

IV New prospect of South African youth's participation in social development

The *National Youth Policy 2015 – 2020* aims to develop youth development plans to address the challenges faced by South African youth and enable youth to have agents and control their future. Based on past youth policies and research on youth conditions, the following areas are prioritized: economic participation, education, skills and correct behavioural change, etc. ②

In order to increase economic participation, the *National Youth Policy 2015 – 2020* proposes measures to improve industrial policy interventions for labor absorption, work exposure measures, provides youth with access to on-the-job experience, connects young job seekers with employers, and supports entrepreneurship interventions, promotes access to opportunities for young companies and cooperatives, business training and markets, and improves public employment programs to reduce inequalities in opportunities. ③

Suggested interventions to improve opportunities and quality of education and skills development include improving the quality of basic education through teacher training, introducing after-school care programmes, strengthening curricula, and gradually providing free basic education to poor learners until the undergraduate level. ④Particular attention will be given to providing a

① News 24. Concerns about rising teenage pregnancies. By Jyothi Laldas, October 17, 2018.

② National Youth Development Agency (NYDA), *National Youth Policy (NYP) 2015 – 2020*, April 2015.

③ Ibid..

④ Ibid..

second opportunity for unskilled and uneducated youth. Recommended health interventions include encouraging behavioral change so that youth develop a good self-image, developing skills that are confident in determining sexual and reproductive health, and using law, policy, and recreational facilities to address drug abuse challenges and related diseases, especially the diseases of youth. The *National Youth Policy 2015 – 2020* calls for the promotion of leadership, active citizenship and values outlined in the Constitution to address social cohesion and positive citizenship issues. ①The Youth Development Mechanism will also be optimized to effectively implement and monitor policies and strategies.

In order to ensure the implementation of this policy, an implementation strategy will be developed with clear objectives to negotiate with different stakeholders. An implementation assessment should be carried out two years after the strategy is issued. ②The implementation assessment will show whether the policy is implemented as planned and where improvements are needed. ③To ensure a good assessment study in 2019, NYDA will work with the Planning, Monitoring and Evaluation Department to ensure that data requirements are mapped and collected immediately after the gazette is published.

In South Africa, youth and organizations have the full potential in the social, economic and political compasses to recognize and develop their responsibilities and create a better life for all. South Africa is embarking on a new journey of national development. President Ramaphosa has led South Africa into a new era of hope and confidence by proposing the goals of developing the economy, creating jobs, improving people's lives and promoting social transformation. China is keen to working with South Africa to strive for faster and

---

① National Youth Development Agency (NYDA), *National Youth Policy (NYP) 2015 – 2020*, April 2015.

② Ibid..

③ Ibid..

better development of a comprehensive strategic partnership.

Under the theme of "African BRICS: Inclusive Growth of the Fourth Industrial Revolution and Cooperation for Common Prosperity", China will deepen its strategic partnership with South Africa and other BRICS countries and strengthen the solidarity and cooperation of the BRICS countries. Promote the development of the interlinkages of the BRICS countries. China will work together with South Africa to create a new era of friendship between the two countries. Of course, youth will become the backbone of the development of the two countries.

Chapter VIII Values for South African Youth's Participation in Social Development

The choice of values and expression of opinions for youth to participate in social development is very important to the development of society. South Africa is a typical representative of the modernization development on the African continent. To see the values of South African youth in terms of personal development feelings, national development expectations and development choices, and personal development attitudes under the dual background of high-risk social development environment and cultural transformation, we can get a new dimension to understand the current state of social development in Africa. The development needs of African youth and the corresponding development values are important indicators for us to observe the environment and conditions of African social development. Studying the values of South African youth's participation in social development will provide reference from theoretical and policy perspectives for benefiting African youth the fruits in building China-Africa community with a shared future and achieving targeted complementarity in China-Africa cooperation.

"Nowadays, the advancement of modernization, especially the emergence of new technologies, is bringing human society into a modern 'risk society' while driving social and economic development. Unlike the traditional risk, the modern risk is characterized by its uncertainty and unpredictability. Its rapid and extensive spread may cause widespread social panic. For example, widespread social tension and social unrest caused by terrorist attacks; social panic caused by unknown epidemics and ecological crises; and large-scale social panic transmission possibly caused by financial risks such as stock market crash, bank failure and debt crisis. "① In the process of social development, the technological revolution and the changes in the economic base lead to changes in the superstructure, and the interaction between the two constantly promotes the development process of human society in various fields.

In fact, "the level of economic development is not isolated, but closely related to the level of political development. It is a relationship of mutual influence, mutual promotion and mutual restraint". ②Recently, "in the case of deteriorating security situation, the voice that the South African people demanded the restoration of the death penalty continues to rise". ③The fact that the South African people petitioned to reinstate the death penalty once again shows that the existence or abolishment of death penalty is a manifestation of values. This change is closely related to the current social development environment in South Africa, and the fight against crime is also an option on values that South African youth are strongly concerned about. This involves the environment of survival and development. The ubiquitous risk and the social development environment in the context of cultural transformation make the changes of values, especially the changes and manifestations of youth values, an important part of the country's cultural, economic and political changes, and a beacon about whether the social development is positive. Generally speaking, "the hierarchy of needs of a country's

① Li Peilin, "Using New Thoughts to Guide Social Governance Innovation in the New Era", *People's Daily*, February 6, 2018.

② Ronald Inglehart, *Quiet Revolution*, Translated by Ye Juanli, Han Ruibo et al., Shanghai: Shanghai People's Publishing House, 2016, p. 1.

③ South African People Petitioned for Death Penalty Reinstatement, Xinhuanet, September 6, 2019, http://www.xinhuanet.com//world/2019-09/06/c_1124968527.htm.

majority is directly related to the country's level of economic development, industrialization, and per capita degree of education. In those underdeveloped countries, physical needs and security needs are overwhelming". [1]Youth values are "only part of a broader cultural transformation from the values of existence to the values of self-performance". [2] Cultural transformation is an important part of the far-ranging social development. It is foreseeable that as a component of cultural transformation, especially political and cultural transformation, changes in values reflect the systematic process of economic, social, and political change. Changes in social development and economics at the macro level reflect the changes in people's perceptions and behaviors at the micro level. The impact of these changes in values is far-reaching.

Youth's participation in social development is a dynamic process, and changes in values correspond to social development. In the African continent with a large youth population, paying attention to the status of African youth's participation in social development, having a deeper understanding of the status quo and needs of African social development, and paying attention to the values of African youth's participation in social development are a rigorous indicator and entry point. Africa is a land of great promise for development with younger force for development. According to forecasts, "the world's population will continue to grow and will reach nearly 10 billion by 2050. Although the population growth rate in other regions will slow down significantly, by 2050, the population of sub-Saharan Africa is expected to increase ninefold compared to 1960, namely from 227 million to 2.2 billion" . [3]The continued growth of

---

① Ronald Inglehart, *Modernization and Post-modernization Cultural, Economic, and Political Changes in 43 Societies*, translated by Yan Ting, Beijing: Social Sciences Academic Press, 2013, p. 15.

② Ibid., p. 3.

③ Emi Suzuki, "World Population to Grow to Nearly 10 billion by 2050", World Bank, July 8, 2019, https://blogs.worldbank.org/zh-hans/opendata/worlds-population-will-continue-grow-and-will-reach-nearly-10-billion-2050.

the population, especially the increase in the proportion of young people, will provide abundant human resources for the development of Africa, and provide sustainable development momentum for the modernization of African continent, especially sub-Saharan Africa.

From the perspective of China-Africa relations, to promote the Chinese and African youth to work together to build a China-Africa community with a shared future, we must have an understanding of African youth and of the values of them.

I Value performance of South African youth's participation in social development

This section will study the values of South African youth's participation in social development from two levels, namely the overall social development trend from a macro perspective and the development of youth groups from a micro level. The analysis of the overall economic and social development environment in South Africa and the distribution of population and employment of youth groups mainly uses the World Bank's survey data and online analysis system (see Table 8 – 1 for details). The performance and analysis of South African youth's values mainly use the survey data of world values and online analysis system (see Table 8 – 2 for details). Regarding the age range for the youth in this article, the criteria of the United Nations are adopted. According to the Population Report released by the United Nations Population Division in 2015, young people are described as population between the ages of 15 and 24.①

Judging from the macro social environment of South African young people's

---

① United Nations, "Population 2030 Demographic Challenges and Opportunities for Sustainable Development Planning", December 19, 2015, https://www.un.org/en/development/desa/population/publications/pd f/trends/Population2030.pdf.

growth, the South African population has continued to grow since the 1960s. Since the 21st century, the growth rate has accelerated. As of 2018, the total population of South Africa was 57.7796 million. ①As the population increases in South Africa, the overall economic development and national income of South African society have also undergone significant changes. According to studies conducted, from 1946 to 2018, South Africa's average GDP and per capita national income experienced significant fluctuations and changes. Since 1980, it has been a general downward trend. The specific changes are as follows:

In 1980, South Africa's average GDP was $25623, the highest point in more than seventy years. From 1980 to 2018, the general trend was in a continuous decline. During the period from 2000 to 2011, it was in a rising range, and in 2011, it reached the highest point since entering the new century, at $23326. After reaching a high point in 2011, it showed a downtrend, with $22098 in 2018.

In 1974, South Africa's per capita national income was $21230, the highest point in more than seventy years. Between 1974 and 1980, there was a fluctuation with a U-shaped decline and rebound process. In 1980, it reached $21074. From 1980 to 2018, the general trend was in a continuous decline, and the some years showed a slight rebound during this period. From 2000 to 2011, it was in an obvious rising range, and in 2011 it reached its high point since the beginning of the new century, at $19261. After reaching a high point in 2011, it showed a downtrend, with $18565 in 2018.

From the perspective of income inequality, from 1963 to 2012, the pre-tax per capita income proportion of the top 10% of South Africa's population accounted for 48.9% in 1963 rose to 69.1% in 2012. There were some years

---

① South Africa's total population, https://data.worldbank.org/indicator/SP.POP.TOTL? end = 2018&lo cations = ZA&start = 1960&view = char. The data is publicly available from the World Bank. The data is updated based on World Bank regulations and website information. The data is retrieved on July 5, 2019.

with a slight decline, but the overall trend was in an upward state with a slow trend. From 2000, the upward trend accelerated significantly. ①

As can be seen from the above data, 2011 was an important turning point in South Africa's economic and social development from the beginning of the new century. The International Monetary Fund published a report entitled "Dilemma of South Africa" in the December 2011 issue of Finance and Development, stating: "South Africa's private sector investment and exports are still well below their levels before the crisis. To make matters worse, the number of jobs in the country has been amazingly greatly reduced. Its unemployment situation is similar to that in countries at the heart of the global economic crisis. Two years after the recession, only a small part of jobs have been restored. This has exacerbated South Africa's already high levels of unemployment and income inequality". ②

Judging from the two indicators of total unemployed population of young people and youth unemployment rate related to youth development in South Africa, from 1991 to 2018, the total number of unemployed young people in South Africa reached a peak of 62.1% in 2003, and from 2003 to 2008, it was in a sustained and significant decline. In 2008, it was 45.178%. In the decade from 2008 to 2018, there were occasional fluctuations, but the overall trend was on the rise, reaching 52.853% in 2018. From the data analysis, the number of laborers who currently have no jobs but can work and are seeking jobs is always in a large proportion, accounting for half of the labor

---

① Average Gross Domestic Product, South Africa, 1946 - 2018, Average National Income, South Africa, 1946 - 2018, Top 10% National Income Share, South Africa, 1963 - 2012, sources of three data: World Wealth & Income Database, website: https://wid.world/country/south-africa/, The data is publicly available from the World Wealth and Income Database. The database updates the data information on an annual basis. The data retrieval time in the text is August 6, 2019.

② [Ethiopia] Abebe Aemro Selassie, Dilemma of South Africa, International Monetary Fund, December 2011, https://www.imf.org/external/chinese/pubs/ft/fandd/2011/12/pdf/selassie.pdf.

force in the group aged 15 – 24, even more than half in some years. In fact, young people aged 15 – 24 in South Africa cannot effectively and fully achieve employment.

The youth unemployment rate of South Africa aged 15 – 24 is generally consistent with the trend of total unemployed population of young people. From 2000 to 2018, the unemployment rate reached a peak of 61.437% in 2003 and began to decline. In 2008, the unemployment rate was 45.607%, and the unemployment rate ended its decline from 2003 and began to rise. It rose to 53.425% in 2018. In the decade from 2008 to 2018, the overall rising trend of the youth unemployment rate in South Africa was stable and there were no marked ups and downs. However, since entering the 21st century, the youth unemployment rate in South Africa has not been below 40%, keeping at a high level. The year with the lowest rate is 2008. Young people aged 15 – 24 in South Africa are in a state of having difficulty in employment. According to gender, the youth unemployment rate of female South African youth aged 15 – 24 is significantly higher than that of male youth, and higher than the total youth unemployment rate.

From the indicators of South Africa's population growth, average GDP, per capita national income, income inequality, youth unemployment rate, and total unemployed population of young people, the basic situation of the social development environment in which South African youth grow is analyzed: (1) The population has continued to grow and grown faster since entering the 21st century; (2) income growth has slowed down and is in decline; (3) income inequality has continued to expand and is on the rise, and the proportion of the top 10% has continued to increase; (4) South African young people have difficulty in employment that the unemployment rate has been high for a long time, the female youth unemployment rate is higher than that of males, and the proportion of unemployed youth aged 15 – 24 is high. In the 21st century, especially around

2008, there is an obvious differentiation in main data. From the data analysis, the social environment in which young South Africans participate in social development needs to be improved to provide young people with adequate employment and a common and prosperous development environment.

Table 8 - 1 **2000 - 2018 South African Youth (Aged 15 - 24) Unemployment Situations**①

(%)

Time (Year) \ Unemployment	total youth unemployment rate (%)	total male youth unemployment rate (%)	total female youth unemployment rate (%)	total unemployed population of young people
2000	53.93	49.598	59.213	54.435
2001	56.274	52.387	60.871	56.924
2002	60.141	55.05	66.042	60.721
2003	61.437	56.939	66.624	62.1
2004	56.84	50.536	64.102	57.446
2005	56.408	49.973	64.131	56.865
2006	54.888	48.664	62.108	55.376
2007	52.732	46.992	59.848	53.351
2008	45.607	41.723	50.315	45.178
2009	48.353	45.093	52.353	47.929
2010	51.189	48.101	55.011	50.789

① The data in Table 8 - 1 is from the public data of World Bank. The data is updated according to the World Bank's regulations and website information. The data retrieval time in the table is July 1 to 20, 2019, source: Unemployment, youth total of total labor force ages 15 - 24, national estimate, Data source: https://data.worldbank.org.cn/indicator/SL.UEM.1524.NE.ZS? locations = ZA; Unemployment, youth male of male labor force ages 15 - 24, national estimate, Data source: https://data.worldbank.org.cn/indicator/SL.UEM.1524.MA.NE.ZS? end = 2018&locations = ZA&start = 2000; Unemployment, youth female of female labor force ages 15 - 24, national estimate, Data source: https://data.worldbank.org.cn/indicator/SL.UEM.1524.FE.NE.ZS? end = 2018&locations = ZA&start = 2000; Unemployment, youth total of total labor force ages 15 - 24, modeled ILO estimate, Data source: https://data.worldbank.org/indicator/SL.UEM.1524.ZS? locations = ZA.

Continued

Time (Year) \ Unemployment	total youth unemployment rate (%)	total male youth unemployment rate (%)	total female youth unemployment rate (%)	total unemployed population of young people
2011	50. 279	46. 255	55. 05	49. 997
2012	51. 698	47. 636	56. 681	51. 499
2013	51. 43	47. 978	55. 546	51. 323
2014	51. 297	48. 022	55. 304	51. 269
2015	50. 143	46. 343	54. 89	50. 156
2016	53. 371	48. 618	59. 313	53. 412
2017	53. 29	48. 906	58. 606	53. 57
2018	53. 425	49. 176	58. 75	52. 853

Data source: World Bank.

There are many ways and means for young people to participate in social development under realistic social conditions, but the main route is employment. Employment is a key step in the integration of young people into society, and it is also the premise and foundation for youth to establish themselves in society. Employment reflects fairness of opportunity. The effective promotion of public policies represented by employment can enhance social mobility and help young people realize their "dreams". "The youth don't lack dreams, ideals, or the spirit of struggle. What they lack is the stage to excel. This stage is economic growth, a stable society, a fair environment, a good education, a skill for making a living, or the hope of development."① Youth participation in social development is influenced by the macro development environment and by the micro adaptability of individuals. The formation and shaping of their values are also the result of the interaction

① Ma Feng, "Work with Youth to Build a Closer China-Africa Community with a Shared Future", September 6, 2018, http://www.cssn.cn/zzx/yc_zzx/201809/t20180906_4555627.shtml.

between the individual and the environment. This process runs through the entire process of socialization, until stable opinions and mature views on the world are formed.

Ⅱ Value choice of South African youth's participation in social development

On the basis of the social development environment, the performance of values of South African youth's participation in social development is worth observing. In the 21st century, there has been an important turning point in the development of South Africa's society. The data of the fourth, fifth and sixth rounds of the World Values Survey will be used to analyze the changes in the values of young people in South Africa since the beginning of the 21st century.

Table 8 – 2 shows the performance of values of young people aged below 29 participating in social development in the dimensions of personal development experience, national development expectations and development choices, and personal development attitudes (work).

1 In the dimension of personal development feeling

(1) Among the five options for "Feeling of happiness", the proportions of the options for "Very happy" and "Quite happy" are high, indicating they have positive subjective feeling of happiness. The proportions of the options for "Not very happy" and "Not at all happy" are lower than the above two options, but they are on the growth trend. The option for "Very happy" in the sixth round is lower than that in the fifth round, with obvious fluctuations of the option data. Around the fifth round of the 2006 survey shows significant changes, where the indicator for "Very happy" is lowering, while the option

for "Not very happy" is on the rise. Changes in economic factors had some impact, and the proportion of "Not at all happy" didn't drop to the level of the fourth round in the survey of 2000. In general, the perception of happiness is positive, the details of change are worthy of attention, and are consistent with the macroeconomic changes in general trend.

(2) For "State of health (subjective)", the option for "Very good" accounted for more than half, and this trend didn't change. The option for "Good" is also basically stable, showing an upward trend, and the changewas obvious. The options for "Fair" and "Poor" accounted for a relatively small proportion and showed a declining trend, and the downward trend of "Fair" was obvious. On the whole, young people in South Africa subjectively believed that they have positive health condition, and this trend was stable. There were some fluctuations for some options, but the overall trend was obvious.

According to the data, young people in South Africa are positive in their happiness and health in terms of the sense of personal development. The options for "Very happy" and "Very good" in terms of happiness and health showed a downward trend, but by a minor extent. Negative factors and feelings increased in the options in happiness. Health does not mean happiness, but happiness must depend on health.

2 In the dimension of national development expectations and development choice

This dimension mainly includes three perspectives: (1) Most important choice: First choice; (2) Aims of country: first choice/Aims of this country should be for the next 10 years; (3) Protecting environment vs. Economic growth. It mainly analyzes what the country's most important development task and goal are in the opinions of South African young people. It is an important

Table 8 – 2 **World Values Survey: Performance of Values of South African Youth's Participation in Social Development**[①]

Classification	Question	Option	Fourth Round (1999 – 2004) 2001	Fifth Round (2005 – 2009) 2006	Six Round (2010 – 2014) 2013	Remarks
Feeling of Personal Development	Feeling of happiness	Very happy	38.70%	45.50%	41.60%	Fourth round V11, Fifth round V10, Six round V10
		Quite happy	39.40%	36.30%	37.00%	
		Not very happy	19.30%	13.70%	16.90%	
		Not at all happy	2.60%	4.40%	4.10%	
		Don't know	*	0.10%	0.40%	

① This part of the data is the World Values Survey data, and is a worldwide values survey project spanning nearly forty years led by American scholar Ronald Inglehart. The data on the World Values survey of young people in South Africa used in this paper were collected from the fourth, fifth and sixth rounds of surveys. The fourth round of surveys spanned from 1999 to 2004, the fifth round of surveys spanned from 2005 to 2009, the sixth round of surveys spanned from 2010 to 2014, and the specific surveys in South Africa were in 2000, 2006 and 2013. The issues selected in this book mainly include three aspects closely related to youth development: personal development feelings, national development expectations and development choices, and personal development attitudes, focusing on happiness, health, employment, economic growth, and national development goals, so as to explore the values of young people in South Africa. Among the questions related to the survey, the same question in different rounds of surveys is numbered differently in the questionnaire. In the Remarks section of Table 8 – 2, the same question in each round is marked in numbers in the different survey rounds. In addition, the average time span of each round of survey is 4 years, with different survey time in each country. The specific survey year in South Africa is marked in Table 8 – 2. In the online analysis process, the age selections include "up to 29", "change crossing variable" options to select age, and "add a second crossing variable" option to select age to select age. In the Display section, 'Show total, all responses" option was selected to get the survey data in Table 8 – 2 and subsequent sections above. The data source and analysis website is: World Values Survey, http://www.worldvaluessurvey.org/WVSOnline.jsp. The retrieval time is July 1 to 20, 2019. The world values survey data used in this article are all from this website. As for the data analysis referred to in this article, the online analysis system of the World Values Survey data divides the age into "under 29 (including 29)", "30 – 49", "above 50 (including 50)". To be in line with the standards of the United Nations, this paper focuses on collecting and analyzing information on age groups below 29 (including 29). The questions and options related to the world values survey in Table 8 – 2 and in this paper are in both Chinese and English. In the process of translating it into Chinese, the relevant contents of the Chinese questionnaire for the sixth round of the world values survey is referenced. Website: http://www.worldvaluessurvey.org/WVSDocumentationWV6.jsp.

Continued

Classification	Question	Option	Fourth Round (1999 - 2004) 2001	Fifth Round (2005 - 2009) 2006	Six Round (2010 - 2014) 2013	Remarks
Feeling of Personal Develop-ment	State of health (subjective)	Very good	53. 90%	51. 40%	51. 10%	Fourth round V12, Fifth round V11, Six round V11
		Good	28. 00%	36. 80%	41. 50%	
		Fair	16. 20%	8. 50%	6. 30%	
		Poor	1. 90%	2. 70%	1. 10%	
		Very poor	*	0. 60%	*	
		Don't know	*	*	*	
national development expectations and devel-opment choices	Most important: first choice	A stable economy	48. 20%	41. 10%	47. 40%	Fourth round V124, Fifth round V73, Six round V64
		Progress toward a less impersonal and more humanes ociety	6. 30%	7. 40%	20. 50%	
		Progress toward a society in which ideas count more than money	6. 60%	9. 60%	8. 60%	
		The fight against crime	37. 70%	41. 40%	23. 50%	
		Not sure	1. 10%	60. 00%	*	
	Aims of country: first choice/Aims of this country should be for the next 10 years	A high level of economic growth	58. 80%	57. 30%	45. 90%	Fourth round V120, Fifth round V69, Six round V60
		Strong defense forces	13. 60%	10. 70%	21. 70%	
		People have more say about how things are done	21. 70%	23. 60%	23. 20%	
		Trying to make our cities and coun-tryside more beautiful	4. 50%	8. 00%	9. 20%	
	Protecting environ-ment vs. Economic growth	Protecting environment	30. 10%	23. 70%	38. 80%	Fourth round V36, Fifth round V104, Six round V81
		Economy growth and creating jobs	59. 80%	66. 60%	59. 50%	
		Other answers	4. 40%	1. 30%	1. 70%	
		Don't know	5. 70%	8. 40%	*	

Continued

Classification	Question	Option	Fourth Round (1999 – 2004) 2001	Fifth Round (2005 – 2009) 2006	Six Round (2010 – 2014) 2013	Remarks
Personal development attitude (work)	Worries: Losing my job or not finding a job	Very much	*	*	43.30%	Only survey of Six round, V181
		A great deal	*	*	23.70%	
		Not much	*	*	9.20%	
		Not at all	*	*	15.80%	
		Don't know	*	*	8.10%	

Data sources: World Values Survey.

reference for examining the relationships between individuals and countries as well as individuals and society. In the design of options for each question, it covers almost the fields of economy, national defense, and society, and the "Most important choice: First choice/Aims of this country should be for the next 10 years" for young people and for the country are of great significance to social development.

The proportion of economic options covered by the three questions is very high. The objective needs and concerns of South African youth for economic growth are universal. Whether it is the "Most important choice: First choice" or the "Aims of this country should be for the next 10 years", a stable economy and a high level of economic growth were the primary goals of youth. In terms of "protecting the environment" and "economic growth", the options for economic growth and creating jobs accounted for an average of 60%, further indicating that South African youth firstly focus on economic growth and environmental protection can be placed in the second choice.

In terms of the social development environment, the South African youth's high concern for the fight against crime indicates that South African youth want social stability. Creating a good social development environment and achieving economic growth and social stability are important choices of values and important expectations for national development goals and choices for South African youth. From the proportions for the two different options "progress toward a less impersonal and more humane society" and "people have more say about how things are done", it can be seen that young people in South Africa hope that, in the process of social development, the state will pay attention to the fairness and justice of social development and that the state must make social development more people-oriented and the people must have more say. The option for "progress toward a less impersonal and more humane society" rose significantly from 6.30% in 2001 and 7.40% in 2006 to

20.50% in 2013, reflecting South African youth have a strong desire for a more people-oriented social development in the country's development.

South African youth are paying more attention to the strong defense forces, which is a direct reflection of external insecurity. It is consistent with expectations of economic growth and social stability. Rapid and steady economic growth, social development and the fight against crime require a strong national defense force, to maintain the stability of the domestic environment and the international environment.

South African youth have a high degree of consistency in the attitudes of national development expectations and development choices. Economic growth, social development, national stability, social equity and justice, and strong national defense are important characteristics in values of South African youth. This performance of values of South African youth is highly consistent with the social development environment in which South African youth live.

3 The dimension of personal development attitude (work)

"Worries: Losing my job or not finding a job" is a new option in the sixth round of the World Values Survey. Just judging from the data of the sixth survey, the South African youth are very worried about employment, the most important issue for reality and future personal development. The option for "very much" accounted for 43.30%, and "a great deal" accounted for 23.70%, which added up to 67%. This data reveals that a large number of young people worry about losing their jobs or not being able to find a job, which directly reflects the long-term realistic problem in social development in South Africa. It is highly consistent with the macro environment of social development, and also indirectly echoes South African young people's choices of values on economic growth and social stability in the dimension of national development expectations and development choices.

Through the three dimensions of personal development feelings, national development expectations and development choices, and personal development attitudes (work), we explore the performance of values of South African youth's participation in social development and outline the overall group image of South African youth group: this is an optimistic group with a high sense of happiness. They are full of expectations for health and the future. They hope for the country's economic growth, social stability, more fairness and equity in social development, and strong national defense. They are full of worries about losing or not being able to find jobs. And this is highly correlated with the reality of the macro social environment in which they grow.

Ⅲ Value analysis of South African youth's participation in social development

The performance of values of South African youth's participation in social development and the social development environment on which their growth depends demonstrate the attitudes of South African youth in social development. It is necessary to look at the essence through the phenomenon and analyze the intrinsic relationship between the performance of this value and the environment of social development from a deeper dimension.

According to the long-term research of the World Values Survey, Ronald Inglehart discovered the inextricable link between macroeconomic and social development and the formation and selection of social group values, and proposed the famous theory of intergenerational transfer of values, and extracted the concept of values of materialism and post-materialism. Ronald Inglehart's theory is based on two important hypotheses: scarcity hypothesis and socialization hypothesis.

"Scarcity hypothesis means that almost everyone is eager for freedom and independence, but people tend to give the most urgent needs the highest value. Material necessities and personal safety are directly related to survival. Once these things are scarce, people will put the 'materialist' goals in the first place. But under wealthy conditions, people are more likely to emphasize 'post-materialist' goals such as belonging, respect, aesthetics and knowledge needs. "①

"Socialization hypothesis means that the relationship between material conditions and priority values is not immediately adjustable. To a large extent, the basic values of the individual reflect the living conditions of their underage period, and the change of values is mainly realized through the intergenerational population replacement. "②

In his later research, Ronald Inglehart also listed materialist values as a new dimension—the values of existence. ③

Through the setting and constitutional conditions of scarcity hypothesis, the current values of South African youth can be summarized into materialist values, that is, survival values. South African youth have placed their material necessities and personal safety, which are directly related to survival, such as economic growth, social stability, more people-oriented social development, fairness, justice, and national defense stability, as priority concerns of values, and are worried about losing or not being able to find jobs. The performance of South African youth's materialist values (survival values) has a direct and close relationship with the macro social environment of South African social development. The basis for the formation of materialist values is the "scarcity performance" of economic and social development.

① Ronald Inglehart, *Cultural Shift in Advanced Industrial Society*, translated by Zhang Xiuqin, Beijing: Social Sciences Academic Press, 2013, p. 3.

② Ibid., p. 3.

③ Ibid., p. 2.

Almost everyone is eager for freedom and independence, and young people in South Africa are no exception. But while freedom and independence exist, the prior options of their values vary with the development of the economy and society. This can also be seen as the important reason why South African youth list economic security as an important national goal and employment as their important concerned option for their own survival security.

In Ronald Inglehart's theoretical framework, the values of materialism and the values of post-materialism are distinguished by survival safety and insecurity, performances of values constituted by which are different. In an unsafe living state, political attitudes and economic attitudes are clearly biased towards the focus on survival. ①

The fourth round, the fifth round, and the sixth round of the data in the option of "progress toward a society in which ideas count more than money" in Table 8 – 2 show that their proportions are respectively 6.60%, 9.60% and 8.60%. In a span of 13 years from 2000 to 2013, this option never exceeded 10% in the choice of young people in South Africa, and after a rise in 2006, it dropped by 1% point in 2013. From the perspective of microdata, in the process of social development, for South African youth, the post-material social development is not the current inevitable demand. The priority demand is the society with economic development as the center and of material priority development. From the perspective of values, the emphasis on the spirit and on environmental protection is the manifestation of post-materialist values, and these two points are not preferred in the choice of South African youth values. The priority option is the materialist value, namely the survival value.

It can be seen from the above that the values of South African youth's

① Ronald Inglehart, Ronald Inglehart, *Modernization and Post-modernization Cultural, Economic, and Political Changes in 43 Societies*, translated by Yan Ting, Beijing: Social Sciences Academic Press, 2013, p. 43.

participation in social development are closely related to the social environment. "Young people involved in globalization need skills training in the face of opportunities for development, need good education in the face of development challenges, need dreams to support in the face of their future and choices of life, and need to see promising future in difficulties of development. The synchronization of these needs with development is what young people need. "①

IV China and South Africa cooperate to create new opportunities for youth development

The third decade of the 21st century is approaching us, and the world's development is undergoing changes unseen in a century. The occurrence of the 2008 international financial crisis brought profound adjustments and greater uncertainty to the world economy. "Currently, we are in an era of endless challenges and increasing risks. "② The transfer of value priorities around the world is taking place in the younger generation. The differences in development stages have led to different responses among young people from different countries and regions around the world, but the hope for economic growth, social stability, and fairness and justice in social development are the common pursuit of young people in this era. However, in "the process of human society moving from an industrial society to a risk society, the rational foundations of industrial society such as science, law, democracy, technological economy, political system, etc. will be questioned and then broken and overthrown, and

① Ma Feng, "Work with Youth to Build a Closer China-Africa Community with a Shared Future", September 6, 2018, http://www.cssn.cn/zzx/yc_zzx/201809/t20180906_4555627.shtml.

② "Xi Jinping Meets with German Chancellor Merkel", Xinhuanet, September 6, 2019, http://www.xinhuanet.com/politics/leaders/2019-09/06/c_1124970182.htm.

the rational foundation of the risk society is still far from being formed, and it needs to be discussed and needs to be rebuilt". ①

Therefore, in the era when resources are most needed, resources for development should be given to support youth growth, provide opportunities for youth development, prevent social risks, and increase opportunities and motivation for youth participation in social development. Jayathma Wickramanayake, United Nations Secretary-General's Envoy on Youth, stated: "According to the World Population Prospects Report released by the United Nations, the median age of the world's population today is 30 years old, that is, half of the world's population are under the age of 30. In Africa, half of the population are under the age of 19, and the average age of political figures is over 60. To bridge this gap, the institutional design needs to be strengthened, and the young people need to start from small things and actively focus on and participate in social governance. "②

The performance of South African youth in participating in social development and their needs in the face of development have a high degree of relevance to the "Eight Major Initiatives" announced at the Beijing Summit of the Forum on China-Africa Cooperation. The "Eight Major Initiatives" link Africa's development, namely industrial promotion, infrastructure connectivity, trade facilitation, green development, capacity building, health care, people-to-people exchange, and peace and security. The "Eight Major Initiatives" are highly compatible with the economic and social development needs of Africa and the development expectations of African youth, and provide a broad development path for China-Africa community with

---

① Ulrich Beck, "From Industrial Society to Risk Society (Part 2) -Reflections on Human Survival, Social Structure, and Ecological Enlightenment", *Marxism and Reality*, No. 5, 2003, p. 67.

② Jayathma Wickramanayake, "Supporting Multilateralism Requires Youth' Voice", Elite Reference, July 19, 2019.

a shared future.

For different countries and nations, youth are the future and hope of national and social development. China and Africa—the cooperation between the world's largest developing countries and the continent with the world's most developing countries, will create opportunities for development and sunshine and upward values for young people in the context of high-risk social and cultural transformation. At the opening ceremony of the 2018 Beijing Summit of the Forum on China-Africa Cooperation, President Xi Jinping pointed out: "The future of China-Africa relations lies in our young people. Many of the measures in the 'Eight Major Initiatives' are designed to help young people in Africa. These measures will provide young Africans with more training and job opportunities and open up more space for their development."① The "Eight Major Initiatives" on China-Africa Cooperation in the new era focus on youth and are committed to providing more employment opportunities and better development space for young people. At the same time, it also opens up a new field for African studies in the new era—focusing on youth development.

Only if we make the youth know their life is promising, our society will be promising. Only if the youth master their future, our society will have a great future. We deeply think about the interactive relationship between social development and youth development. We must pursue development with the people as the center, constantly satisfy the youth group's yearning for a better life, and provide and build a stage for young people to excel. The performance of values of South African youth's participation in social development is profound. From the perspective of world youth development, on the one hand,

---

① Xi Jinping, "Work Together for Common Development and a Shared Future—Keynote Speech at the 2018 Beijing Summit of the Forum on China-Africa Cooperation", *Guangming Daily*, Sept. 4, 2018.

we must pay attention to the deep-seated social development issues such as economic growth, social mobility, income distribution, and social security that affect youth development; on the other hand, we must pay attention to the needs of young people in future personal development, namely employment, education, house purchasing and entrepreneurship. The social development environment and the needs of youth development constitute two aspects of the whole. It is necessary to both continuously solve the deep-seated problems of social development that affect youth development, shape a good environment for economic and social development, and guide young people to integrate into and participate in social development and enable young people to promote social development in participation and sharing.

In terms of China's youth development, we must further do a good job in youth work. On the one hand, from the perspective of macro-social development and environment, we must always adhere to economic development as the center and promote high-quality economic development. "We will provide extensive public employment services to open more channels for college graduates and other young people as well as migrant rural workers to find jobs and start their own businesses. We must remove institutional barriers that block the social mobility of labor and talent and ensure that every one of our people has the chance to pursue career through hard work. "① Moreover, we must always combat crime, maintain social stability, and create a favorable environment for the development and growth of young people. On the other hand, from the perspective of youth development needs, we must continue to meet the youth's yearning for a better life, provide and build a stage for young people to excel, and actively guide young people to integrate

① Xi Jinping, "Secure a Decisive Victory in Building a Moderately Prosperous Society in All Respects and Strive for the Great Success of Socialism with Chinese Characteristics for a New Era—Delivered at the 19th National Congress of the Communist", *Guangming Daily*, Sept. 4, 2018.

into social development.

China and South Africa are both developing countries that play important leading roles in the process of building a China-Africa community with a shared future. The yearning for a better life for young people in China and South Africa is a common performance of the values of the two countries' young people. The "Eight Major Initiatives" on China-Africa cooperation meet the development needs and expectations of South African youth and the expectations of the African continent for modernization. In the new era, in the process of China and Africa together building a community with a shared future for mankind, it is necessary for young people in China and Africa to work together.

Appendix

I China-Africa Relations in the New Era: A Summary of the Academic Dialogue on China-South Africa Youth Social Development

Co-sponsored by the National Institute of Social Development, the Chinese Academy of Social Sciences and Cape Peninsula University of Technology, and funded under the project of the China-Africa Institute, the Chinese Academy of Social Sciences, "China-Africa Relations in the New Era: Academic Dialogue on China-South Africa Youth Social Development" for celebrating the 40th Anniversary of Reform and Opening-up was held in Beijing on August 27, 2018.

At this academic dialogue, Chinese and South African scholars had extensive and in-depth discussions and exchanges on the interaction mechanism of South African youth's participation in social development, the thirty years of youth cultural change, African youth in China, employment structure and youth employment in China, China's urbanization and the mobility of intergenerational career status of young people, the goals and realization ways of the new social organization's youth talent development strategy, and the fourth industrial revolution and youth development.

Chris Nhlapo, president of Cape Peninsula University of Technology, South Africa, expounded the interaction mechanism of South African youth's participation in social development from the aspects of age structure and development of young people in South Africa, the national support policy of and institutions for youth development in South Africa, and the mechanisms of Cape Peninsula University of Technology in students' participation in social development and promoting employment, and analyzed the policies and mechanisms between South Africa's promotion of industrial development and the promotion of youth employment in the fourth industrial revolution. In addition, Chris Nhlapo stated that youth development is a common topic in the social development of both China and South Africa as countries of the BRICS. In promoting youth participation in social development, China has many successful experiences that are worth learning from for South Africa, especially in the promotion of youth employment.

Dr. Ma Feng from the National Institute of Social Development, the Chinese Academy of Social Sciences emphasized on the important impact of the fourth industrial revolution on youth development. He said that the fourth industrial revolution is both an opportunity for youth development and a survival choice for youth development. On the one hand, young people should actively participate in the global replacement of old growth drivers by new ones brought about by the fourth industrial revolution, and realize the improvement of skills and the reversal of fate in the replacement of growth drivers and become the backbone of the new technological revolution; on the other hand, we should prevent the appearance of "forgotten people and marginalized people" brought about by the development of the new technological revolution. We should pay attention to the role of human resources, especially young talents.

Yan Bingwen, professor at Cape Peninsula University of Technology,

South Africa, expounded on the South African government's youth development policies from South Africa's youth development strategies, the age and gender structure of youth, the structure of South African youth in population growth, and the participation of South African youth in economic and social development. Yan Bingwen noted that it is necessary to further promote the development of young people in South Africa and achieve the development goals for South African youth in 2020 so that young people can master their own future. In addition, it is necessary to further reduce youth unemployment rate, promote youth integration into society in development, let youth become a driving force for social development, share the fruits of development, and focus on solving such problems as employment, poverty, and income inequality that affect youth development.

Xie Sujun, director of the Guangdong Youth Talent Institute, said that in recent years, along with the promotion and extension of the Belt and Road, the seemingly faraway Africa has been drawn closer to China, and that African youth are the "wave riders". They entered into China, and mainly engaged in business activities. This has led to the gradual trend that China-Africa people-to-people exchanges have become the main force in China-Africa exchanges. The Chinese style African youth have shown in terms of "words, actions, food, and feeling" has become a true portrayal of a China-Africa community with a shared future. We can uphold the principle of seeking common ground while reserving differences, embracing each other's living habits to romote African youth's development in China to promote China-Africa friendship and youth exchanges.

Chen Chen, associate researcher at the China Youth & Children Research Center, introduced the development of Chinese youth culture for 30 years. Chen Chen believes that youth cultural changes can be understood from four perspectives: first, the development of media technology has profoundly affected the personality and values of young people; second, the rise of emerging groups in the new class reflects the diverse cultural mentality of the youth; third, domestic and foreign situations have shaped the environment of youth behavior; fourth, the memory of major historical events has become the carrier of youth emotional condensation and cultural reflection. Since entering the new era, with a more positive attitude, Chinese youth have integrated themselves into the development of the era and the creation of new youth culture in the new era. Chinese youth have become more individualized, creative, and independent in the development, which reflects the synchronization with contemporary China's economic and social development and the new characteristics of cultural development.

Sun Zhaoyang, associate researcher at the National Institute of Social Development, the Chinese Academy of Social Sciences, elaborated on China's employment structure and youth employment. He noted that since the reform and opening up, China's employment structure transformation has had four characteristics: first, the transfer from the primary industry to the secondary and tertiary industries; second, the transfer from rural areas to urban areas; third, the transfer from employment mainly in state-owned enterprises and collective enterprises to multiple employment forms; fourth, the transfer from the demographic dividend society to an aging society. In the 40 years of reform and opening up, China has gone through the century-long modernization development path of the West and achieved remarkable historical achievements. However, we still face contradictions of imbalance and inadequacy in its development. We still lack high-quality jobs, the structural contradictions in employment are prominent, and youth employment faces new development bottlenecks. It is necessary to further promote comprehensively deepening reforms and remove institutional barriers that block the social mobility of labor and talent and ensure that every one of our people has the chance to pursue career through hard work."

II A summary of the Symposium on China-South Africa Youth Development

Sponsored by the National Institute of Social Development, the Chinese Academy of Social Sciences and funded by the first batch of projects of the China-Africa Institute, the Symposium on China-South Africa Youth Development was held in Beijing on May 22, 2019. This symposium held academic discussions around the theme of youth development in China and South Africa, and achieved fruitful academic results.

The convening of this symposium coincided with the establishment of the China-Africa Institute. This symposium had academic discussions on and formed rich academic achievements in many topics, including Chinese youth's social development and social participation, poverty alleviation legislation and youth development in the new era, factors affecting South African youth development and some important intervening measures, youth and Chinese social organization development, youth and China's grassroots social management core issues, social innovation and youth development, the employment situation of migrant workers in large cities under the new business and the countermeasures, and the transformation of employment structure since the reform and opening up. Through academic exchanges, the content of international studies has been further enriched. It showed the achievements of China's youth development in the 70 years since the founding of the People's Republic of China and the achievements of youth development in South Africa. This symposium also conducted in-depth exchanges on policies, measures and experience of China and South Africa in helping young people integrate into social development, focusing on the synergy of the eight major initiatives with South African and African youth, the Chinese and African youth's joint building of China-Africa community with a shared future, and strengthening the dialogue, exchanges and cooperation among civilizations.

In his speech at the opening ceremony, Kou Wei, deputy director of the National Institute of Social Development, the Chinese Academy of Social Sciences, pointed out that although China and Africa are far apart, the Chinese and African peoples have kept a good relationship just as what Chinese often say: "Distance cannot separate true friends who remain close even when thousands of miles apart." This is the second time that the Symposium on China-South Africa Youth Development was held at the National Institute of Social Development, the Chinese Academy of Social Sciences. The convening of this symposium coincided with the establishment of the China-Africa Institute, the Chinese Academy of Social Sciences. As for the first batch of joint research projects, we hope the teams from the two sides can carefully collaborate, seriously discuss, strive to do the jobs with high-quality research results, and give full play to the intellectual support of academic circles and think tanks, so as to make our contribution to the joint building of a China-Africa community with a shared future.

Professor Yan Bingwen from Cape Peninsula University of Technology, South Africa pointed out in his speech: "Nothing, not even mountains and oceans, can separate Chinese and the African people with shared goals and vision." China has got more and more popular in Africa. President Xi Jinping puts forward the "Eight Major Initiatives" which focus on youth development and capacity building in China, injecting impetus for the modernization cause in Africa. Joint research on the youth development in China and Africa is of great significance for the youth of the both sides to get to know each other and for African youth to learn from China's development experience. Through this symposium, we can better understand the youth development in South Africa and China, and promote academic exchanges and cooperation.

Yu Shaoxiang, an associate researcher at the National Institute of Social Development, the Chinese Academy of Social Sciences, pointed out in his speech entitled Poverty Alleviation Legislation and Youth Development in the New Era that the youth group is the important target for poverty alleviation. It is of great significance to further strengthen and improve poverty alleviation legislation on the occasion of building a well-off society in an all-round way, so as to provide stages for young people to excel and to satisfy the youth group's yearning for a better life.

Yan Bingwen, a professor of Cape Peninsula University of Technology of South Africa, highlighted the facilitation mechanisms, policies and measures in South African youth development in his speech entitled "Factors Affecting Youth Development in South Africa and Some Important Intervening Measures". Professor Yan Bingwen emphasized, in the "Eight Major Initiatives", President Xi Jinping attached great importance to the issue of youth and development issue of African youth. For example, in implementing the industrial promotion initiative, China has decided to send 500 senior agricultural experts to Africa, through various channels to help Africa train a group of young farmers who can lead other farmers out of poverty to carry out localization technology demonstration, promote China's agricultural production technology and rural economic development experience and drive local farmers to increase production and income. This will play a positive guiding role for young farmers to start their own businesses and become rich. In addition, Matamela Cyril Ramaphosa, president of South Africa, delivered an opening speech at the Beijing Summit of the Forum on China-Africa Cooperation, praised China's "excellent economic achievements", including lifting millions of people out of poverty.

Sun Zhaoyang, an associate researcher of the National Institute of Social

Development, the Chinese Academy of Social Sciences, elaborated on the issue of youth employment development in China from three aspects, namely a historical review of the transformation of China's employment structure, the main features of China's employment structure transformation, and the main challenges faced by China's employment structure, in a speech entitled Transformation of Employment Structure Since Reform and Opening up. This speech analyzes the four stages and characteristics of China's labor mobility, including shifting from primary industry to secondary and tertiary industries; productivity improvement brought about redeployment of human resources factors; while accelerating urbanization, we have promoted the transfer of labor from rural to urban areas, from state-owned enterprises and collective enterprises to multiple employment forms, and from the central and western regions to the southeastern coastal areas. In addition, as China's employment faces structural contradictions, to promote youth employment and development, we must take multiple measures and create new macroeconomic policies, so as to integrate youth development into social development and national progress through employment.

Ma Feng, assistant researcher of the National Institute of Social Development, the Chinese Academy of Social Sciences, focused on the social development and social participation of Chinese youth in his speech entitled "China's Youth Social Development and Social Participation", demonstrating the achievements of China's youth development in the past 70 years from the perspective of the youth development of the new China. Dr. Ma Feng introduced China's historical transition from an illiterate country to a large human resource country in the past seven years from such aspects as historical achievements in youth development, the synchronization of youth development and national progress, continuous advancement on youth development in "dream-chasing" and "dream-realizing", and youth development in the new era of national rejuvenation. This speech points out that having more individuality and more emphasis on participation and initiative becomes the distinctive features of youth development in this era. At the same time, the pressure of work, family, marriage, child-rearing and old-age care also puts contemporary young people under the pressure when they pursue career development. Therefore, there is obvious volatility in their outlook on life, world outlook and values. The emergence of words such as "young empty nester", "antizen" and "left-behind youth" also reflects the multi-faceted and pluralistic nature of today's youth development, as well as the differentiation and structural composition within the youth group. Each generation of youth has their own image of struggle. Each generation of youth has a different time and space background to grow and develop.

Lin Hong, an assistant researcher of the Institute of Sociology, the Chinese Academy of Social Sciences, focused on the history, current situation and future of China's youth development and the development of Chinese social organizations in a speech entitled Review, Status and Prospects of Youth Development and China's Social Organization Development. Dr. Lin Hong analyzed the development mechanisms and paths for youth's participation in social organization development and social development in the development process of Chinese social organizations from the development history, status, and prospects of Chinese social organizations. The development of social organizations have provided a broad space for China's youth development from the specialized path, industry norms and institutionalization, the third sector's participation in the institutionalization of public affairs, and the sharing of experience and participation in global environmental governance. General Secretary Xi Jinping's speech at the 100th anniversary of the May Fourth Movement pointed out: "Young people should not only care about their family and country, but also have concerns for humanity. They should carry forward the spirit of concern for the common good of humanity in the Chinese culture, struggle for the great rejuvenation of the nation, work hard to promote the building of the Belt and Road, and promote the construction of a community with a shared future for mankind. "

Ge Yanxia, assistant researcher of the National Institute of Social Development, the Chinese Academy of Social Sciences, gave a lecture entitled "Commuting Pressure on Migrant Youth in Megacities and Its Causes and Countermeasures", focusing on the influence of commuting pressure in megacities on migrant youth's participation in social development, and analyzing its causes and proposing countermeasures. Dr. Ge Yanxia analyzed the current situation of commuting pressure of migrant talents in Beijing and the causes of it. The quantitative analysis method was used to analyze the family and personal factors that affect commuting, and the theoretical hypothesis was put forward and verified. The analysis found that residential location, family structure, occupational factors and personal factors have significant impact on commuting time. Among the many influencing factors, the residential location and family size structure have greater impact on commuting pressure. Generally speaking, the main reason for the excessive pressure on commuting of migrant talents is the excessive spatial separation of the employment area and the residential area, and the rigid demand for housing space and quality by family members. It is necessary to take various measures to ease the commuting pressure of migrant talents and promote the healthy and sustainable development of the city.

Liu Xue, assistant researcher at the National Institute of Social Development, the Chinese Academy of Social Sciences, focused on the important significance and mechanism of social innovation in promoting youth development in his speech entitled "Social Innovation and Youth Development". From the current situation and problems, new business forms and social development, poverty alleviation and human development mechanism, and enterprise public welfare innovation and youth development, Dr. Liu Xue discussed that social innovation and development are faced with new requirements in the new era. We need to focus on creating new forms and contents, increase the intensity of comprehensively deepening reforms, open up the space for young people to participate in social innovation and development, rationally define the boundaries of corporate boundaries of interests and responsibility, and promote the innovative development of corporate public welfare, so as to help with youth development and the modernization of social governance.

Zhang Shuwan, assistant researcher and postdoctor of the National Institute of Social Development, the Chinese Academy of Social Sciences, in a speech entitled "The Employment Status and Countermeasures of Migrant Workers in Large Cities in New Business Situations", focused on the employment situation of migrant workers in large cities in the context of new business conditions and deeply revealed the internal mechanism of migrant workers in social participation and social development. Through the field investigation and questionnaire analysis of the staff engaged in the delivery industry in big cities, the portrayal of the group image of the employed young people in new business is constructed, and the hidden development problems of the explicit group was deeply analyzed. He proposed measures to promote the healthy development of new forms of business and the healthy growth of migrant youth, including strengthening social security coverage, improving the building of mobile Party organizations and improving social integration mechanisms.

The Symposium on China-South Africa Youth Development achieved fruitful results and reached broad academic consensus. In-depth and meticulous academic discussions as well as exquisite and delicate academic exchanges were held at the symposium.

The participation of young people from China and South Africa is of great significance to the growth of youth. Youth is an important source of human resources. Only if the youth development has a bright future can national development and world development have a bright future. Social development must provide a broad stage and space for youth development.

We need to promote the synergy of China's youth experience in youth development, China's wisdom and the needs for African youth development, and implement the "Eight Major Initiatives". Young people of China and Africa should work together to build China-Africa community with a shared future. We need to make African young people have a better understanding of China, promote the wider participation of Chinese youth in the cause of African development and the building of the Belt and Road.

We need to promote mutual exchanges between China and Africa. Civilizations are beautiful because of their diversity. The splendid Chinese civilization and the unique African civilizations should deepen exchanges and mutual understanding. We need to uphold the beauty of each civilization and the diversity of civilizations in the world, which will more effectively promote China-Africa exchanges and mutual learning, and build a closer China-Africa community with a shared future.

Afterword

This book is the research results of the first batch of research projectstitled "China-South Africa youth participation in social development mechanism and tendency" (CAI2017004) that are funded by China-Africa Institute. In the process of writing, the members of the research group of China and South Africa worked together and achieved the research goals set by both sides. Among them, as a member of the research group, Dr. JIANG Ningning contributed the second chapter titled "Social Organization Mechanisms and Talent Strategy of Chinese Youth's Participation in Social Development" of the first part of this book, and shared the research results in the social organization mechanism of Chinese youth's participation in social development. The other parts and chapters of this book were completed respectively by Dr. MA Feng of the National Institute of Social Development, CASS, and Dr. YAN Bingwen of Cape Peninsula University of Technology, South Africa.

We would like to express our sincere thanks to all the colleagues who have supported, cared and participated in this research. We hope that the research results can contribute to the promotion of Sino-African friendship and the deepening of Sino-African academic exchanges and cooperation, and play a role of "casting a brick to attract jade".

The Research Group

Beijing, November 2020